D0945846

THE
AMERICAN EXPRESS
POCKET GUIDE TO
AMSTERDAM

Derek Blyth

PRENTICE HALL PRESS
NEW YORK

The Author

Derek Blyth has lived in Holland since 1980, working as a writer, journalist and translator. His work on several Dutch cities includes *A Walk Through Maastricht* (written with Mary Maclure; 1984), and he has also written on Scotland.

Acknowledgments

The author wishes to thank in particular Mary Maclure, who provided essential moral support and suggested innumerable improvements to the text. The author and publisher also wish to thank the following for their invaluable help and advice: Helen Bannatyne, Sharon Belden, Alan Blyth, Abi Daruvalla, Jules Farber, Mark Fuller, Jane Hedley-Prôle, Yvette Rosenberg and Menno Spiering.

Quotations

The author and publishers are grateful to Doubleday & Co. Inc. for their kind permission to reprint the extract from *Anne Frank's Diary* on page 52.

Few travel books are without errors, and no guidebook can ever be completely up to date, for telephone numbers and opening hours change without warning, and hotels and restaurants come under new management, which can affect standards. While every effort has been made to ensure that all information is accurate at the time of going to press, the publishers will be glad to receive any corrections and suggestions for improvements, which can be incorporated in the next edition, but cannot accept any consequences arising from the use of the book, or from the information contained herein. Price information in this book is accurate at the time of going to press, but prices and currency exchange rates do fluctuate. Dollar amounts reflect exchange rates in effect in mid-1987.

Editor Elizabeth Hubbard

Assistant Editors Alison Franks, Elizabeth Newman, Jean Gordon
Series Editor David Townsend Jones
Project assistant Anderley Moore
Proof reader Sue McKinstry
Indexer Hilary Bird
Gazetteer Catherine Palmer

Art Editor Nigel O'Gorman
Design assistant Christopher Howson
Illustrator Karen Cochrane
Map Editor David Haslam
Jacket illustration Christian Broutin
Production Androulla Wakefield

Edited and designed by
Mitchell Beazley International Limited,
14–15 Manette Street, London W1V 5LB
for the American Express Pocket Travel
Guide Series

© American Express Publishing
Corporation Inc. 1988
All rights reserved including the right of
reproduction in whole or in part in any
form
Published by Prentice Hall Press
A Division of Simon & Schuster, Inc.
Gulf & Western Building
One Gulf & Western Plaza
New York, New York 10023
PRENTICE HALL PRESS is a
trademark of Simon & Schuster, Inc.
Maps in 2-color and 4-color by Lovell Johns Ltd, Oxford, England
Typeset by Vantage Photosetting Co. Ltd, Eastleigh and London, England
Printed and bound in Hong Kong by
Mandarin Offset

Library of Congress Cataloging-
in-Publication Data.
Blyth, Derek.
The American Express pocket
guide to Amsterdam / Derek Blyth.
  p. cm.
Includes index.
ISBN 0-13-025081-3
1. Amsterdam (Netherlands)—
Description—Guide-books.
2. Amsterdam (Netherlands)—
Description—Tours.
I. American Express Company.
II. Title.
DJ411.A53B53 1988
914.92′3—dc19   87-20894
                            CIP

Contents

How to use this book

The American Express Pocket Guide to Amsterdam is an encyclopedia of travel information, organized in the sections listed on the previous page. There is also a comprehensive index (pages 193–201), which is accompanied by a gazetteer (pages 202–204) of the most important streets that are shown in the full-color maps at the end of the book.

For easy reference, all major sections (Sights and places of interest, Hotels, Restaurants) and other sections are arranged as far as possible alphabetically. For the organization of the book as a whole, see *Contents*. For places that do not have separate entries in Sights and places of interest, see the *Index.*

Abbreviations

As far as possible only standard abbreviations have been used. These include days of the week and months, points of the compass (N, S, E and W), street names (Ave., Pl., Sq., St.), Saint (St), rooms (rms), century (C), and measurements.

Bold type

Bold type is used in running text primarily for emphasis, to draw attention to something of special interest or importance. It is also used to pick out places – shops or minor museums, for instance – that do not have full entries of their own.

Cross-references

Whenever a place or section title is printed in *sans serif italics* (for example, *Rijksmuseum* or *Basic information*) in the text, this indicates that you can turn to the appropriate heading in the book for further information. Cross-references in this typeface refer either to sections in the book – *Basic information* or *Planning*, for example – or to individual entries

---

How entries are organized

Grachtengordel

Maps 6, 7, 8, 9 and 10. Tram 13, 14, 17 to Westermarkt (early 17thC area); tram 1, 2, 5 to Keizersgracht (middle section); tram 16, 24, 25 to Keizersgracht (Golden Bend) or tram 4 to Keizersgracht (Amstel area).

Amsterdam's magnificent semicircle of canals and cross-streets (literally, the "canal girdle") was built under the ambitious "Plan of the Three Canals" drawn up by the city carpenter Hendrick Staets in the early 17thC. The three canals – *Herengracht, Keizersgracht* and *Prinsengracht* – were built in two stages: initially from Brouwersgracht to Leidsegracht during the first half of the 17thC, and then from Leidsegracht to the *Amstel* after 1665. The different stages can be detected in the architecture: picturesque brick buildings such as the Renaissance **Bartolotti House** (see *Nederlands Theater Instituut*) in the older part and sober sandstone palaces such as the *Museum Van Loon* in the final stretch. Subtle differences can also be discerned between the aristocratic town houses on Herengracht, the smaller middle-class dwellings on Keizersgracht and the modest artisan homes and workshops on Prinsengracht.

The best introduction to the Grachtengordel is to take a canal boat tour, since this shows the buildings as they were

in the *A to Z* of Sights and places of interest, such as *Rijksmuseum* or *Oude Kerk*. For convenient reference, use the headings printed at the top corner of the page (examples: *Basic information* on pages 8–18, *Oude Kerk* on page 67).

Ordinary italics are used to identify sub-sections. For instance: see *Architecture* in *Culture, history and background*.

Map references

Each page of the color maps at the end of the book has a page number (2–12), and each map is divided into a grid of squares, which are identified vertically by letters (A, B, C, D, etc.) and horizontally by numbers (1, 2, 3, 4, etc.). A map reference identifies the page and square in which the street or place can be found – thus *Rijksmuseum* is located in Map **6G3**.

Price categories

Price categories are denoted by the symbols □ ⬜ ▥ ▦ and ▦ which signify cheap, inexpensive, moderately priced, expensive and very expensive, respectively. In the cases of hotels and restaurants these correspond approximately with the following actual prices, which give a guideline at the time of printing. Although actual prices will inevitably increase, the relative price category will be likely to remain the same.

Price categories	Corresponding to approximate prices	
	for **hotels**	for **restaurants**
	double room with bath; single slightly cheaper	*meal for one with service, taxes and house wine*
□ cheap	under $50	under $25
⬜ inexpensive	$50–100	$25–32
▥ moderate	$100–150	$32–40
▦ expensive	$150–200	$40–50
▦ very expensive	over $200	over $50

Bold blue type for entry headings.

Blue italics for address, practical information and symbols, encapsulating standard information and special recommendations.
For list of symbols see page 6.

Black text for description.

Sans serif italics used for cross-references to other entries.

Bold type used for emphasis.

Entries for hotels, restaurants, shops, etc. follow the same organization, and are usually printed across a narrow measure.
In hotels, symbols indicating special facilities appear at the end of the entry, in black.

Toro ♣
Koningslaan 64 ☎ *(020) 737223. Map **6**H1* ▥ *12 rms* AE ⊕ ⬤ VISA
Tram 2 to Valeriusplein.
Location: In a quiet street on the s side of the Vondelpark, a short tram-ride from Leidseplein. This bright, elegant 19thC villa filled with plants and flowers exudes an English air. The bedrooms are spacious and comfortable (some with views of the *Vondelpark*), and the attractive breakfast room is furnished with antiques and family portraits. This is an ideal hotel for families, and parking in the area is relatively easy.
🛏 🚗

Key to symbols

- ☎ Telephone
- ⊕ Telex
- ★ Recommended sight
- ♣ Good value
- *i* Tourist information
- ⛟ Parking
- 🔲 Free entrance
- 🔲 Entrance fee payable
- ♿ Facilities for disabled people
- 📷 Photography forbidden
- ✗ Guided tour
- 🍽 Cafeteria
- ✳ Special interest for children
- ⋘ Good view
- 🛏 Hotel
- ☐ Cheap
- ⊓ Inexpensive
- ⊓⊓ Moderately priced
- ⊓⊓⊓ Expensive
- ⊓⊓⊓⊓ Very expensive
- 🛁 Rooms with private bathroom

- AE American Express
- Ⓓ Diners Club
- 🅜 MasterCard/Eurocard
- VISA Visa
- 🚘 Secure garage
- ☁ Quiet hotel
- ⬆ Elevator
- ☐ TV in each room
- ☎ Telephone in each room
- 🏋 Gym/fitness facilities
- 👥 Conference facilities
- 🍴 Restaurant
- 🍷 Good wines
- ♠ Casino/gambling

An introduction to Amsterdam

"On a desolate marsh overhung by fogs and exhaling diseases," wrote the historian Thomas Macaulay, "a marsh where there was neither wood nor stone, neither firm earth nor drinkable water, a marsh from which the ocean on one side and the Rhine on the other were with difficulty kept out by art, was to be found the most prosperous community in Europe." A 17thC artist from Haarlem captured the essence of Amsterdam more briefly when he exclaimed: "O glorious morass!"

To Descartes, who lived in Amsterdam from 1628–49, Amsterdam was a city of endless opportunities: "Where else in the world," he wrote, "could one choose a place where all life's commodities and all the curiosities one could wish for are as easy to find as here?"

"Where else in the world . . . . ?" is a phrase that constantly springs to mind as one wanders along the canals and streets of Amsterdam savoring the myriad exotic details. Where else, for example, do people walk their dogs by bicycle, or hoist furniture into apartments from the street? Where else does one see herons perched on the roofs of parked cars, or hurdy-gurdies in the streets? Where else would you find a floating refuge for stray cats moored opposite one of the most expensive hotels in town?

Statistics confirm that Amsterdam is a remarkable city: a population of 740,000; 1.6 million foreign visitors; 100km (62 miles) of canals; 2,800 houseboats; 7,000 protected monuments; 500,000 bicycles; 1,250 cafés; 350 bookshops; 30 cinemas; 35 museums; 720 registered charities (including one for the improvement of false teeth); one doll doctor; three pet crematoria; and just one building more than 20 stories high.

Amsterdam became a storehouse of curiosities after the voyages to the East and West Indies in the early 17thC, when ships returned laden with unknown spices, rare plants, coffee beans, tobacco bales, Chinese porcelain and furs. Still standing are the warehouses on Brouwersgracht, Prinseneiland and Keizersgracht where these goods were stored. Evocative names survive, such as the Greenland and Rhineland Warehouses. The N fringe of the old city still retains the mood of seafaring days, especially in remote corners such as Oude Schans, the Zandhoek and the Entrepôtdok. More romantic still is the panoramic view of the harbor obtained from the ferries that ply between Centraal Station and Amsterdam Noord.

For all that it is an exotic city, there is also an unmistakably Dutch flavor to Amsterdam's gentle life style and peaceful mood, which recall paintings by 17thC Dutch Masters such as Ruisdael and Vermeer. This quiet mood, tinged with a certain nostalgia, can be felt most strongly in brown cafés on rainy Sunday afternoons, when the only sound to break the silence is the clunk of a chess piece being moved.

Not everyone, however, has been seduced by the city's charms. "Amsterdam did not answer our expectations," grumbled the English writer Hazlitt in 1826, "it is a kind of paltry, rubbishy Venice."

Despite its faults, Amsterdam retains the qualities so admired by Descartes – tolerance and diversity, freedom to worship and experiment – which have attracted Jews, Huguenots, Pilgrim Fathers, Armenians and, most recently, the world's youth. Perhaps the key to enjoying this city, then, is to discover those places where you feel most comfortable – and let the rest go its own way.

Before you go

Documents required

For citizens of the EEC, USA, Canada, Australia and New Zealand, a valid passport is the only document required for visits not exceeding three months. For some other nationals a visa must be obtained in advance from a Dutch consulate in the country of departure. Vaccination certificates are not normally required. Foreign visitors not staying in a hotel, pension, camp site or youth hostel must register with the local Aliens Police (*Vreemdelingenpolitie*) within eight days of arrival. Visitors arriving by private boat should report to the nearest customs office on entering and leaving the Netherlands.

If you are driving a vehicle in the Netherlands, you must have a valid national driver's license, the vehicle registration certificate and a national identity plate.

Travel and medical insurance

It is advisable to take out an insurance policy covering loss of deposits paid to airlines, hotels, tour operators, etc., and emergency costs, such as special tickets home, as well as a medical insurance policy.

The IAMAT (International Association for Medical Assistance to Travelers) has a list of English-speaking doctors in the Netherlands who will call for a fee. Membership of IAMAT is free. For information and a directory of doctors and hospitals, write to: IAMAT, 736 Center St., Lewiston, NY 14092.

Money

The unit of currency is the guilder (Fl.), divided into 100 cents (ct). There are coins for 5ct (known as *stuivers*), 10ct (*dubbeltjes*), 25ct (*kwaartjes*), Fl. 1 (*guldens*) and Fl.2.5 (*rijksdaalders*). Brightly-colored banknotes, with embossed markings for the blind, are issued in denominations of Fl.5, Fl.10, Fl.25, Fl.50, Fl.100, Fl.250 and Fl.1,000. There are no restrictions on the amount of currency that may be imported or exported.

Travelers cheques issued by all major companies are widely recognized. Make sure you read the instructions included with your travelers cheques. It is important to note separately the serial numbers of your cheques and the telephone number to call in case of loss. Specialist travelers cheque companies such as American Express provide extensive local refund facilities through their own offices or agents.

Currency may be changed and travelers cheques and Eurocheques cashed at all banks and at the *Grenswisselkantoren (GWK)* found in many railway stations and at frontier posts. These have the advantage of being open longer hours than ordinary banks. Post offices, some tourist offices, long-distance trains and major department stores will also handle foreign exchange.

The major credit cards such as American Express, Diners Club, Eurocard (Mastercard) and Visa are widely, although not universally, accepted in shops, hotels and restaurants. Eurocheques, written in guilders, are the most common method of payment for larger sums. American citizens who also bank in Europe can make use of the Eurocheque Encashment scheme whereby they can cash personal checks with a Eurocheque Encashment card.

8

Customs

If you are visiting the Netherlands for less than six months, you are entitled to bring, free of duty and tax, all personal effects that you intend to take with you when you leave, with the exception of tobacco goods, alcoholic drinks, perfume, toilet water, coffee and tea. Make sure that you are carrying dated receipts for more valuable items, or you may be charged duty.

In the following list of duty-free allowances, the figures in parenthesis show the increased allowances for goods obtained duty and tax paid in EEC countries. All limits apply to travelers over 17.

Tobacco goods 200 (300) cigarettes *or* 100 (150) cigarillos *or* 50 (75) cigars *or* 250g (400g) tobacco if you are coming from an EEC country. If you are coming from outside Europe, 400 cigarettes *or* 200 cigarillos *or* 100 cigars *or* 500g tobacco, while visitors arriving from non-EEC European countries are allowed half this amount.

Alcoholic drinks 1 (1.5) liters spirits (over 22% alcohol by volume) *or* 2 (3) liters of alcoholic drink under 22% alcohol *plus* 2 (4) liters still wine and 8 liters of still Luxembourg wine.

Perfume 50g/60cc/2fl.oz (75g/90cc/3fl.oz).

Coffee and tea 500g (1,000g) coffee *plus* 100g (200g) tea.

Other goods Goods to the value of Fl.125 (Fl.890).

Prohibited or restricted goods include drugs, weapons, meat, fruit, plants, flowers and protected animals. Dogs and cats brought into the Netherlands from countries other than Belgium and Luxembourg must have a certificate of vaccination from the official veterinary service of the country of departure.

Getting there

Amsterdam's Schiphol Airport (regularly voted one of the world's most popular) is a major international airport with direct flights from all over the world, including many cities in the USA. Cities in North America that are connected by direct non-stop flights to Amsterdam include New York, Chicago, Toronto, Montreal and Vancouver. Flights from other major US cities usually involve stop overs in London. For travelers interested in visiting other parts of the Netherlands, Virgin Atlantic flies (via London Gatwick) from Newark to Maastricht (2½hrs by train from Amsterdam).

Getting there from Britain

For those who are traveling to the Continent from Britain several options are available. There are frequent shuttle services from London Heathrow and Gatwick airports as well as daily flights from other major UK cities. In addition, regular train-and-ferry and train-and-hovercraft services operate from London's major railway stations. The total journey time to Amsterdam from London is about 12hrs by boat on any route, 10hrs by Jetfoil. For car and foot passengers traveling by ferry or hovercraft, there are several different routes across the North Sea: from Sheerness to Vlissingen (7hrs by day, 9hrs by night); from Hull to Rotterdam (14hrs by night); and from Dover to Oostende (3¾hrs). The fastest crossing is via the Jetfoil from Dover to Oostende, which takes 1¾hrs. The cheapest means of getting to Amsterdam from England is by bus. Inquire at a travel agent for all further details.

Climate

Holland has a breezy maritime climate with mild winters and cool summers. The driest months are, surprisingly, in the spring, while the warmest months tend to be July and Aug. Although the Dutch may apologize for the wet, unreliable weather, it does create exceptional cloud formations reminiscent of landscape paintings by Jacob van Ruisdael and the Hague School.

Clothes

Be prepared for rain and wind and bring comfortable shoes for walking; high-heeled and thin-soled shoes spell disaster on the uneven, bricked sidewalks of Holland. The Dutch are colorful, casual dressers, and Amsterdammers particularly flamboyant and creative. Dress up by all means for the smarter hotels and for restaurants and concerts, but few places, apart from casinos, will insist on formality.

General delivery (poste restante)

Letters to be collected should be marked *poste restante* and addressed to Hoofdpostkantoor PTT, Nieuwe Zijds Voorburgwal 182, 1012 SJ Amsterdam (☎ *(020) 5558911)*. These can be collected at the main post office: take identification. **American Express** (*write to: Client Mail, American Express Travel Service, Damrak 66, 1012 LM Amsterdam* ☎ *(020) 262042*) and **Thomas Cook**, which has several branches in Amsterdam, offer the same service to their customers.

Getting around

From Schiphol Airport to the city

There is a main railway station at Schiphol Airport, lying on the line from Amsterdam to Leiden, Den Haag and Rotterdam. There are two separate lines to Amsterdam, one to Centraal Station (18mins), the other to Zuid WTC (7mins) and RAI (10mins) on the southern rim of the city. During the day there are four trains an hour on each line, while one train per hour runs through the night to Centraal Station only. The night train service links the main cities of Holland, namely Utrecht, Amsterdam, Leiden, Den Haag and Rotterdam. (*For train information* ☎ *(020) 202266, Mon–Fri 8am–10pm, Sat and Sun 9am–10pm.*)

Taxis are a convenient and not unduly expensive alternative to public transport.

Public transport

All Dutch cities have excellent integrated public transport systems. City buses (*stadsbussen*) are usually maroon, while buses serving outlying districts or other towns (*streekbussen*) are yellow. Amsterdam, Rotterdam and Den Haag have extensive tram (streetcar) networks, and Amsterdam and Rotterdam also have metros. It is worth obtaining a public transport map when you visit any of these cities.

The same tickets are used on buses, trams and metro throughout the Netherlands. You can buy a ticket for a single journey (*eenritskaart*) from the driver, but it is much cheaper to buy in advance a multi-strip ticket – known as a *strippenkaart* – sold in units of 15. These can be bought at post offices, railway stations, public transport offices, VVV tourist offices and in newsagents and tobacconists displaying the *strippenkaart* symbol. Drivers also sell 6- and 10-strip tickets, but at a higher price.

The country is divided into zones and the *strippenkaart* has to be folded and stamped according to the number of zones traveled, plus a flat rate of one strip per journey. Therefore if you are traveling within a single zone (e.g., from Dam to Spui) you should stamp the ticket on strip 2, and if you travel through two zones (e.g. from RAI to Dam), the ticket should be stamped on strip 3. One ticket can be used for more than one person – just stamp the required number of strips for each person. The machine for stamping tickets is usually located at the back of the tram.

If you need to begin a new card, simply stamp the last strip of the old card and then the remaining strips required on the new card. As well as stamping the zone in which you begin your journey, the machine records a time on the ticket. Your ticket is then valid for connections on any tram, bus or metro for one hour after the time stamped if you are traveling 1–3 zones, or 1½hrs if you are traveling 4–6 zones.

The system works on the basis of trust in trams and on the metro, while in buses the driver will check your ticket as you enter. However, random checks are made by inspectors who can fine you on the spot if you do not have a valid ticket.

If you are baffled, you should state your destination to the driver, who will then stamp your ticket. You can also avoid headaches in Amsterdam by purchasing a *daagkaart* for unlimited travel, valid for one or more days.

A route map is usually displayed above the doors on trams, while the name of the stop is given on a signpost, together with the zone number, timetable and map of zones. Stops are requested by pressing a red button.

Trams and metros usually run until midnight, while night buses (*nachtbussen*) run throughout the night on certain routes.

The transport information office is located opposite Centraal Station (☎ *(020) 272727*). There is also a small office at Leidseplein. Other cities: Rotterdam (☎ *(010) 4546890*), Den Haag (☎ *(070) 824141*), Utrecht (☎ *(030) 317962*).

Buses
The smaller villages N of Amsterdam can be reached by regional buses (*streekbussen*), operated by NZH from Centraal Station (☎06-8991177).

Taxis
Taxis can be ordered by telephone (☎ *(020) 777777*), in which case they arrive almost immediately, or picked up at one of the taxi stands in the city, which are located at rail stations, hotels and near major sights and museums. Taxis cannot be hailed in the street. The charge displayed on the meter will include a service charge, but a small tip should be added.

Getting around by car
To paraphrase a famous New York slogan, don't even *think* of driving in Amsterdam. The picturesque streets and narrow bridges that are a delight to the cyclist and pedestrian make driving a nightmare. Drivers will find their way constantly blocked by roadworks, one-way streets and removal vans, while pedestrians and manic cyclists add to the general chaos.

Parking is also difficult and illegally parked cars may be wheel-clamped or towed away to a remote corner of the dock area. To make matters worse, cars with foreign license plates are often broken into, so never leave valuables inside the car.

The best thing to do is to park your car and travel by public transport. Beyond Singelgracht, you can usually find safe parking in the street, but if you are staying within the canal area, you should park your car at **Europarking** multistory parking garage (*next to the police station at Marnixstraat 250 ☎ (020) 236694*). You can easily walk from here through the peaceful Jordaan to the city center, or take tram 7 or 10 for Leidseplein, or tram 17 for Dam and Centraal Station.

The speed limit in built-up areas is generally 50kph (31mph), in some designated areas 30kph (19mph), and in special residential districts known as *woonerven* (indicated by a blue sign showing a white house) cars are restricted to a crawl. Main roads outside the city have a limit of 80kph (50mph), and freeways 100kph (62mph).

Traffic coming from the right has priority unless otherwise indicated. Drivers should take particular care when turning right, as cars must give way to cyclists on their inside that are proceeding straight ahead. Trams have priority and pedestrians on a pedestrian crossing must be given right of way. Seat belts are compulsory.

Renting a car
Most major international car rental firms have branches in Amsterdam and at Schiphol Airport. Payment by credit card avoids the need for a large cash deposit. A current driver's license is required, and the minimum age is usually 18.

Railway services
Travel by rail in the Netherlands is quick, efficient and reasonably priced. NS (Netherlands Railways) operates frequent services between all the main towns, as well as night trains between Utrecht, Amsterdam, Schiphol, Leiden, Den Haag and Rotterdam. An *Intercity* is a fast train linking main cities, while a *stoptrein* calls at intermediate stations as well. A full timetable (*spoorboekje*), with explanatory notes in English, can be purchased at railway stations.

One-way tickets (*enkele reis*) and round-trip tickets (*dagretours*) are valid in the Netherlands on the day of issue only. There are various special tickets such as weekend round trips (*weekendretours*, for outward travel on Sat, returning on Sun); evening round trips (*avondretours*, valid after 6pm); day tickets (*dagkaarten*, for unlimited travel throughout the Netherlands for one day); 3- and 7-day Rovers entitling the holder to unlimited train travel for a specified length of time (for an extra charge, these can be used on other forms of public transport); and group tickets (*meer man's kaart*, for unlimited travel on one day for 2–6 people traveling together). Children under 3 travel free, while those aged 3–9 pay a reduced fare.

The NS also offers bargain trips (*dagtochten*) to popular sights, museums, exhibitions and parks, which include the round-trip rail fare, any bus or boat fares necessary, entrance charges and perhaps a refreshment. These make excursions easy and economical, while leaving you free to decide when to travel and how long to stay. A free brochure *NS-Dagtoerisme*, available only in Dutch, lists special excursions, and further information can be obtained from NS (☎ (020) 238383).

Information on train services can be obtained from
Netherlands Board of Tourism (*355 Lexington Ave., 21*ˢᵗ
Floor, New York, NY 10036 ☎*370–7360; 25–28 Buckingham
Gate, London SW1E 6LD* ☎*630–1735*). In the Netherlands,
NS Travel Information Offices provide full information:

Amsterdam CS   ☎(020) 202266
Eindhoven   ☎(040) 448940
Den Haag CS   ☎(070) 824141
Haarlem   ☎(023) 323551
Leiden   ☎(071) 125890
Rotterdam CS   ☎(010) 4117100
Schiphol   ☎(020) 141959
Utrecht CS   ☎(030) 315814

Domestic airlines
Domestic flights are operated by **NLM City Hopper**
(☎*(020) 493252*) and by **Netherlines** (☎*(020) 170931*).

Getting around by boat
Holland's dense web of rivers, canals and lakes makes it
possible to reach almost anywhere by boat. The IJsselmeer,
which can be reached from Amsterdam via the IJ, is ideally
suited to sailboats, and its coastline is dotted with historic
towns offering mooring facilities. The Loosdrechtse plassen
(an area of lakes between Amsterdam and Utrecht) offer more
sheltered sailing conditions. One of the most attractive routes
for cruising is from Amsterdam to Utrecht via the Amstel,
Holendrecht, Angstel and Vecht rivers. The NBT publishes
an excellent guide to sailing in the Netherlands, *Holland
Watersports Paradise*, available from **Netherlands Board of
Tourism** (see *Railway services* for ☎ and address).

Getting around on foot
Dutch cities tend to be compact and traffic-free, which makes
walking a pleasure. Outside cities, however, public footpaths
are rare and the only areas suited to walking in the vicinity of
Amsterdam are the woods near Hilversum and the dunes w of
Haarlem.

On-the-spot information

Public holidays
New Year's Day, Jan 1; Easter Monday; Queen's Birthday,
30 Apr; Ascension Day (sixth Thurs after Easter); Whit
Monday (second Mon after Ascension); Dec 25; Dec 26. All
banks and most stores are closed on these days, although
museums are sometimes open. Good Friday is also a bank
holiday, but most stores open for at least part of the day. Some
government offices close on Liberation Day (May 5).

Time zones
The Netherlands, like most Western European countries, is
1hr ahead of GMT in the winter and 2hrs ahead in the
summer, i.e., 6hrs ahead of the eastern USA most of the year.

Banks and currency exchange
Banks in Amsterdam are open Mon–Fri 9am–4pm and
sometimes later on Thurs (late-night shopping). The

Basic information

Grenswisselkantoor (GWK) at Centraal Station
(☎ *(020) 272731*) is open daily 7am–10.45pm. There are also
branches at Schiphol's NS Station (☎ *(020) 179881*) and
Amstelstation (☎ *(020) 934545*).

Shopping hours

Store opening hours are strictly regulated in the Netherlands.
Normally, stores are open Mon 1–6pm, Tues–Fri 9am–6pm
and Sat 9am–5pm. Stores in city centers may also remain open
late one evening a week (*koopavond*): Thurs in Amsterdam,
Den Haag and Utrecht, Fri in Rotterdam and Delft.

Postal and telephone services

Post offices (*postkantoren*), marked PTT, are normally open
Mon–Fri 8.30am–5.30pm. The main post office in Amsterdam
(*N.Z. Voorburgwal 182*) is just behind the Royal Palace on
Dam, and is open Mon–Fri 8.30am–6pm (Thurs until
8.30pm), Sat 9am–noon. International telephone calls,
telegrams, fax and telex are handled by the Telehuis
(*Raadhuisstraat 48*).

Stamps can be obtained in post offices, from coin-operated
machines and from many newsstands selling postcards. Mail
boxes are red and marked PTT; the slot marked *streekpost* is
for local mail only. Allow 7 to 10 days for letters between the
Netherlands and the USA. There is also an express mail
service (*expresspost*) for urgent mail. Call for information on
postal services, (☎*0017 — free*). Telegrams can be sent from
any post office or over the telephone (☎*009*).

Public telephones are green and marked *telefoon*. They are
found in post offices, cafés, museums, large department stores
and occasionally in the street. Dialing instructions are given in
numerous languages (including Esperanto). Some telephones
take only 25ct coins, while others take 25ct, Fl.1 and Fl.2.5
coins. Coins must be inserted before dialing. The dialing code
for Amsterdam and Schiphol is 020, which should be omitted
when dialing within the city. The ringing signal is a long, low
intermittent tone, the busy signal a higher and more rapid
tone. A three-tone sound indicates the number is not available.
Public telephones have an amplifying button.

International calls should be preceded by 09 and the country
code (e.g., 1 for the USA), then the number minus the initial 0
digit of the area code. Country codes are listed in the telephone
directory, which contains instructions in English. See also
Telephone services in *Useful Addresses*.

Museums

Most museums are closed on Sun morning, all day Mon and on
certain public holidays. If planning to visit several museums,
buy a *Museumkaart* (museum card), which gives free access to
the 300 museums listed on the card (although for some special
exhibitions, an entrance fee may be charged). The
Museumkaart, valid from Jan 1–Dec 31, is sold at VVV
(tourist) offices and in major museums.

Public rest rooms

There are very few public rest rooms in Amsterdam. You will
find clean rest rooms in railway stations, museums, art
galleries, cafés and major department stores such as the
Bijenkorf and Vroom en Dreesmann. Expect to pay about 25ct
in railway stations and department stores.

Electric current
The electric current is 220V. Plugs are two-pin round, standard European.

Laws and regulations
The Dutch Criminal Code certainly does not read like a manifesto for license, yet many visitors are astonished, even shocked, by the permissive attitude adopted in Amsterdam and other large cities toward soft drugs, prostitution and pornography, which are to a large extent decriminalized. There are limits, however, and you should not assume that a practice is legal simply because it is widespread.

Customs and etiquette
Holland is relaxed about etiquette and there are few unusual conventions. People usually say: "*dag* (good morning/afternoon)," on entering or leaving a store; in restaurants you will usually be exhorted to: "*eet smakelijk* (enjoy your meal)," on being served; and at the end of the meal asked: "*heeft het gesmaakt?* (did you enjoy your meal?)." Other cultural quirks include leaving front-room curtains undrawn at night and treating dogs with the reverence other countries bestow on holy cows.

Tipping
In restaurants and cafés in the Netherlands, service charges and sales tax are almost invariably included in the price (*inclusief btw en bediening*) and you need not leave any additional tip unless you want to show your appreciation for the service. Taxi fares also include service and taxes, but drivers still expect an additional tip. Small tips are given to hairdressers, porters and cloakroom attendants, but not cinema ushers.

Disabled visitors
The provisions for disabled people in Holland are generally good, although in cities such as Amsterdam there are numerous obstacles to mobility such as steep, narrow staircases in old buildings, and uneven, narrow sidewalks often blocked with cars. Netherlands Railways (NS) will provide information and assistance for disabled people on request (☎(030) 351253 Mon–Fri 8.30am–4pm). General information and advice can also be obtained from **Mobility International Nederland** (*Postbus 165, 6560 AD Groesbeek* ☎(08891) 1744). There is a useful booklet available, called *The Handicapped*, listing hotels, restaurants and sights accessible to the disabled, published by the Netherlands Board of Tourism.

Local and foreign publications
The monthly *Uitkrant*, which is available at the **Uit Buro** (*Leidseplein 26*), provides a comprehensive listing in Dutch of theater, dance, galleries, music and other events happening in Amsterdam. The VVV's weekly English guide *Amsterdam This Week* is available at tourist offices, hotels, etc. and lists selected events.

KLM's magazine *Holland Herald* contains a short listings section and some restaurant tips.

Newsstands and English bookstores are listed under *Books and newspapers* in *Shopping*.

Useful addresses

Tourist information
The VVV (tourist office) is located opposite Centraal Station
(*Stationsplein 10* ☎ *(020) 266444* ● *12324; write to: Postbus
3901, 1001 AS Amsterdam. Open Oct 1–Easter Mon–Sat 9am–
7pm, Sun 10am–1.30pm, 2.30–5.30pm; Easter–Sept 30 daily
8.45am–11pm*). There are also VVV offices at Leidsestraat 104
and on the A2 as you drive into the city, both open Easter–
Sept 30. Tourist offices outside Amsterdam usually close Sun.
    American Express Travel Service (*Damrak 66*
☎ *(020) 262042*) is a valuable source of information for any
traveler in need of help, advice or emergency services.

Telephone services
Directory inquiries   Holland ☎008, abroad ☎0018
Travel information   ANWB ☎(070) 313131
Telegrams   ☎009 (free number)

Post offices
Central Post Office (Hoofdpostkantoor PTT)   Nieuwe Zijds
Voorburgwal 182 ☎(020) 5558911
Branch post offices are often located in large department stores
such as the Bijenkorf and Vroom en Dreesmann.
Telehuis   Raadhuisstraat 48 (for international telephone calls,
telegrams, fax and telex facilities).

Tour operators
The following companies organize bus excursions in and
around Amsterdam:
American Express   Damrak 66 ☎(020) 262042
Holland International   Damrak 7 ☎(020) 222550
Lindbergh   Damrak 26 ☎(020) 222766

Canal boats
Most canal tours last 1hr.
Holland International   Prins Hendrikkade, opposite Centraal
Station ☎(020) 227788
Kooy   Oude Turfmarkt 125, near Spui ☎(020) 233810
Lovers   Prins Hendrikkade, opposite Centraal Station
☎(020) 222181 (facilities for disabled)
Noord-Zuid   Stadhouderskade 25 (departs from near the
Rijksmuseum and follows an attractive and unusual route)
☎(020) 791370

Airlines
British Airways   Stadhouderskade 2 ☎(020) 852211
British Caledonian   Rokin 134 ☎(020) 262440
KLM   Leidseplein 1 ☎(020) 493633
Pan Am   Leidseplein 29 ☎(020) 262021
TWA   Singel 504 ☎(020) 262277

Coaches and youth fares
Magic Bus   Rokin 38 ☎(020) 264434
Budget Bus   Rokin 10 ☎(020) 275151
Transalpino   Rokin 34 ☎(020) 239922
NBBS   (youth fares) Dam 17 ☎(020) 237686

Major libraries
British Council Library   Keizersgracht 343 ☎(020) 223644

Openbare Centrale Bibliotheek   Prinsengracht 587
☎(020) 265065 (the central public library)
Rijksmuseum   Stadhouderskade 42 ☎(020) 732121 (reference
books on art and artists; closed Sat and Sun)

Places of worship
Begijnhofkapel (Catholic)   Begijnhof 30 ☎(020) 221918
English Church (Anglican)   Groenburgwal 42 ☎(020) 248877
English Reformed Church (Presbyterian)   Begijnhof 48
☎(020) 249665

Consulates in Amsterdam
Many countries have a consulate in Amsterdam.
Austria   Weteringschans 106 ☎(020) 268033
Belgium   Herengracht 541 ☎(020) 248771
Denmark   De Ruyterkade 139 ☎(020) 234145
Finland   Herengracht 462 ☎(020) 249090
France   Vijzelgracht 2 ☎(020) 248346
Germany, West   De Lairessestraat 172 ☎(020) 736245
Greece   Keizergracht 411 ☎(020) 243671
Iceland   Herengracht 176 ☎(020) 262658
Italy   Herengracht 609 ☎(020) 240043
Japan   Keizersgracht 634 ☎(020) 243581
Luxembourg   Herengracht 507 ☎(020) 231486
Norway   De Ruyterkade 107 ☎(020) 242331
Portugal   Noorderstraat 7 ☎(020) 270885
Spain   Jacob Obrechtstraat 51 ☎(020) 796591
Sweden   De Ruijterkade 107 ☎(020) 242699
Switzerland   Johannes Vermeerstraat 16 ☎(020) 644231
United Kingdom   Koningslaan 44 ☎(020) 764343
United States   Museumplein 19 ☎(020) 645661

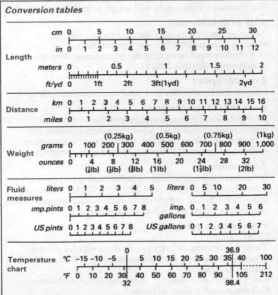

17

Emergency information

Emergency services
Police ☎222222
Ambulance ☎5555555
Fire ☎212121

Hospital
The main hospital is the Academisch Medisch Centrum, Meibergdreef 9 ☎(020) 5669111 (general) or (020) 5663333 (first-aid team). Take the metro to Holendrecht.

Medical emergencies
Doctors' and dentists' 24hr service ☎(020) 642111

First aid
First aid can be obtained from the Eerste Hulp kruispost, Oude Zijds Voorburgwal 127 ☎(020) 249031

All-night pharmacy
Pharmacists are open Mon–Fri 8am (or 9am)–5.30pm. For information on weekend services and all-night pharmacists ☎(020) 948709

Help line
SOS Telefonische Hulpdienst ☎(020) 161666

Automobile accidents
— Do not admit liability or incriminate yourself.
— Ask any witness(es) to stay and give a statement.
— Contact the police.
— Exchange names, addresses, car details and insurance company details with any other drivers involved.
— Give a statement to the police who will compile a report that insurance companies will accept as authoritative.

Car breakdowns
— Put on flashing hazard warning lights, and place a warning triangle 50m (55yds) behind the car.
— Telephone police or ring the Stadsdienst Wegenwacht (road patrol) ☎(020) 268251

Lost passport
Contact the local police and your consulate immediately.

Lost travelers cheques
Notify the local police immediately, then follow the instructions provided with your travelers cheques, or contact the issuing company. Contact your consulate or American Express if you are stranded with no money.

Lost property
If you have lost something on public transport, go to GVB, Prins Hendrikkade 108–114 ☎(020) 5514911. Report all losses to the police immediately as insurance companies may not accept a claim without a police report.

Emergency phrases
Help! *Help!*
There has been an accident. *Er is een ongeluk gebeurd.*
Where is the nearest telephone/hospital? *Waar is hier een telefoon/ziekenhuis?*
Call a doctor/ambulance! *Roep een dokter/ambulance!*
Call the police! *Roep de politie!*

Time chart

The Counts of Holland

c.1225	Small settlement of fishermen on the Amstel.
c.1270	Construction of a dam on the Amstel.
1275	Count Floris V of Holland granted Amsterdam exemption from tolls – the first document to refer to Amsterdam.
Late 13thC	Conflict between Counts of Holland and Bishops of Utrecht; Count Floris V of Holland was assassinated and his son died 2yrs later; Holland then passed to John of Hainault, who defeated the Bishop of Utrecht and installed his brother Gwijde as Bishop. In 1300 Gwijde granted Amsterdam its first charter.
1317	Amsterdam was finally annexed to Holland.
1345	The Miracle of the Host brought pilgrims to Amsterdam; in the same year Count William IV of Holland died and the county passed to the son of his sister, Margaretha, wife of Ludwig of Bavaria. This led to feuds between "Hooks" and "Cods".
Mid-14thC	Amsterdam became an important entrepôt for goods from N Germany, the Baltic and Flanders, especially beer and grain.
c.1400	First election of burgomasters; town hall built.

The Burgundians

1428	Philip the Good, Duke of Burgundy, acquired Holland from his cousin Jacoba of Bavaria. Burgundy, now controlling much of the Low Countries, pursued a policy of centralization that eroded the privileges enjoyed by the cities; but the *Pax Burgundica* brought stability and prosperity to trading cities, especially Amsterdam, which vied with the Hanseatic League for Baltic trade.
1477	Death of Charles the Bold, son of Philip the Good. He was succeeded by his daughter, Mary of Burgundy, who restored the privileges to the cities in the *Groote Privilegie* to secure the loyalty of the Low Countries. She married Maximilian Hapsburg, later Holy Roman Emperor, who in 1489 granted Amsterdam the privilege of placing the imperial crown above its coat of arms.
1496	Philip the Fair, son of Mary and Maximilian, wed Juana the Mad, heiress to Castile and Aragon.
1500	Birth of Charles V, their son.
1515	Charles V assumed control of the Low Countries and of Spanish and German territories.
1535	A group of Anabaptists (radical Protestants), following the example of Münster (1533), seized Amsterdam town hall, but were evicted the following day and executed.
1555	Charles V abdicated in favor of his son, Philip II of Spain. Philip pursued an increasingly intolerant policy towards Protestantism and tried to assert the power of the crown over cities and nobles.
1566	The Iconoclasm (*Beeldenstorm*), an outburst of popular unrest, during which numerous Catholic works of art were destroyed.
1568	William of Orange led the Dutch Revolt against Spain; beginning of the Eighty Years' War.

1576	Pacification of Ghent briefly united 17 provinces of the Low Countries, but stalled on religious grounds.
1578	Amsterdam, previously loyal to the Catholic (Spanish) side, finally converted to the Protestant side in a peaceful revolution (*Alteratie*).
1579	Union of Utrecht was signed by the seven northern provinces of the Netherlands, guaranteeing mutual assistance yet leaving provinces with considerable independence.
1581	Northern provinces renounced Philip II as their sovereign.
1585	Antwerp fell to the Spanish and Amsterdam seized the chance to attract trade; the influx of refugees from Antwerp also benefited Amsterdam economically.

The Republic

1588	The defeat of the Spanish Armada eroded Spanish naval power. Beginning of Holland's Golden Age, a period of economic prosperity and scientific and artistic brilliance.
1594–97	Willem Barents made several unsuccessful attempts to discover a northern route to China.
1594	Nine Amsterdam merchants established the Compagnie van Verre to exploit the spice trade; Cornelis de Houtman discovered Java.
1599	The Compagnie's second expedition to the East Indies yielded 400 percent profits.
1602	Dutch East India Company established.
1603–11	Construction of Amsterdam's Zuiderkerk, the first Dutch Protestant church to be built.
1604	Publication of *De Jure Praedae* by Hugo Grotius proclaimed freedom of the seas.
1609	The plan of the three canals was drawn up.
1609–21	A 12yr truce with Spain was concluded; during this period a dispute flared up between two Protestant factions – the Remonstrants and Counter-Remonstrants – leading to the execution of Van Oldenbarnevelt and the imprisonment of Grotius.
1620	The Pilgrim Fathers departed from Delfshaven on the *Speedwell*, bound for the New World.
1621	Dutch West India Company established.
1626	Peter Minuit purchased Manhattan from Indians for 60 guilders ($24) and built a fort at the s end of the island. This became the settlement of New Amsterdam, which in 1664 ejected the Dutch governor Pieter Stuyvesant in favor of the English; the settlement was then renamed New York.
1628	Descartes settled in Amsterdam.
1632	A university, the Athenaeum Illustre, was established in Amsterdam.
1634–37	Tulip fever led to spectacular price increases, which then collapsed causing many bankruptcies.
1642	Rembrandt painted the *Night Watch*; his wife Saskia died in the same year.
1642–43	Abel Tasman, searching for a route to S America through the East Indies, discovered Tasmania and New Zealand.
1648	The Treaty of Münster concluded the Eighty Years' War; in the same year work began on a new town hall for Amsterdam.

1652	Dutch settlement established at Cape Town.
1652–54	First Anglo-Dutch War broke out as a result of the English Navigation Act.
1665–67	Second Anglo-Dutch War, during which Admiral de Ruyter sailed up the Medway and set fire to the English fleet.
1672	Louis XIV invaded the Netherlands.
1672–74	Third Anglo-Dutch War.
1683–88	John Locke, the English philosopher, in Holland.
1685	Revocation of the Edict of Nantes by Louis XIV brought a flood of Huguenot refugees from France.
1688	The Glorious Revolution: Stadholder William III of Holland and his wife Mary became King and Queen of Great Britain.
1697	Czar Peter the Great visited Amsterdam to study shipbuilding.
18thC	Decline of Amsterdam's role as an entrepôt due to competition from France and England.
1747	French invasion; civil unrest in Amsterdam.
1780–84	Fourth Anglo-Dutch War caused by Dutch assistance to American rebels.
1782	Persuaded by John Adams, the Netherlands was the first European government to recognize the United States.
1792–95	Batavian Republic established by Dutch radicals aided by French revolutionary troops.
1806	The Kingdom of the Netherlands was established with Louis Napoleon as head of state.

The Kingdom of the Netherlands

1813	Liberation of the Netherlands; creation of a Kingdom under William I; this briefly reunited the N and S Netherlands.
1830	The Belgian Revolt; Belgium (formerly S Netherlands) became an independent state.
1848	In the Year of Revolutions a new Dutch constitution drafted by Thorbecke was approved.
1876	Construction of the North Sea Canal brought new prosperity to Amsterdam.
1901	The Housing Act led to dramatic improvement in the design of public housing.
1928	Olympic Games held in Amsterdam.
1932	Completion of the Afsluitdijk, a dike enclosing the Zuider Zee, to create the IJsselmeer.
1934	Riots in the Jordaan.
1940	Holland capitulated to the invading German army after the bombing of Rotterdam.
1941	Amsterdam dock workers went on strike in protest at the deportation of Jews.
1942	Japan occupied the Dutch East Indies.
1944–45	Liberation of Holland.
1949	Dutch East Indies achieved independence; the Republic of Indonesia was created.
Mid-1960s	Provo demonstrations in Amsterdam resulted in short-lived radical policies such as free municipal bicycles and public electric cars (*Witcars*).
1970s	Clashes in Amsterdam over metro construction, housing, squatting and new opera house.
1986	Completion of new opera house (*Muziektheater*) at Waterlooplein.
1987	Completion of new town hall (*Stadhuis*).

Architecture

As befits a trading city, Amsterdam's principal buildings are merchants' homes, warehouses, shops, weigh houses, banks, exchanges and insurance offices. Small-scale architecture has always flourished in Amsterdam and most styles are to be found here, trimmed to fit the narrow facades on the canals. What is delightful about Amsterdam is the profuse detail, from the sculpture that adorns gable tops to the witty facade stones illustrating the trade or name of the house owner. Interior design in shops, cafés and restaurants is equally diverse, ranging from creaking, brown, wooden interiors of traditional cafés to ultramodern buildings.

Gothic relics

The street pattern of the Middle Ages – and something of the social pattern as well – is preserved in the narrow lanes around Amsterdam's two pre-Reformation parish churches, the Oude Kerk and Nieuwe Kerk (old and new churches). After Amsterdam's conversion to Protestantism in 1578, the numerous convents and monasteries of the old city were used for secular purposes – as orphanage, university, hospital or barracks – leaving only the lovely Begijnhof on Spui and the two chapels s of Oude Hoogstraat as reminders of the city's Catholic origins. Stringent town-planning regulations in the 17thC also led to the virtual extinction of the picturesque wooden Gothic houses, which were a notorious fire hazard in

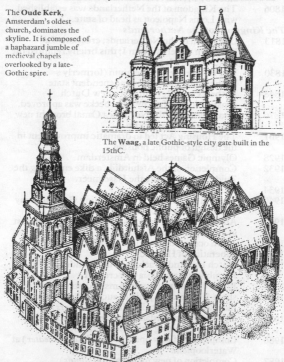

The **Oude Kerk**, Amsterdam's oldest church, dominates the skyline. It is composed of a haphazard jumble of medieval chapels overlooked by a late-Gothic spire.

The **Waag**, a late Gothic-style city gate built in the 15thC.

the crowded, industrious city. Here and there, however, the odd glimpse of a jettied wall indicates a resilient medieval framework to which a more modern facade has been attached.

Dutch Renaissance

Dutch Renaissance architecture was a late and rather eccentric development of Italian and French Renaissance styles. The early Dutch Renaissance emerged under the Emperor Charles V, when Dutch architects were able to travel to Italy, while Italian architects were often employed by Dutch patrons. The Revolt of the Netherlands severed these links with Italy, however, and architects of the late Dutch Renaissance had to rely largely on books of engravings. The most influential of these source books was published by Hans Vredeman de Vries in Antwerp in 1577, illustrating a style that had much in common with the explosive Mannerism of Michelangelo. The best examples of this neurotic style in Amsterdam are the ornate gates of the Orphanage (now the Amsterdams Historisch Museum) and the Athenaeum Illustre.

Hendrick de Keyser (1565–1621) was city architect at just the moment Amsterdam's economy began to take off, and he was appointed to build three new Protestant churches, several spires, the first stock exchange and many private houses. One soon learns to spot a De Keyser building by its animated step-gabled facade of whitened sandstone set off against rosy red brick. Lieven de Key's Stadhuis in Leiden and Vleeshal in Haarlem are other striking examples of this style.

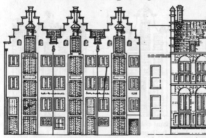
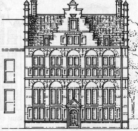

The **Groenland Pakhuizen** and **House on the Three Canals**, two elegant examples of 17thC architecture distinguished by their fine step gables.

The **Westerkerk**, begun in 1620 by Hendrick de Keyser, built in Dutch Renaissance style.

The **Montelbaanstoren** (1512), with 17thC spire.

Culture, history and background

Dutch Classicism

De Keyser's Mannerism was a touch too swashbuckling and jovial for the humorless temperament of the Dutch Calvinist rulers of the second quarter of the 17thC. They much preferred the sober and rational Classicism of Jacob van Campen (1595–1657). Constantijn Huygens, the powerful secretary to Prince Frederik Henry, put his weight behind Van Campen because he "admonished Gothic curly foolery with the stately Roman, and drove old Heresy away before older Truth." Van Campen's stately style can be seen in the house at Keizersgracht 177 built in 1624 for the Coymans brothers, the pleasingly compact Mauritshuis in Den Haag (1633–44) and the Royal Palace (formerly Town Hall) in Amsterdam (1648–55). These simple, reserved buildings reflect the quiet dignity of the Dutch Golden Age as perfectly as do the paintings of Vermeer.

Philips Vingboons (1608–75) developed a less austere Classicism that retained a lingering fondness for the Gothic gable. Vingboons' distinctive contribution to the Amsterdam skyline was the neck gable – a simplified step gable with ornate claw pieces – as in his four stately houses built for the Cromhout family at Herengracht 364–70. His brother Justus Vingboons' 1660 Trippenhuis on Kloveniersburgwal shows an even more stately form of Dutch Classicism.

Daniel Stalpaert (1615–76) had a significant impact on Amsterdam as city architect during the mid-17thC. His first

A 1638 **neck-gabled house** on Herengracht, built by Philips Vingboons.

An elegant example of a 17thC **bell-gabled house**.

A stately 18thC **canal house** with a Louis XIV-style cornice.

The balanced classical lines of the **Stadhuis** (town hall), begun by J. van Campen in 1648, express the solid confidence of the Dutch Golden Age.

task was to complete the Town Hall after Jacob van Campen mysteriously dropped out of the project, and he then went on to design a number of massive public buildings such as the austere 1656 Admiralty Arsenal on Prins Hendrikkade, the 1661 Prinsenhof on Oude Zijds Voorburgwal, the German Synagogue on Waterlooplein and the Amstelhof on the River Amstel.

Even more sober were the residences built by Adriaen Dortsman in the 1660s and 1670s on fashionable sites close to the Amstel. Dortsman's houses stand out sharply against the colorful pluralism of Amsterdam, with their grim, gray sandstone facades purged of all decoration – except for lithe sculptures of Grecian gods perched on the balustrades. Few Dortsman houses have survived intact, but there is a splendid pair at Keizersgracht 672–74, housing the Museum Van Loon.

French styles of the 18thC

After the decline of Classicism at the end of the Golden Age, Dutch architecture fell under the spell of French styles introduced by Protestant refugees who fled from France after Louis XIV's Revocation of the Edict of Nantes in 1685. Daniel Marot (1661–1752) brought the grand Baroque style of Louis XIV to Holland, carefully compressing its features to fit the modest proportions of Dutch houses. This Dutch Louis XIV style is characterized by monumental double staircases, splendidly decorated centerpieces, grand entrances, and cornices laden with heavy, symmetrical decoration. A handsome example of this style is the Museum Willet-Holthuysen at Herengracht 605. The gorgeous frothy tops of Keizersgracht 244–46 and the haughty pair of neck gables at Keizersgracht 606–8 illustrate the tendency at this time for architects to be over-zealous in their work.

During the mid-18thC, the heavy Baroque symmetry of Louis XIV softened into the delicious Rococo style of Louis XV. The Herengracht and Keizersgracht élite had already spent their money on Louis XIV improvements, and so Louis XV details tend to appear on more modest dwellings on the less prestigious canals such as Singel, Prinsengracht and Kloveniersburgwal. The style is characterized by capricious bell gables and other touches of whimsy. Prinsengracht 126 shows this style at its most flamboyant.

After the sensual abandon of Rococo, a sober reaction set in – the Louis XVI style – which reached Amsterdam from France in the 1770s. During this cooling-off period, exactly 100 years after the gray sobriety of Dortsman and Stalpaert, necks, bells and crests were brutally chopped off to be replaced by flat cornices. This resulted in the permanent ruin of large tracts of Amsterdam's skyline, though the consequences were far more dire in Utrecht, Delft and Den Haag.

The French occupation in the late 18th and early 19thC brought the Empire style to Holland. This was a continuation of the geometrical Louis XVI style, with various oddities such as cushion doors and palm motifs. The economy of Amsterdam was in poor shape at this time, however, and the Empire style had little impact beyond the decoration of fanlights with attractive geometrical designs.

Eclecticism

A somber tone persisted through to the Greek Revival architecture of the early 19thC, as seen in the horrendous law courts at Prinsengracht 436 and the solid 1840 Willemspoort at the w end of Haarlemmerstraat.

Culture, history and background

After the economic doldrums of the French occupation, Amsterdam's economy began to take off with the opening of the North Holland Canal in 1823 and the Amsterdam-Haarlem railway in 1839. The palaces on the Golden Bend of Herengracht ceased to be fashionable and new mansions were commissioned on the edge of the Vondelpark or overlooking the Amstel. Architects flirted with various historical styles, from the musty Old Dutch Renaissance style to the fussy neo-Gothic.

Architects of public buildings tended to adopt a diplomatic compromise between these two styles, although P. J. H. Cuypers (1827–1921) could not fail to conceal his strong Catholic prejudices in his neo-Gothic designs for the Rijksmuseum (1876–85), Centraal Station (1881–89) and numerous churches. On the other hand, A. N. Weissman's Stedelijk Museum is a solid piece of neo-Renaissance design. Eventually, the dispute was solved by the adoption of a haughty international Classicism, seen in A. L. van Gendt's dignified 1888 Concertgebouw, which could almost belong in Vienna.

Art Nouveau architecture failed to make much headway in Amsterdam. The finest Art Nouveau work in Amsterdam was produced by the versatile Gerrit van Arkel, who skipped deftly from neo-Renaissance (Heiligeweg 35) and neo-Gothic (Plantage Middenlaan 36) to outrageous Art Nouveau in his 1905 office building overlooking Keizersgracht at Leliegracht.

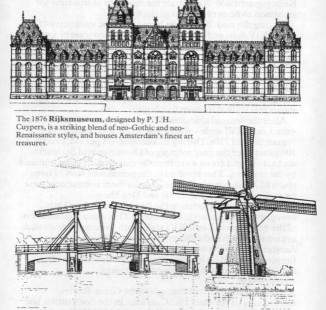

The 1876 **Rijksmuseum**, designed by P. J. H. Cuypers, is a striking blend of neo-Gothic and neo-Renaissance styles, and houses Amsterdam's finest art treasures.

The **Magere Brug**, the only traditional wooden drawbridge still standing over the Amstel.

An example of an octagonal **poldermolen**.

Modern architecture

The Amsterdam Beurs (stock exchange) on Damrak, completed in 1903 by H. P. Berlage (1856–1934), represents a decisive break with 19thC eclecticism and a firm assertion of a new architectural ethic based on rigorous proportions and an honest use of building materials.

Berlage was also responsible for drawing up the Expansion Plan for Amsterdam Zuid (1905–17), which brought an end to the ruthless urban growth of the 19thC and a return to the harmonious ideals of the 17thC. The Plan was drawn up under the 1901 Housing Act, which required municipal authorities to subsidize and control the construction of working-class housing. The first wave of new housing after the 1901 Act was designed by the Amsterdam School, a group of passionately idealistic socialist architects who developed a brilliantly inventive organic style and launched it with gusto in the 1911–16 design for the Scheepvaarthuis. This large office block on Prins Hendrikkade is encrusted with fabulous seafaring motifs. Dazzling blocks of surreal workers' housing were later designed by Michel de Klerk (1884–1923) at Spaarndammerbuurt in west Amsterdam and at Henriette Ronnerplein in the south. P. L. Kramer (1881–1961) displayed similarly restless energy in his matching blocks on P. L. Takstraat, and in many highly unusual bridge designs.

Despite its unbounded creative vitality, the Amsterdam School style lasted barely a decade. It lost much of its impetus

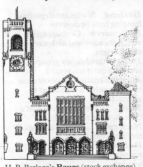

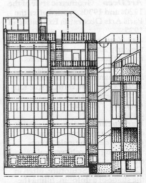

H. P. Berlage's **Beurs** (stock exchange), built in 1903, heralds the modern age of architecture.

The **Moederhuis**, a colorful, functional building designed by A. van Eyck in 1978.

The **Muziektheater** (opera house) is a modern design created by Cees Dam and Wilhelm Holzbauer and was opened in 1986.

with the early death of De Klerk in 1923, but there were deeper reasons for its demise, such as its high production costs and its concentration on surface decoration.

The Dutch Modern Movement architects roundly renounced the theatrical flights of the Amsterdam School. They were inspired by a rational, rather than romantic, socialism and sought to design spacious, light-filled buildings that were crisply functional. The Cinétol at Tolstraat 154 (recently converted to a public library) is one of the best examples of Modern Movement architecture in Amsterdam, designed in 1926 by J. A. Brinkman and L. C. van der Vlugt. A much later building in this same tradition is the Van Gogh Museum, designed by Gerrit Rietveld (1888–1964).

The key figure in the development of postwar Amsterdam architecture is Aldo van Eyck, whose 1978 Moederhuis combines functionalism with an enchanting rainbow of colors. The city council's "compact city" policy in the 1980s has led to the filling in of numerous gap sites in the Nieuwmarkt and the Jordaan areas with imaginative small-scale housing projects, and there are signs of a new school of Amsterdam architecture emerging in buildings such as Theo Bosch's P. C. Hooftgebouw on Singel and Hertzberger's Montessorischool on Apollolaan.

Glossary of architectural terms

Art Deco Geometric style of the 1920s and 1930s, named after the Paris Arts Décoratifs Exhibition of 1925

Art Nouveau Sinuous style of the early 20thC, deriving inspiration from natural forms

Basilica Church with nave higher than the flanking aisles

Bell gable An 18thC gable top in the shape of a bell

Capital The carved top of a column

Cartouche A decorative frame enclosing a window or panel

Caryatides Female figures supporting an architectural element

Claw piece Sculpture, often in the shape of a dolphin, filling the steps of a gable

Cornucopia Sculpture depicting a horn overflowing with fruit, symbolizing abundance

Entablature The horizontal structure supported by the columns in Classical architecture, comprising architrave, frieze and cornice

Facade stone A decorative stone attached to the front of a house to indicate the address; the stones often refer to a trade or are puns on the owner's surname

Fanlight Window above a door, admitting light to the hallway

Gable Ornate upper part of a wall between the sloping roofs

Garland Sculpture depicting hanging fruit or flowers

Hall church Gothic church in which the nave and aisles are of equal height

Hofje Almshouses grouped around a quiet courtyard

Mask Renaissance decoration showing either a human or an animal face

Nave The central section of a church, running w to E

Neck gable A gable with an elevated centerpiece

Pediment Triangular or rounded form above door or window

Pilaster A flat column projecting slightly from a wall

Putto Cute sculpture representing a small boy, cherub or cupid

Sash window An 18thC window that slides up and down in its frame

Spout gable A simple triangular gable often used on warehouses

Step gable A Gothic gable ascending by a series of steps

Strapwork Mannerist decoration curled at the edges like old parchment or leather

Tracery Pattern of intersecting ribs in windows and walls of Gothic buildings

Transepts Transverse arms of a cruciform church

Dutch painting

To most people Dutch painting means the art of the Golden
Age: the peaceful landscapes of Jacob van Ruisdael and
Hobbema, the quiet domestic interiors of Vermeer and De
Hoogh, the merry banqueting scenes of Frans Hals and the
vibrant portraits by Rembrandt.

The Rijksmuseum in Amsterdam boasts the world's finest
collection of Dutch art of the Golden Age, and there are also
excellent collections at the Mauritshuis in Den Haag and at the
Museum Boymans-van Beuningen in Rotterdam. Other well-
known Dutch artists are Van Gogh, to whom a museum is
devoted in Amsterdam, and the abstract painter Piet Mondrian,
whose work can be studied in Den Haag's Gemeentemuseum.

It is also interesting while in Holland to explore some of the
less well-known areas of Dutch art, such as the exquisite Delft
Masters of the 15thC, the Haarlem Mannerists of the 16thC and
the Impressionists of the 19thC.

Early Netherlandish painting

Early Dutch painting has its roots in the realism of Flemish
Masters such as Jan van Eyck and Hans Memling, who were
active in the Southern Netherlands (present-day Belgium)
during the 15thC. The most notable Dutch artist of this period
was Geertgen tot Sint Jans (1460s–90s), whose fascination
with rich jewelry and clothes is typically Flemish.

The most bizarre artist of the 15thC was Hieronymus Bosch
(c.1450–1516), whose paintings present a disturbing vision of
burning cities, erotic fantasies and fabulous beasts, often
verging on the surreal.

Renaissance

Hints of the Renaissance can be detected in early 16thC
paintings by Jan Mostaert (c.1475–c.1555) from Haarlem,
whose works abound in delightful details, and Jacob Cornelisz.
van Oostsanen (c.1470–1533): But it was Van Oostsanen's
pupil Jan van Scorel (1495–1562) who introduced the
techniques of the Renaissance to the Northern Netherlands.
As keeper of the Vatican art collection from 1522–23 under the
Dutch Pope Adriaen IV, Van Scorel was able to study the
works of Leonardo da Vinci and Raphael. Paintings such as his
Mary Magdalene in the Rijksmuseum are unmistakably Italian
in style, although lingering traces of Flemish realism can be
detected in the group portraits he painted in Utrecht and
Haarlem. His pupil Maerten van Heemskerck (1498–1574)
displays a similar blend of Renaissance and Flemish styles in
his portraits.

A more dynamic and fluid style was achieved by Lucas van
Leyden (1494–1533) in works such as *The Last Judgment*,
which hangs in the Lakenhal in his home town of Leiden, and
the *Dance around the Golden Calf* in the Rijksmuseum. A
strange, exotic Mannerism was developed in the nearby town
of Haarlem by artists such as Cornelis Cornelisz (1562–1638).

The Golden Age

The Golden Age, which lasted for much of the 17thC,
produced the type of art that is thought of as typically Dutch:
placid landscapes with grazing cattle, tranquil domestic scenes,
dramatic sea battles, empty white churches, and portraits of
civic guards sporting magnificent mustaches. During this
period, the church ceased to be an important patron of the arts,
and merchants, burgomasters and even shopkeepers became
avid collectors of paintings. This led to a shift from religious

themes to mundane subjects such as quacks, prostitutes, household tasks and local landscapes.

The mood of the Golden Age is faithfully reflected in group portraits by Frans Hals (c.1580–1666), which range from merry civic guards on festive occasions to grim, tight-lipped governors of hospitals and old people's homes.

Holland's greatest artist is Rembrandt van Rijn (1606–69), who in 1632 moved from Leiden to Amsterdam. He painted a number of group portraits, such as *The Anatomy Lesson of Dr Tulp* (1632), *Night Watch* (1642) and *The Wardens of the Amsterdam Drapers' Guild* (1661). The mysterious golden light that suffuses these works is also present in his numerous portraits, historical scenes and biblical episodes. Rembrandt was also a skilled etcher, as can be seen in the remarkable collection of portraits and landscapes in the Rembrandthuis.

Numerous pupils studied under Rembrandt in his atelier on Jodenbreestraat, including Gerrit Dou, Ferdinand Bol, Nicholas Maes and the mysterious Carel Fabritius (1622–54). Fabritius may have influenced Johannes Vermeer (1632–75), whose meticulous paintings convey a serene, almost spiritual quality. Vermeer produced about 30 paintings in his lifetime, of which six remain in Holland. Perhaps the most extraordinary is the *View of Delft* (c.1658) in the Mauritshuis, which the French writer Marcel Proust praised as "the most beautiful painting in the world." The Mauritshuis also owns the simple, enthralling *Head of a Girl* (c.1660), while the Rijksmuseum boasts another fond view of Delft, and two tranquil portraits – *The Kitchen Maid* (c.1658) and *Woman Reading a Letter* (c.1662) – that demonstrate Vermeer's exceptional skill at capturing the elusive qualities of light.

Other Delft painters of the 17thC include Pieter de Hoogh (1629–c.1684), who painted domestic interiors rich in spatial complexity, and Gerrit Houckgeest (1600–61), painter of whitewashed church interiors. The purity of Protestant churches also preoccupied the supremely fastidious Haarlem artist Pieter Saenredam (1597–1665).

Landscape painting also flourished during the Golden Age, when artists acquired a taste for the low horizons, cloudy skies and watery meadows of Holland. Salomon van Ruysdael (c.1600–70) was fond of depicting tranquil, windless days, while his nephew Jacob van Ruisdael (c.1628–82) preferred stormy, changeable skies as a romantic backdrop to his scenes. Hobbema (1638–1709) was more drawn by tranquil vistas, while Jan van Goyen (1596–1656) portrayed the bleak, desolate scenery of the eastern provinces. Under the influence of the Italianizing landscape painters of Utrecht such as Jan Both, Albert Cuyp (1620–91) from Dordrecht produced idealized Dutch scenes in which the mellow golden light and the rolling landscape do not ring quite true. Much more realistic are the merry winter skating scenes painted by Hendrick Avercamp (1585–1634) of Kampen.

Still-life paintings came into vogue in the 17thC, reaching a peak of technical virtuosity in the works of Pieter Claesz. (c.1597–1661) and Willem Claesz. Heda (1599–c.1680). These somewhat academic paintings tended to conceal some hidden meaning such as transience (a tumbled glass, a history book, an extinguished pipe) or deception (a peeled lemon).

The paintings of Jan Steen (1625–79) are also packed with hidden messages, sometimes surprisingly erotic, such as the red stockings in *Woman at her Toilet* in the Rijksmuseum, which symbolized prostitution, and the oysters (a popular aphrodisiac) in *Girl Eating Oysters* in the Mauritshuis, which symbolized copulation. Other familiar symbols in these *genre* paintings (which were moralistic reminders of death or the folly of infidelity) include dead birds (symbolizing impotence), musical instruments (vanity) and needlework (domesticity).

18thC–19thC painting

Dutch art of the 18thC was a pale reflection of French styles, and perhaps the most pleasing artists were Jan de Beijer and Isaac Oudewater, who confined themselves to the careful portrayal of charming urban scenes.

A fresh vitality entered Dutch art in the middle of the 19thC when the artists of the Hague School (Haagse School), inspired by French painters of the Barbizon School, turned their attention to the peculiarities of Dutch landscape and light. The leading figure of the Hague School was Josef Israels (1824–1911), whose paintings display a sad, pensive quality, while his son Isaac Israels (1865–1934) painted cheerful impressionistic views of the dunes at Scheveningen. Other artists of the Hague School include Hendrik Weissenbruch (1824–1903), painter of watery meadows and luminous skies; Hendrik Willem Mesdag (1831–1915), a prolific marine painter; and Jacob Maris (1837–99), who depicted rainswept Dutch skies.

The Amsterdam artist George Breitner (1857–1923) used Impressionism to capture the bustle of Amsterdam in the heady days of the Industrial Revolution, while at other times his paintings showed the sad melancholy of the old port area, where he had a studio.

The languid style of the Hague School stands in sharp contrast to the feverish vitality of Vincent van Gogh (1853–90), born in the village of Nuenen near Eindhoven. Van Gogh's earliest works show the same dark tones and somber mood as the works of Josef Israels, but later, after moving to Paris and falling under the spell of Impressionism, his works became increasingly colorful and at times dazzling, particularly after his move to Arles in 1888. The Provençal landscape, which initially inspired the famous series of apple blossom paintings, quickly seems to have become oppressive, however, for two years later Van Gogh killed himself, shortly after completing the desolate *Crows over the Wheatfield*.

Modern art

Modern art in the Netherlands began with Piet Mondrian (1872–1944), a methodical artist whose lifestyle developed in perfect harmony with his art. In the early 20thC, Mondrian affected a thick bohemian beard, inhabited a cluttered atelier in Amsterdam and exhibited dreamy moonlit Symbolist paintings, but in 1912 he moved to Paris, shaved off his beard, and began to develop an increasingly abstract style. After helping to set up the De Stijl (The Style) movement in 1917, he slowly evolved his distinctive use of horizontal and vertical lines enclosing vivid blocks of primary color. Other De Stijl artists were Theo van Doesburg and Bart van der Leck.

Contemporary Dutch artists continue to experiment with a series of colors and abstractions, and the innocent optimism of the postwar years is reflected in the delightfully colorful and childlike works of Karel Appel, Constant, Corneille and Brands, who formed the Dutch branch of the international COBRA group. Works by COBRA artists and other modern Dutch artists can be seen at the Stedelijk Museum in Amsterdam and in many small commercial galleries.

Amsterdam gallery guide

There are more than 150 small commercial art galleries in Amsterdam, featuring a broad range of Dutch and international art. Many galleries are located close to the Rijksmuseum, along the streets and canals running from Leidsestraat to Vijzelstraat. Others are clustered around hotels such as the Pulitzer, which has its own gallery, and the Sonesta, which owns a superb collection of modern painting and sculpture. Events worth watching out for include Kunst RAI in June, when many Dutch and European galleries mount exhibitions at the RAI center, and the spring art fair in the Nieuwe Kerk, where several hundred major Dutch galleries exhibit works.

The *Uitkrant* (available free of charge from the Uit Buro at Leidseplein 26) provides a monthly galleries listing. Gallery owners lead unpredictable lives and it is worth phoning to check that a gallery is open before visiting. Generally, major galleries open Tues–Sat noon–6pm. A few galleries are also open Sun.

ABN Bank
Vijzelstraat 68–78. Tram 16, 24, 25 to Keizersgracht.
A long arcade with an art gallery and sidewalk neon-art installations.

Aorta
Spuistraat 189 ☎ (020) 271287 Open Wed–Sun 1–6pm. Tram 1, 2, 5, 13, 14, 17 to Dam.
A bleak post-industrial ruin – formerly the printing works of the *Algemeen Handelsblad* newspaper – featuring shows by young, experimental European artists.

Art & Architecture
J. Verhulststraat 109 ☎ (020) 626652. Open Tues–Sat 12.30–5.30pm. Tram 16 to Cornelis Schuytstraat.
For anyone interested in architectural design, it is worth tracking down this small gallery exhibiting architectural photographs and drawings, plexiglass sculpture and furniture.

Art & Project
Prinsengracht 785 ☎ (020) 220372. Open Tues–Sat 1–5pm. Tram 1, 2, 5 to Prinsengracht.
Large exhibition space featuring interesting Dutch artists such as Ger van Elk, as well as international stars such as Richard Long and Barry Flanagan.

Arti et Amicitiae
Rokin 112 ☎ (020) 233508. Open Tues–Sun 11am–5pm. Tram 4, 9, 14, 16, 24, 25 to Muntplein.
The artists' club where Mondrian exhibited his earliest works.

Elisabeth den Bieman de Haas
Nieuwe Spiegelstraat 44 ☎ (020) 261012. Open Tues–Sat 11am–5pm. Tram 6, 7, 10 to Spiegelgracht.
A pleasant gallery in the antiques district, specializing in landscapes by the Dutch Bergen School and COBRA graphics.

Canon Photo Gallery
Leidsestraat 79 ☎ (020) 254494. Open Tues–Fri noon–5.45pm, Sat 11am–4.45pm. Tram 1, 2, 5 to Keizersgracht.
A spacious gallery spread over several floors of a corner building overlooking Keizersgracht, exhibiting contemporary international photography and selling books and postcards.

Collection d'Art
Keizersgracht 516 ☎ (020) 221511. Open Tues–Sat 1–5pm. Tram 1, 2, 5 to Keizersgracht.
A major gallery exhibiting works by COBRA artists such as Appel and Abstract Expressionists including De Kooning.

'd Eendt
Spuistraat 272 ☎ (020) 265777. Open Tues–Sat 10am–6pm. Tram 1, 2, 5 to Spui.
This busy gallery specializes in international modern painting and ethnic art.

Barbara Farber
Keizersgracht 265 ☎ (020) 276343. Open Tues–Sat 1–6pm. Tram 13, 14, 17 to Westermarkt.
Barbara Farber travels regularly to

New York and delves into the studios of SoHo and the East Village to discover exciting new talents. Her Amsterdam canal house gallery, with its incongruous Old World Baroque ceiling, is often the first European gallery to show New York's shocking new.

Gamma
Keizersgracht 429
☎ *(020) 230767. Open Tues–Sat 11.30am–5.30pm. Tram 1, 2, 5 to Keizersgracht.*
Painting, sculpture and graphics, are shown here, including attractive examples of lyrical Abstractionism.

Krikhaar
Spuistraat 330 ☎ *(020) 267166. Open Tues–Sat 10.30am–6pm. Tram 1, 2, 5 to Spui.*
This well-established gallery close to Spui specializes in Dutch artists of the COBRA group such as the jovial Appel and the sensitive Corneille, together with works by older moderns such as Picasso, Chagall and Miro.

Lageman
Prinsengracht 260
☎ *(020) 220695. Open Tues–Sat 11am–5pm. Tram 13, 14, 17 to Westermarkt.*
A conventional gallery, exhibiting inexpensive works, including attractive watercolors of misty Dutch landscapes.

Lieve Hemel
Vijzelgracht 6–8
☎ *(020) 230060. Open Tues–Sat noon–6pm. Tram 16, 24, 25 to Prinsengracht.*
The full title of this gallery, Lieve hemel stoot je hoofd niet (For goodness sake don't bang your head), is not just another piece of Amsterdam whimsy, but an attempt by the gallery owners to avoid a devastating liability action brought by customers who stun themselves on the low lintel. Despite its hazards, however, this is a beautiful gallery in an atmospheric 17thC interior with low beams and precarious staircases, which specializes in contemporary Dutch Realist painting and sculpture.

Mokum
Oude Zijds Voorburgwal 334
☎ *(020) 243958. Open Tues–Sat 11am–5pm. Tram 4, 9, 14, 16, 24, 25 to Spui.*
A small gallery specializing in melancholy Dutch Surrealist works.

Nieuw Perspectief
Amstel 34 ☎ *(020) 263952. Open Tues–Fri 10am–6pm, Sat 1–5pm. Tram 4, 9, 14, 16, 24, 25 to Muntplein.*
A conscientious gallery displaying painting, photography, ceramics and jewelry produced by young Amsterdam artists who might otherwise starve in bell-gabled garrets. The prices charged are very reasonable.

Petit
Nieuwe Zijds Voorburgwal 270
☎ *(020) 267507. Open Tues–Sat noon–6pm. Tram 1, 2, 5 to Spui.*
Larger than its name suggests and presenting interesting lyrical Realist paintings and sculpture on its three floors.

Pulitzer Art Gallery
Prinsengracht 323
☎ *(020) 228333. Open Mon–Sun 9am–10pm. Tram 13, 14, 17 to Westermarkt.*
The Pulitzer Hotel's art exhibitions are held in a beautiful sunlit gallery that zigzags through the leafy garden, from the hotel entrance on Prinsengracht to the bar on Keizersgracht. Look out for other interesting galleries in the vicinity of the Pulitzer, especially on Reestraat.

Ra
Vijzelstraat 80 ☎ *(020) 265100. Open Tues–Fri noon–6pm, Sat 11am–5pm. Tram 16, 24, 25 to Prinsengracht.*
This is an exciting gallery presenting a selection of modern experimental jewelry with designs ranging from the bizarre to the outrageous.

Stichting Wonen
Leidsestraat 5 ☎ *(020) 230984. Open Mon–Fri 10am–5pm, Sat 1–5pm. Tram 1, 2, 5 to Koningsplein.*
The Stichting Wonen is a small gallery with some interesting exhibitions on architecture and town planning.

Swart
Van Breestraat 23
☎ *(020) 764736. Open Wed–Sat 2–6pm, Sun 3–5pm. Tram 2 to Jacob Obrechtstraat.*
Dynamic gallery showing recent abstract art, along with video and sculpture.

Orientation map

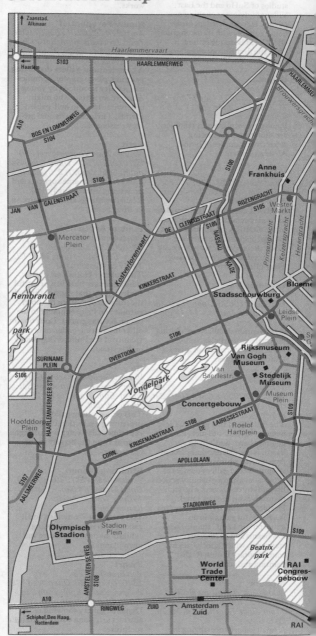

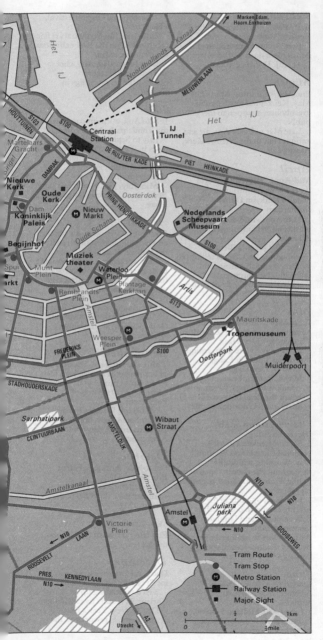

Legend:
- — Tram Route
- Tram Stop
- Ⓜ Metro Station
- ▦ Railway Station
- ◼ Major Sight

Calendar of events

February

Early Feb, International Film Festival, Rotterdam.

Feb 25, commemoration of Amsterdam dock workers' strike, 1941, at J. D. Meijerplein.

March

End Mar/beginning Apr to late May, Keukenhof gardens and greenhouses are open to the public.

Late Mar to Early Apr, art and antiques fair in the Nieuwe Kerk, Amsterdam.

April

Mid-Apr to mid-May, World Press Photo exhibition in the Nieuwe Kerk, on Dam in Amsterdam.

Late Apr to mid-Sept, cheese market on Fri mornings in Alkmaar.

Apr 30, Queen's Birthday (Koninginnedag). Stalls selling old clothes, books, furniture and ethnic food throughout Amsterdam. Lively street parties in the Jordaan.

May

Early May to mid-June, public admitted to the Japanese Garden, Clingendael, Den Haag.

Early May to late Sept, antique market on Thurs at Lange Voorhout, Den Haag.

May 4, Remembrance Day (Dodenherdenking). Ceremonies to honor the dead of World War II at the National Monument, the Dam.

May 5, Liberation Day (Bevrijdingsdag).

Second weekend in May, National Bicycle and Windmill Day. Working windmills throughout the country open to the public. Demonstrations, organized bicycle trips.

End May, opening of the herring season in ports such as Scheveningen and IJmuiden. Gourmets eagerly crowd around the fish stalls to sample the first batch of *maatjes* (cured young herring).

June

June to Aug, Royal Palace, Amsterdam, open to the public.

June 1–30, Holland Festival. International festival of music, dance and theater.

International Organ Festival, Haarlem.

Mid-June, international art fair (Kunst RAI) at the RAI exhibition center, Amsterdam.

Late June to late Aug, cheese and craft market takes place on Thurs mornings in Gouda.

July

July to Aug, open-air concerts in the Vondelpark, Amsterdam.

July to Sept, beautiful display of roses in Westbroekpark, Den Haag.

July, festival of alternative theater, Amsterdam (Zomerfestijn).

Mid-July, JVC North Sea Jazz Festival at Congresgebouw, Den Haag.

August

End Aug on Fri, open-air concert on Prinsengracht, sponsored by the Pulitzer Hotel.

Last weekend in Aug, Uitmarkt in Amsterdam. Promotion of forthcoming cultural attractions, with drama and music performances.

Late Aug to early Sept, Festival of Ancient Music (Festival van Oude Muziek) at Vredenburg, Utrecht.

September

Third Tues in Sept, State Opening of Parliament (Prinsjesdag), Den Haag. Royal procession; Queen addresses joint session of Parliament.

Mid-Sept, Jordaan Festival.

Last Sat in Sept, floral parade proceeds from Aalsmeer to Amsterdam.

October

Oct to Nov, Antiques Fair at Prinsenhof, Delft.

Oct 3, parade in Leiden to commemorate the relief of the siege in 1574.

November

End Nov, arrival of St Nicholas celebrated.

December

Dec 5, celebrations in preparation for St Nicholas Day (Dec 6).

Ten days leading up to Christmas, Gouda by candlelight.

Dec 31, New Year's Eve celebrations. Fireworks on the Dam.

When and where to go

Amsterdam is at its best in the spring, when the tulips bring color to the streets and the skies are filled with billowy clouds. In summer, Amsterdam tends to become congested and the weather is often unreliable, but there are also attractions such as open-air concerts in the *Vondelpark*.

Amsterdammers mostly go on vacation in July and many theaters, small restaurants and boutiques close at that time. Autumn can be mild and pleasant, while a visit in winter might be rewarded by the sight of animated skating scenes on the frozen canals and lakes.

Amsterdam is a compact city with a distinctive pattern of canals and streets, which, once mastered, is never forgotten. The most pleasant area for exploring is the 17thC ring of canals, the *Grachtengordel* (canal girdle), which encloses the old city in a sweeping arc. The main canals, *Herengracht*, *Keizersgracht* and *Prinsengracht* offer an endless parade of architectural styles from Renaissance to Post Modern, while the side streets, radiating from the center like the spokes of a wheel, contain many of Amsterdam's most interesting shops.

The main museums are located beyond here in the 19thC ring, which extends in a broad arc around the old city, whose boundary is marked by Singelgracht. The architecture in this area ranges from the opulent to the utilitarian and the streets tend to lack the animation of the central area.

The 20thC ring and the outlying suburbs are of considerable interest architecturally, but are otherwise somewhat dull and suburban.

Area planners and visits

The following list gives an idea of the character of Amsterdam's different areas.

Oude Zijde (Old Side — *Map 11C-E5*). Between Damrak/ Rokin and Kloveniersburgwal: Amsterdam's oldest, most historic area, packed with interest but becoming seedy N of the line of Damstraat-Oude Doelenstraat-Oude Hoogstraat, which marks the boundary of the red-light district.

Nieuwe Zijde (New Side — *Map 11C-E4*). Between Damrak/ Rokin and *Singel*: somewhat bleak due to the filling in of its canals, but still full of historic interest, especially around the Dam; has a slightly dilapidated air N of Dam, though the construction of several new hotels is helping to restore morale.

Jodenbuurt (Jewish Quarter — *Map 12E-F6*). Waterlooplein and J. D. Meijerplein: melancholy relics of Amsterdam's once-flourishing Jewish community, interspersed with controversial modern architecture. With the completion of the Muziektheater (Opera House), the area is beginning at last to recover from the bitter memory of the war and may soon become fashionable.

Grachtengordel (Canal Girdle — *Map 6, 7, 10, 11*). Amsterdam's great arc of canals: an area of outstanding architectural interest — every visit to this area reveals some new delight or detail.

Jordaan (*Map 10*). w of *Prinsengracht*: a baffling maze

of streets and canals possessing a dilapidated charm that
Amsterdammers find irresistible; jammed with small ateliers
and businesses ranging from the bohemian to the bizarre, good
brown cafés and intimate restaurants.

Plantage (*Map 8E-F7*). E of Waterlooplein: an unusual, almost
rural area of the 17thC *Grachtengordel*, with parks, gardens, a
zoo and elegant 19thC villas.

Westelijke Eilanden (*Map 11A-B4/5*). N of
Haarlemmerhouttuinen: a peaceful area of crumbling
warehouses, canals jammed with old boats, and white wooden
drawbridges; ideal for a gentle stroll on Sun morning while
waiting for the museums to open.

Oostelijke Eilanden (*Map 12C7*). E of the
Scheepvaartmuseum: interesting maritime details; various
new developments may inject fresh vigor into this somewhat
sad area.

Oud Zuid (*Map 6*). S of Singelgracht: the 19thC ring, opulent
and prosperous around the *Vondelpark* and *Rijksmuseum*;
somewhat dreary w of Hobbemakade and N of Overtoom.

Nieuw Zuid (*Map 8*). Around the Amstelkanaal: the 20thC
ring, rich in Amsterdam School architecture of the 1920s and
De Stijl buildings of the 1930s. A new business district is
developing along the S edge of the city, especially around the
World Trade Center.

Amsterdam Noord (*Map 5C4*). N of the IJ inlet: this isolated
area of Amsterdam retains a distinctive North Holland
identity, with bright green wooden houses strung out along
ancient dikes such as the Nieuwendammerdijk and
Buiksloterdijk.

On a short visit to Amsterdam, try not to cram in too much
sightseeing. Visit one or two museums, of course, and take a
boat trip on the canals, but you would be missing an important
dimension of Amsterdam if you did not sample the quiet
conviviality of a Dutch brown café or while away an hour or
two exploring small shops and boutiques. It is generally a good
idea to spend cold or wet days in museums, and hope for sunny
weather to explore the canals.

Remember that most museums are closed on Sun morning
(with the exception of the *Anne Frank Huis*) and all day Mon,
with the exception of the *Stedelijk Museum* and
Tropenmuseum in Amsterdam, the Frans Hals Museum in
Haarlem and, during the summer, the Zuiderzee Museum in
Enkhuizen (see *Excursions*). You may already have a clear idea
of what you want to see in Amsterdam; if not here are some
suggested programs for a two-day and a four-day visit.

Two-day visit
Day 1 Begin with a visit to the *Rijksmuseum*, if possible
arriving early to enjoy the Dutch Masters before the crowds.
While in this area, you might also visit the *Van Gogh Museum*
or *Stedelijk Museum*. Have lunch on P.C. Hooftstraat. In the
afternoon take a boat trip from Stadhouderskade and then walk
to *Leidseplein* to find a brown café.
Day 2 In the morning visit the *Amsterdams Historisch
Museum* (Historical Museum), then the *Koninklijk Paleis*
(Royal Palace) and the *Nieuwe Kerk*. Have lunch near the Dam
and in the afternoon explore the area of canals to the w of Dam.
End the afternoon with a visit to a *proeflokaal* (see *Introduction
to Cafés*).

Try sampling a *rijsttafel* (Indonesian rice table) for dinner.

Four-day visit

Day 1 Follow *Walk 1*, then take a canal-boat tour from Centraal Station. If you are not sure where to eat, take tram 4 to Rembrandtsplein and investigate the restaurants on Utrechtsestraat.

Day 2 Visit the *Nederlands Scheepvaartmuseum* (Maritime Museum) in the morning, then walk down Nieuwe Herengracht to reach the *Amstel*. Lunch in the vicinity of Waterlooplein, then visit the *Rembrandthuis*. Walk down Oude Schans to the Montelbaanstoren. If you are feeling adventurous, try booking a table for dinner in one of the restaurants on Reguliersdwarsstraat.

Day 3 Walk along Brouwersgracht and then turn off down Korte Prinsengracht to reach the Westelijke Eilanden (Western Islands). Take tram 3 to De Clercqstraat, then tram 13 or 14 to Westermarkt to visit the *Anne Frank Huis*. In the afternoon, explore the *Jordaan*, pausing in a brown café. Make sure to note down the addresses of any interesting restaurants where you might dine later.

Day 4 Select a trip out of Amsterdam (see *Excursions*). *Gouda* is at its best on Thurs, *Alkmaar* on Fri and *Utrecht* on Sat, while *Haarlem* is the only town with much to offer on Mon. Most small towns are also bleak on Sun, although the IJsselmeer ports of *Enkhuizen* and *Hoorn* are cheerful on windy, summer days.

Walks in Amsterdam

Walk 1/The old town
*Allow 1 hr. Maps **11** and **12**. Tram 1, 2, 4, 5, 9, 13, 14, 16, 17, 24, 25 to Dam.*

"Holland," observed the writer Ethel Portnoy, "is the smell of *patates frites* [french fries] mingled with jasmine." This jarring contrast provides a foretaste of Amsterdam's oldest quarter, where you find a perplexing mixture of beauty and ugliness.

The walk begins at the historic center of Amsterdam, the Dam, where the former town hall retains an aloof dignity amid a rather chaotic scene. Walk down Rokin, an elegant shopping street, and turn right down Wijdekapelsteeg. This leads to the Renaissance gateway of the municipal orphanage. Enter the leafy courtyard of the orphanage, which is an unexpected surprise after the crush of Kalverstraat, Amsterdam's busiest shopping street.

Turn left beyond the courtyard to reach the Schuttersgalerij, a unique public passage hung with 17thC paintings from the collection of the *Amsterdams Historisch Museum*. Take the first right to enter the *Begijnhof*, a medieval religious community that has managed against all odds to retain an atmosphere of gentle piety. Leave by the passage between no. 37 and no. 38 to reach Spui, an animated square famous in the 1960s for Provo happenings and political protests.

Turn left and cross Rokin, pausing on the bridge over Grimnessesluis (a former sluice) to catch one of Amsterdam's

Planning

most picturesque views, which includes the Renaissance
House on the Three Canals and the tower of the *Zuiderkerk*.
Walk down Langebrugsteeg to reach Grimburgwal.

Turn left down the second canal, Oude Zijds
Achterburgwal, and then take the first right through the
bookshop-lined passage Oudemanhuispoort to reach the canal
Kloveniersburgwal. Turn right, then left over the bridge and
straight ahead down Staalstraat. Then turn left down the canal
Groenburgwal, which is splendidly terminated by the tower of
the 17thC *Zuiderkerk*. Turn right at the next canal,
Raamgracht, then left down Zanddwarsstraat and right to
enter the attractive Zuiderkerkhof. The houses here are built
on replaceable rubber shock absorbers to deaden vibrations
from the metro, which passes below. Leave this square by the
Renaissance gateway, which once gave access to the
Zuiderkerk churchyard. Turn right, then take the first left,
passing a gateway that once belonged to the Amsterdam
leprosy asylum. Descend the steps by the sluice (which is
closed every night while the canals are pumped out) and walk
around the canal to reach Oude Schans. Walk down to the
Montelbaanstoren, and turn left along Binnenkant to reach
Centraal Station, where there are trams that depart to most
parts of the city.

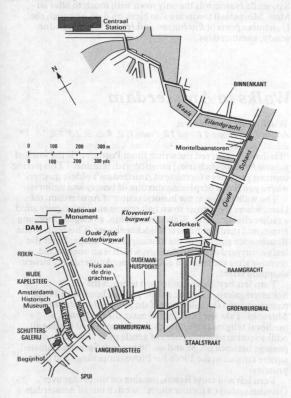

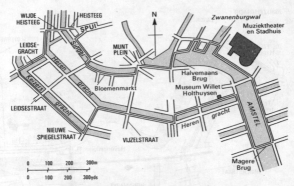

Walk 2/Canals and the River Amstel

Allow 2hrs. Maps 11 and 12. Tram 1, 2, 5 to Spui.

"Have you noticed that Amsterdam's concentric canals resemble the circles of hell?" inquired the narrator in Albert Camus' *The Fall*. Other observers have responded more positively to Amsterdam's stately canals; "Nothing can be more pleasing," wrote John Evelyn in 1641, "being so frequently planted and shaded with the beautifull lime trees, which are set in rowes before every mans house." In recent years the canals have been the scene of fierce battles between developers and conservationists, yet the unique Baroque framework remains virtually intact.

Begin at Spui and walk down Heisteeg to reach *Singel*, continue down Wijde Heisteeg to *Herengracht* and turn left on the far side of the canal. This takes you past a splendid row of 17thC gable houses, interrupted by a remarkable 19thC palace (no. 380–82). Turn right down Leidsegracht to reach an elegant area of *Keizersgracht*. Cross this canal and turn left to reach Leidsestraat, then continue along the next stretch of Keizersgracht. On reaching Nieuwe Spiegelstraat, turn left to return to Herengracht. This stretch of canal was much coveted by merchants in the late 17th and 18thC and became known as De Bocht in de Herengracht (The Bend in Herengracht).

Turn right to reach Vijzelstraat and continue along Herengracht to the Museum *Willet-Holthuysen*. Then continue to the river Amstel, and turn right to reach the wooden drawbridge known as the Magere Brug (Narrow Bridge). Cross the bridge and turn left down the *Amstel*, past an interesting cross section of houseboats. Located on the bend in the Amstel is Amsterdam's controversial Muziektheater (Opera House) and Stadhuis (Town Hall), a curious combination that one acerbic Dutch critic attributed to "that cut-rate philosophy of two for the price of one that is so dear to the Dutch commercial soul."

Follow the Amstel on the opera house side, cross the bridge over Zwanenburgwal and turn left. Keep to the edge of the river and cross at the first bridge, the Halvemaansbrug ("Half-Moon Bridge"). Turn right, still following the Amstel, to reach the floating flower market on Singel, where the narrator in *The Fall* exclaimed: "How beautiful the canals are this evening! I like the breath of stagnant waters, the smell of dead leaves soaking in the canal and the funereal scent rising from the barges laden with flowers."

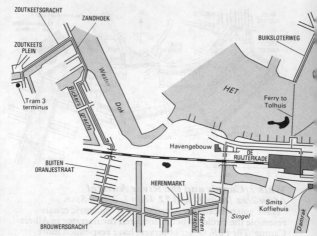

Walk 3/The harbor

Allow 2–3 hrs. Maps 6, 7 and 11. Tram 3 to Zoutkeetsgracht.

The peculiar charm of Amsterdam's port area was discovered by Vincent van Gogh during his stay here. "I like to wander through the old, narrow and rather somber streets," he wrote, "with their shops occupied by chemists, lithographers and ships' chandlers, and browse among the navigation charts and other ships' supplies. I cannot tell you how beautiful the area is at twilight."

This walk follows in the footsteps of Van Gogh along the old harbor front, where there are still numerous echoes of Amsterdam's seafaring past.

From the tram terminus at Zoutkeetsgracht, cross the bridge to Zoutkeetsplein, a small square, and turn right along the canal to reach *Zandhoek*, an evocative corner of the old city rarely penetrated by tourists. Turn right along Zandhoek, cross the bridge and turn right onto Bickersgracht, a canal where boats, bridges and warehouses blend into a picturesque confusion. At the end of Bickersgracht, turn left, pass under the railway viaduct and continue straight ahead down Buiten Oranjestraat. On reaching Brouwersgracht, a canal lined with sturdy warehouses, cross the bridge, turn left and follow the canal.

Overlooking Herenmarkt – a small square on the N side of Brouwersgracht between *Keizersgracht* and *Herengracht* – is the former headquarters of the Dutch West India Company, which established the Dutch colony of Nieuw Amsterdam on Manhattan, having bought the island from the Indians in 1626 for 60 guilders ($24). The company was not so astute in its other ventures, however, and almost went bankrupt in 1674.

Continue along Brouwersgracht to *Singel* and turn left. Cross the street and walk under the railway viaduct. On reaching the Havengebouw, whose 12th-floor restaurant enjoys a panoramic view of the port, turn right and walk along the quay to the pier marked *Pont naar Tolhuis*, where you can take the free municipal ferry across the IJ to Amsterdam Noord to catch a glimpse of the port. You can then catch a second ferry (which only runs Mon–Fri) back to Centraal

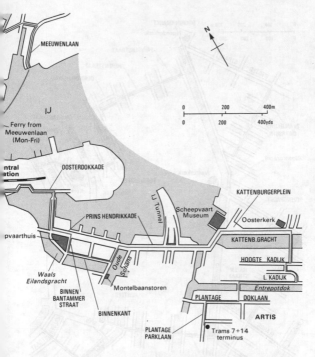

Station. To reach this ferry, walk down Buiksloterweg, take the first right to cross the Noord Hollandsch Kanaal at the lock, then turn right on reaching Meeuwenlaan.

After this brief detour, walk through Centraal Station, perhaps pausing for refreshment at Smit's Koffiehuis (see *Cafés*), which overlooks Damrak, the last vestige of Amsterdam's oldest harbor. Continue E along Oosterdokskade and turn right to reach Prins Hendrikkade. On the opposite side of the street is the splendid Scheepvaarthuis, with its row of mariners' heads gazing purposefully seaward. Turn right down the picturesque Binnen Bantammerstraat, then left along Binnenkant. The old harbor front once ran along the opposite side of Waalseilandsgracht, and the Montelbaanstoren, at the end of this canal, protected the NE corner of the city.

At Oude Schans, turn left, then right, to pass the West India Company warehouses at 's Gravenhekje and the East India Company warehouses at Prins Hendrikkade 176. After crossing the IJ-tunnel approach road, take the underpass to reach the *Nederlands Scheepvaart Museum* and the attractive cluster of 17thC houses on Kattenburgerplein. Continue E along Kattenburgerstraat to the 17thC Classical Oosterkerk and then cross the bridge opposite this church to reach Hoogte Kadijk, a former dike. Go down the street that is almost directly staight ahead of you and turn left along Laagte Kadijk to discover the recently renovated Entrepôtdok, comprising some 84 warehouses named in alphabetical order after Dutch cities. Turn right to reach the bridge that leads to the terminus of trams 7 and 14.

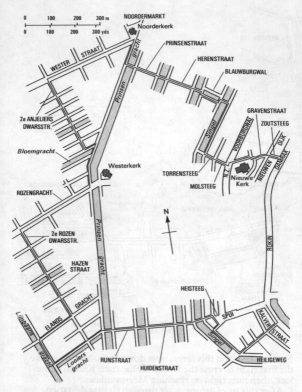

Walk 4/Shopping in Amsterdam
*Allow 1hr. Maps **10** and **11**. Tram 4, 9, 16, 24, 25 to Dam.*
Amsterdam's past as a trading city is still much in evidence in
the variety of shops stocked with exotic goods from all over the
world. Some shops resemble private collections of rarities and
many are worth visiting simply for their interiors.

Begin at the elegant department store **De Bijenkorf** (see
Shopping) cross Damrak and walk down the narrow alley
Zoutsteeg, then cross Nieuwendijk and continue down
Gravenstraat. Some interesting shops are located around the
Nieuwe Kerk, including a few tiny premises squeezed into gaps
in the outside walls of the church. Cross Nieuwe Zijds
Voorburgwal and continue down the medieval alley Molsteeg,
then cross Spuistraat and head down Torensteeg to *Singel*.

Turn right and walk down this canal, then cross the first
bridge on the left and head down Blauwburgwal to reach the
lively shopping streets Herenstraat and Prinsenstraat. On
reaching *Prinsengracht*, cross the bridge and turn right to
reach **Noordermarkt** (see *Shopping*), scene of a bustling flea
market on Mon mornings. Turn left along Westerstraat, a
filled-in canal that on Mon is lined with stalls selling clothing.
Turn left at Tweede Anjeliersdwarsstraat (one of many short
streets in the *Jordaan* with uncommonly long names). Follow
this street, which changes its name many times, until you

reach an attractive canal, Bloemgracht; then turn left to reach
Prinsengracht again. Turn right to reach Rozengracht, cross
the street and turn right again to reach Tweede
Rozendwarsstraat. This leads into Hazenstraat, one of the
Jordaan's most buoyant shopping streets. At the end of
Hazenstraat, turn right along Elandsgracht, a former canal that
lost its sparkle when it was filled in during the 19thC. The
indoor antique market **De Looier** (*Elandsgracht 109, open
Sat–Thurs 9am–5pm*) sells old books, Art Nouveau vases,
postcards, coins, records and toys.

At the end of Elandsgracht, turn left along Lijnbaansgracht,
which marks the western limit of the 17thC city. Then take the
first left down the canal Looiersgracht, where there is a small,
shabby, indoor flea market (*Looiersgracht 38, open Sat–Thurs
11am–5pm*). Cross Prinsengracht and continue down
Runstraat and Huidenstraat, which are lined with interesting,
unusual shops of every description. Now continue down
Heisteeg to reach Spui, which is good for bookshops, then
head right down Singel, and left down Heiligeweg. Cross
Kalverstraat and carry on straight ahead to reach Rokin.

Walk 5/Nightlife
*Allow 1–2hrs. Maps **6**, **7** and **11**. Tram 1, 2, 4, 5, 9, 13, 16, 17,
24, 25 to Centraal Station; or tram 9, 14 to Waterlooplein to
avoid the red-light district.*

Amsterdam's most celebrated nocturnal attraction is, of
course, the red-light district, where prostitutes pose in
seductive lingerie at the windows of 17thC gable houses, while
the police stroll nonchalantly by. The walk described below
includes an optional detour through this strangely surreal
quarter of the city, where you should obviously proceed with a
certain amount of caution and keep to the crowded streets.
(Those who would prefer to stay clear of this area should begin
the walk at the Muziektheater on Waterlooplein.)

Begin at Centraal Station and walk down Damrak. The red-
light district lies E of here and can be reached by turning left
down Oude Brugsteeg, left again at Warmoesstraat and then
right into Lange Niezel. This street was favored in the Middle
Ages by Amsterdam's richest merchants but, as the 17thC
Amsterdam playwright Bredero was fond of reminding his
audiences, "things can change", and Lange Niezel is now
jammed with sex shops and cramped striptease joints. On
reaching the canal Oude Zijds Voorburgwal, turn right
towards the *Oude Kerk*, Amsterdam's finest Gothic church,
now encircled by brothels. Cross the canal by the bridge facing
the church and walk straight ahead down Oude Kennissteeg,
across Oude Zijds Achterburgwal and down Molsteeg. Then
turn right down Zeedijk to reach *Nieuwmarkt*. This marks the
limit of the red-light district. To continue the walk, cross the
market square, walk down Sint Antoniesbreestraat, and at the
sluice turn right down Zwanenburgwal. Cross the bridge on
the left and continue past the opera house (which looks its best
at night) to the Blauwbrug, a stately bridge from which there is
a good view of the Magere Brug (Narrow Bridge) outlined in
lights. Cross the Blauwbrug and continue straight ahead down
Amstelstraat to reach Rembrandtsplein, lined with somewhat
nostalgic-seeming cafés, such as the traditional brown café **De
Populair** (*Reguliersbreestraat 51*). This mood spills over into
the topless bars on adjacent Thorbeckeplein, where even the
striptease shows have an old-fashioned flavor.

Planning

Walk down Reguliersbreestraat, pausing to glance into the Art Deco lobby of the *Tuschinski* cinema, then cross over to *Singel*, walk down the left side of the canal and take the first left to reach Reguliersdwarsstraat. This is Amsterdam's most fashionable street at night, its restaurants always packed, its cafés spilling out into the street. On reaching Leidsestraat, turn left and follow the crowds. After crossing *Prinsengracht*, turn left down Lange Leidsedwarsstraat, take the first right along a side street and then turn right again down Korte Leidsedwarsstraat. This short detour provides a glimpse of some of Amsterdam's nightspots, ranging from crowded discos to highbrow jazz cafés.

A pleasant way to end the evening is in a peaceful brown café, such as **Eijlders** (*Korte Leidsedwarsstraat 47*) or **Pieper** (*Prinsengracht 424*).

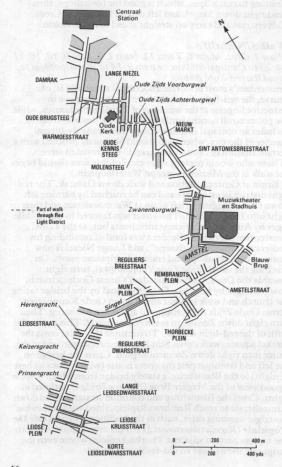

Tram rides

Amsterdam's extensive tram network can be used to reach many of the city's remoter sights. If possible avoid the rush hour (4.30–5.30pm). (For practical information on using public transport, see *Getting around* in *Basic information*.)

Route 1/The old city

Take tram 9 from Centraal Station to Mauritskade. Cross the street and catch tram 10 to Rozengracht. Walk round the corner and take tram 13 or 17 back to Centraal Station. Allow 1½hrs.

The first stage of this tour provides a glimpse of Berlage's Beurs, the Dam, Muntplein, the Art Deco *Tuschinski* Theater, Rembrandtsplein, the *Amstel*, Waterlooplein, the Synagogues and finally the *Tropenmuseum*. The second stage of the journey follows the outer edge of the 17thC city past several monumental buildings. The final stage leads down the rather shabby Rozengracht – where Rembrandt spent his final years – past the *Westerkerk*, the main canals, the main post office, the *Koninklijk Paleis* (Royal Palace) and the *Nieuwe Kerk*.

Route 2/Eccentric architecture

Take tram 4 from Centraal Station to Victorieplein. Walk down Rijnstraat to Churchilllaan, turn right through the arcade and continue on to Waalstraat. Turn right to reach P. L. Takstraat, which begins on the far side of the Amstelkanaal. Walk down P. L. Takstraat, turn left down Burg. Tellegenstraat, left again along Willem Passtoorstraat and soon afterwards left into Therese Schwartzestraat, which leads to a small square. Leave the square at the opposite end and turn left to recross the bridge over the canal.

Return to Churchilllaan and take tram 12 to Roelof Hartplein. Walk down J. M. Coenenstraat and turn left into Harmoniehof. Return to Roelof Hartplein and take tram 3 or 12 to Overtoom. Walk back along 1ᵉ Constantijn Huygensstraat to Vondelstraat and turn right to reach the Vondelkerk, where a path leads left into the *Vondelpark*. Leave the park by the path beside the Filmmuseum. Follow Roemer Visscherstraat, turning left into Tesselschadestraat, then left along Vondelstraat. Take tram 1, 2 or 5 on Overtoom to return to Centraal Station. Allow 2hrs.

After crossing the major canals, the tram leaves the old city to pass through first the 19thC ring and then the early 20thC ring. At Victorieplein there is a solitary 1930s skyscraper by J. F. Staal and a robust statue of H. P. Berlage who planned Amsterdam Zuid. The short walk N leads through the remarkable De Dageraad housing scheme from the early 1920s.

The next stage of the tour ends at Roelof Hartplein, designed as a ceremonial entrance to Amsterdam Zuid with some late Amsterdam School-style buildings dating from just before the Depression. J. F. Staal designed the block Harmoniehof, on the right-hand side of J. M. Coenenstraat.

The final short walk from Overtoom takes you past P. J. H. Cuypers' neo-Gothic Vondelkerk and other 19thC architectural delights of the Vondelpark area. Look out in particular for the astonishing row of houses at Roemer Visscherstraat 20–30a known as De Zeven Landen (The Seven Countries).

Sights and places of interest

Amsterdam has only a few major sights (the Rijksmuseum, the Van Gogh Museum and the Anne Frank Huis) and much of its charm lies in the small details and unexpected curiosities. Many of these are mentioned under the area descriptions and can be found in the *Index*.

Most museums are closed on Sun morning and all day Mon. See individual museums for opening times. Certain departments in the Rijksmuseum are occasionally closed because of staff shortages.

Major sights classified by type	
Major museums	Westerkerk
Amsterdams Historisch Museum	Zuiderkerk
Anne Frank Huis	**Other sights**
Het Rembrandthuis Museum	Begijnhof
Rijksmuseum	Hollands Schouwburg
Stedelijk Museum	Koninklijc Paleis
Van Gogh Museum	Leidseplein
Other museums	Madam Tussaud
Allard Pierson Museum	Tuschinski
Aviodome	**Districts**
Bijbels Museum	Amstel
Electrische Museum Tramlijn	De Dageraad public housing
Informatiecentrum	Grachtengordel
Dienst Ruimtelijke Ordening	Herengracht
Joods Historisch Museum	Jodenbuurt
Nederlands Scheepvaart	Jordaan
Museum	Keizersgracht
Nederlands Theater Instituut	Nieuwe Zijde
NINT Technisch Museum	Nieuwmarkt
Six Collection	Oude Zijde
Spaarpotten Museum	Prinsengracht
Tropenmuseum	Singel
Period houses	Spaarndammerbuurt
Amstelkring, Museum	Zandhoek
Van Loon, Museum	**Parks and gardens**
Willet-Holthuysen, Museum	Amstelpark
Churches	Amsterdamse Bos
Nieuwe Kerk	Artis
Oude Kerk	Hortus Botanicus
	Vondelpark

Air Museum See *Aviodome.*

Allard Pierson Museum
Oude Turfmarkt 127 ☎ (020) 5252556. Map 11E5 ▨ Open Tues–Fri 10am–5pm, Sat, Sun, hols 1–5pm. Tram 4, 9, 14, 16, 24, 25 to Spui.
The extensive archeological collection of the University of Amsterdam is located in a Neoclassical building which once belonged to the Nederlandsche Bank. The interior has been completely modernized, leaving only the curious 19thC lamps as a memento of the bank. The collection includes some unusual Coptic finds, a large section of Greek relics and some objects from Crete and Cyprus. The labeling is mainly in Dutch and the non-specialist may find the collection rather unenlightening.

Amstel
Tram 9, 14 or metro to Waterlooplein, or tram 6, 7, 10 to Oosteinde.
The meandering river Amstel, a remote distributary of the Rhine, once formed the main axis of the city, although now it is

a tranquil backwater popular for Sun afternoon walks.

The finest stretch is s from the 19thC bridge, the Blauwbrug, an attempt by W. Springer to copy the Belle Epoque allure of Paris. Look s towards the restored wooden drawbridge known as the Magerebrug (Narrow Bridge), which seems a more fitting symbol of Amsterdam's antique charm. An eccentric touch is added to the scene by the barge – constructed by the American artist, Victor Bulgar – that sits below the Blauwbrug like a raft that has floated in from the South Seas. On the right are several splendid mansions, including a sober Doric house built by Adriaen Dortsman at Amstel 216 and, at no. 218, the discreet Baroque building in which the *Six Collection* is housed. On the opposite bank is the **Amstelhof**, a 17thC old people's home.

Overlooking a picturesque complex of sluices is the splendid **Theater Carré**, originally built as a circus in 1887. Continuing beyond the Hogesluis – another of Springer's opulent bridges – you pass the legendary **Amstelhotel** built in 1867. Some of its splendor rubs off on Weesperzijde, as can be seen in the **IJsbreker Café** (see *Cafés*). Cross the Nieuwe Amstelbrug – built in 1902 by Berlage – to reach the fairy-tale 19thC house complete with giant gnomes on the roof at Ceintuurbaan 251–55.

Continuing s takes you past the highly ornate neo-Renaissance **Gemeentearchief**, which often exhibits prints from the city's archives. A short detour right down Tolstraat is the technical museum *NINT*, while opposite is the brilliantly revitalized **Cinétol** library, built by J. A. Brinkman and L. C. van der Vlugt in 1926 as a Theosophical Hall and later used as a cinema. The modern interior is particularly striking.

Farther down the Amstel a ceremonial effect is created by the twin blocks of Amsterdam School housing facing the bridge Berlagebrug, one of Berlage's last projects. From here, continue down the Amstel, past scenes sketched by Rembrandt, to reach the *Amstelpark*, or pick up a tram back to the center.

Amstelkring, Museum

Oude Zijds Voorburgwal 40 ☎ (020) 246604. Map 12C6 ▨
Open Mon–Sat 10am–5pm, Sun, hols 1–5pm. Tram 4, 9, 16,
24, 25 to Dam, then a 5mins walk.

This delightful museum is unfortunately located on a shabby patch of canal in the red light district. Once safely inside, however, the visitor is plunged back into the Dutch Golden Age, with its sober virtues and solid furniture. The private foundation responsible for restoring this building has gone to great lengths to create the appearance of an Old Master painting, and the neat arrangements of fruit and casually discarded clay pipes give the impression that the owner has just stepped out to supervise the arrival of a consignment of spices from the East Indies. One of the house's most attractive rooms is the kitchen, which persuades light into its darkest corners by means of ingenious windows and gleaming tiles.

The house is full of unexpected surprises: windows in strange locations, labyrinths of creaking staircases and a concealed priest's room in the belly of the building. But the biggest surprise is the bulky church constructed in the attic, which gives the house its memorable name: Onze Lieve Heer Op Zolder – Our Lord in the Attic.

The original owner was a Catholic merchant who built a

clandestine church here after the outlawing of Catholicism by
the Calvinist authorities in 1581. The museum contains an
interesting map showing just how many of these ostensibly
secret churches there were in Amsterdam in the 17th and
18thC. It also reveals the astonishing variety of religions
practiced in the tolerant climate of Amsterdam. The present
church – which extends over no fewer than three houses – was
built in the 1730s. Its ingenious foldaway pulpit is a typical
Amsterdam space-saving solution.

Looking from the upper windows towards the harbor, you
can see the Baroque domes of **St Nicolaaskerk**, which the
congregation of Onze Lieve Heer Op Zolder erected in the
19thC when the ban on the Catholic church was finally lifted.
Religious enthusiasm waned almost completely sometime in
the 20thC and, sadly, the church is now used only for
occasional concerts.

Facing the museum is a magnificent neck gable in
Vingboons style dating from 1656. Fabulous dolphins
wreathed with strings of pearls decorate the claw pieces,
though few people in this part of Amsterdam take much
interest in such detail.

Amstelpark

Europaboulevard 🖼 ⇌ ☂ 🛥 *Open dawn–dusk. Tram 4 to
Station RAI. On leaving the station turn right – the park
entrance is just beyond the Novotel.*
This restful park on the s edge of the city near the exhibition
center RAI contains an art gallery (**Het Glazen Huis**), a
rosarium, a maze and sauna, as well as various animals such as
seals and donkeys.

Amsterdams Historisch Museum *(Amsterdam Historical Museum)* ★

Kalverstraat 92 🕾 *(020) 255822. Map* **114E** 🖼 ⇌ ✗
*Guidebooks in English, French or German can be borrowed.
Open Mon–Sat 11am–5pm, Sun, hols 1–5pm. Entrances at
Kalverstraat 92, St Luciensteeg 27, Nieuwezijds Voorburgwal
357, Gedempte Begijnensloot and Begijnhof. Tram 1, 2, 5 to
Spui.*
How did a tiny fishing village on the Amstel develop into one
of the world's richest and most beautiful cities? What were
Amsterdam's achievements and failings? How did its citizens
live? Amsterdam's historical museum attempts to answer
questions such as these by means of a fascinating collection of
maps, portraits, utensils, clothes, globes, models, books,
sculpture and topographic views.

The bustling, cosmopolitan spirit of Amsterdam is best seen
in the various views of the Dam in the 17thC (rm 6), and the
languid stillness of its great canals in the 18thC is reflected in
the attractive urban scenes of Jan de Beijer and H. P. Schouten
(rms 9, 10). The most remarkable map is Cornelis
Anthoniszoon's 1544 woodcut showing the medieval city in
minute detail (rm 1), while Amsterdam's finest moment is
captured in H. C. Vroom's *Return of the Second East Indies
Expedition* (rm 5), depicting the dramatic scene in the inlet of
water, the IJ, in 1599 as a flotilla of small boats (including a
gondola) surround the four returning galleons. The painful,
slow decline of the city is symbolized by the models of the
unbuilt Nieuwe Kerk tower (rm 10), the paintings of the
Napoleonic army entering Amsterdam (rm 16), the melancholy

Impressionist works by Witsen and Breitner, and the scenes of the 1930s Depression and war years (rm 17).

The museum, which is housed in the splendid 17thC municipal orphanage, retains the **Regentenkamer**, a beautiful 17thC Classical room in which the governors met. The small adjoining room commemorates one of the orphans, Jan van Speyk, who heroically blew up his ship during the 1830 Belgian revolt to prevent its falling into enemy hands.

Even if you do not visit the museum, be sure to glance into the two courtyards and walk through the unique **Schuttersgalerij**, a covered public thoroughfare lined with 17thC Civic Guard group portraits. Other interesting details include the original orphanage entrance – dating from 1581 – at Kalverstraat 92 and the collection of facade stones displayed along St Luciensteeg (including a delightful scene of the Montelbaanstoren, and a giant tooth). Finally, the shaded café terrace in the Boys' Courtyard and the benches in the Girls' Courtyard are pleasant places to escape the crush of Kalverstraat.

Amsterdamse Bos

Amstelveenseweg ⇌ ◢ *CN bus 170, 171, 172 from Amsterdam Centraal Station to Van Nijenrodeweg; for details of summer tram service, see Electrische Museum Tramlijn on page 53.*

Amsterdam's largest park was built in the sw suburbs in the 1930s as an employment creation scheme. Although inspired by the Bois de Boulogne in Paris, the Amsterdamse Bos has an unmistakably Dutch flavor, with carefully segregated routes for cars, bicycles, horses and pedestrians. The park even includes an artificial hill (signposted *heuvel*). Notice also the distinctive wooden bridges, built in Amsterdam School style by P. L. Kramer between 1937 and 1957. The park has a rowing racecourse, the Bosbaan, which was built for the 1928 Amsterdam Olympics.

The Amsterdamse Bos can also be reached on bicycle, by following the Amstel to the café Kleine Kalfje (see *Cycle trips* in *Excursions*), then turning right and following the cycle path along Kalfjeslaan, which leads straight into the park. There is a small cycle rental shop at the Van Nijenrodeweg entrance to the park (*Fiets-o-fiets* ☎ *(020) 445473*), and canoes and water bicycles can also be rented (follow signs to *kano- en waterfietsen verhuur*).

Anne Frank Huis *(Anne Frank House)*

Prinsengracht 263 ☎ *(020) 264533. Map* **10***C3* ▨ *Open Mon–Sat 9am–5pm, Sun, hols 10am–5pm. Tram 13, 14, 17 to Westermarkt.*

During the Nazi occupation of the Netherlands, eight Jewish Amsterdammers hid for 25 months in the annex of this house near the *Westerkerk* to avoid deportation to concentration camps. Among them was the 14-year-old schoolgirl, Anne Frank, who kept a diary recording her experiences in meticulous detail. Her observations ranged from complaints about the food to lyrical descriptions of the bells of the Westerkerk. Anne Frank and her family were eventually betrayed to the Germans and in 1945 she died in Bergen-Belsen concentration camp. Her diary was published in 1947 under the title *Het Achterhuis*.

The house has been kept in the same state as when the

Franks were in hiding, and on the wall of the room occupied by Anne are photographs of Deanna Durbin and the British princesses, which she cut out of magazines, together with pencil marks indicating the growth of Anne and her sister.

Special exhibitions are organized by the Anne Frank Foundation to focus on contemporary manifestations of fascism, racism and antisemitism.

> From my favorite spot on the floor I look up at the blue sky and the bare chestnut tree, on whose branches little raindrops glisten like silver, and at the seagulls and other birds as they glide on the wind.
>
> *The Diary of Anne Frank*, February 25 1944

Artis *(Zoo)*
*Plantage Kerklaan 40 ☎(020) 262833. Map **9**F8 ☒ ⅋ ⇌ ✳*
Open 9am–6pm (buildings close at 5pm). Tram 7, 9, 14 to Plantage Kerklaan.
Natura Artis Magistra (Nature is the Teacher of the Arts) is the official title of Amsterdam's zoo, although it has always been known simply as Artis. It was opened in 1838 in a garden on the unfashionable E side of the city and grew to become one of the world's largest zoos.

Its delights include the reptile house, which is landscaped like a steamy jungle, a nocturnal house, an aquarium and a glass-walled seal pool. The owls peer out from a ruined city wall as in the paintings of Hieronymus Bosch. There is also a small farmyard, where children can wander freely among domestic animals.

Animals in Artis are given generous amounts of space, which does not leave a great deal for humans, and on Sun it can become rather crowded.

Aviodome
Schiphol ☎(020) 173640 ☒ ✳ ⇌ Open 10am–5pm; Nov–Mar closed Mon. Train to Schipol, then 10min walk.
The Dutch national air museum is located near Schiphol airport in a futuristic dome which shudders each time a jumbo takes off. Some 20 historic aircraft and spaceships are on display, ranging from the Wright Brothers' fragile 1903 *Flyer* to the Spacelab, together with models and memorabilia. The salvaged fragments from the bomber of Captain McVie, a World War II pilot, whose last words to his crew were "No panic, don't forget the pigeons," are particularly haunting.

Begijnhof ★
*Spui. Map **11**E4 ☒ Begijnhof open dawn–dusk; Begijnhofkapel (Begijnhof 30) open 9am–5pm; English Church (Presbyterian) open for concerts Sat 4pm. Tram 1, 2, 5 to Spui. Disabled people are advised to use the side entrance on Gedempte Begijnensloot.*
The convent Begijnhof was founded by the Catholic sisterhood of Beguinages in the 14thC near the S limit of the city, at a safe distance from the noise and confusion of the harbor. It is entered from the N side of Spui through a modest doorway which leads unexpectedly into an enchanting courtyard filled with birdsong – like a secret Garden of Eden in the center of the bustling city.

The sisters of this attractive religious order popular in the Low Countries took no vows but otherwise lived as nuns. The

Mother Superior occupied the tall house at no. 26, and services were held in the charming Begijnenkerk, which dates from 1419.

After Amsterdam's conversion to Protestantism in 1578, the church was handed over to Scottish Presbyterians and, to their chagrin, renamed the English Church. Opposite, concealed behind a domestic facade, is the clandestine chapel built in 1665 for the Catholic Begijnhof residents, who had been allowed to retain their property after the Reformation. Both churches continue to coexist amicably.

Although most of the houses in the Begijnhof have 17th and 18thC facades, there is one splendid 15thC survival at no. 34, with a tarred wooden front and a simple spout gable. This is Amsterdam's oldest house, built with stone side walls to prevent the spread of fire. The small courtyard alongside contains several facade stones illustrating religious themes.

Bijbels Museum *(Bible Museum)*
*Herengracht 366 ☎ (020) 247949. Map **10E3** ▦ Open Tues–Sat 10am–5pm, Sun 1–5pm. Tram 1, 2, 5 to Spui.*
A somewhat evangelical collection of objects relating to the Old Testament, housed in two handsome canal houses built in 1662.

Botanical Garden   See *Hortus Botanicus*.

De Dageraad public housing
s of the Sarphatipark. Tram 4 to Lutmastraat.
This small patch of utopian public housing, built in bold Amsterdam School style from 1918–23 for De Dageraad (The Dawn) housing association, produces a thrilling impact in an otherwise rather dull area of Amsterdam Zuid. The main axis of P. L. Takstraat, designed by P. L. Kramer, embodies the confidence of early 20thC socialism in its magnificently sculpted twin corner blocks standing sentinel over the street like a medieval city gate. Notice also the surging waves of roof tiles, the ornate hoist beams for lifting furniture into the houses, the sculpture by Hildo Krop and the heavily protective doorways.

Two secluded squares E and W of P. L. Takstraat–Th. Schwartzeplein to the W of P. L. Takstraat and Henriette Ronnerplein to the E – feature astonishing mock-villas (each containing eight apartments) built by Michel de Klerk for De Dageraad.

Electrische Museum Tramlijn *(Electric Tramline Museum)*
Haarlemmermeerstation, Amstelveenseweg 264
☎ (020) 272727 ▦ ⚥ Open Apr–Oct Sun, hols only 10am–6pm; July, Aug Sat noon–6pm as well; antique trams depart every 20min, last ride 6pm. Tram 6, 16 to Haarlemmermeerstation.
A group of tram enthusiasts has built up a collection of some 60 antique trams from Amsterdam, Den Haag, Rotterdam, Groningen, Kassel and Vienna, and on summer weekends operates services from the former Haarlemmermeer railway station to the Amsterdamse Bos and Amstelveen. The period detail is fastidiously maintained, to the extent that the conductor is required to descend at each crossing to control the traffic with a red flag.

Grachtengordel

Maps 6, 7, 8, 9, 10. Tram 13, 14, 17 to Westermarkt (early 17thC area); tram 1, 2, 5 to Keizersgracht (middle section); tram 16, 24, 25 to Keizersgracht (Golden Bend) or tram 4 to Keizersgracht (Amstel area).

Amsterdam's magnificent semicircle of canals and cross-streets (literally, the "canal girdle") was built under the ambitious "Plan of the Three Canals" drawn up by the city carpenter Hendrick Staets in the early 17thC. The three canals – *Herengracht, Keizersgracht* and *Prinsengracht* – were built in two stages: initially from Brouwersgracht to Leidsegracht during the first half of the 17thC, and then from Leidsegracht to the *Amstel* after 1665. The different stages can be detected in the architecture: picturesque brick buildings such as the Renaissance **Bartolotti House** (see *Nederlands Theater Instituut*) in the older part, and sober sandstone palaces such as the *Museum Van Loon* in the final stretch. Subtle differences can also be discerned between the aristocratic town houses on Herengracht ("The Gentlemen's Canal"), the smaller middle-class dwellings on Keizersgracht ("The Emperors' Canal") and the modest artisan homes and workshops on Prinsengracht ("The Princes' Canal").

The best introduction to the Grachtengordel is to take a canal boat tour, since this shows the buildings as they were meant to be seen: from the water. The tour also gives you an idea of the sights and areas that are worth exploring in greater detail. To obtain a glimpse of a typical canal house, the *Museum Willet-Holthuysen* or the *Six Collection* is worth a visit. It is also fascinating to view the canal web from above, which is possible by climbing the *Westerkerk* tower (*summer only*), or by visiting the café-restaurant on the 6th floor of Metz & Co., at Keizersgracht 455.

The tree-lined canals are also pleasant to walk along – particularly on Sun when there is scarcely any traffic. Don't try to cover too much distance – Prinsengracht is 3.5km (2 miles) long, Keizersgracht 3km (1¾ miles) and Herengracht 2.5km (1½ miles). Select a short stretch of canal and take time to stop and look at the wealth of detail in gables, doorways, staircases and decorated facade stones.

Be sure also to explore the cross-streets, which still fulfill their original function as shopping streets. Between Raadhuisstraat and Leidsestraat is the liveliest area of the Grachtengordel; the **Weteringbuurt** – between Spiegelgracht and Reguliersgracht – is the most peaceful and forgotten.

Herengracht ★

Maps 7, 11. Tram 1, 2, 5 to Dam or Koningsplein, or tram 4 to Herengracht.

No visit to Amsterdam would be complete without at least a glimpse of Herengracht, the inner canal of the 17thC *Grachtengordel*. Though the older section of the canal – from Brouwersgracht to Leidsegracht — is hardly distinguishable from the parallel sections of *Keizersgracht* and *Prinsengracht*, the later stretch – from Leidsegracht to the *Amstel* – contains many of Amsterdam's most handsome 17th and 18thC town houses. These were built during the second phase of the canal web developments, when Herengracht was envisaged as a mainly residential area from which many industries were banned, such as sugar refining (which was a notorious fire hazard), brewing (which produced unpleasant smells), and coopery (which was noisy). Clearly the patrician families who moved here from the E side of the Amstel wanted to withdraw from the noise and smells of the trading city into an environment that was as rural as possible. Yet this absence of shops and warehouses produced a somewhat sterile atmosphere, not improved by the numerous banks and insurance companies that now occupy these houses.

Measuring about 2.5km (1¼ miles), Herengracht can be walked from end to end without too much difficulty; if you have only a short time to spare, concentrate on the short stretches from Huidenstraat to Leidsestraat, and Leidsestraat to Vijzelstraat (the Golden Bend).

From Brouwersgracht to Raadhuisstraat

The old end of Herengracht retains the flavor of the medieval city, especially on its E side, which was developed shortly after the construction of the 1585 city wall. Notice the curious sculleries attached to many of the corner houses, such as **Herengracht 1**. The most attractive relics from Herengracht's earliest period are the two warehouses **De Fortuyn** (Fortune) and **d'Arcke Noach** (Noah's Ark) at no. 43–45, probably dating from around 1600.

A much grander style of architecture begins to appear on the first bend in Herengracht, particularly the **Bartolotti House** at no. 170–72. This splendid Renaissance house, built by Hendrick de Keyser in 1617, is one of the finest facades in Amsterdam, and canal boats pause reverently on *Singel* to admire its jaunty red and white facade through the gap of Drie Koningenstraat. Its first owner was a brewer with the unremarkable name of Willem van den Heuvel, which he changed to the more catchy Guillielmo Bartolotti. The building now accommodates the *Nederlands Theater Instituut*. Its rather more austere neighbor at **no. 168**, built in 1638 by Philips Vingboons, provides further accommodation for the museum. Notice the spectacular coat of arms in the neck gable, placed there by its first owner, Michiel Pauw, who in 1630 played a major role in the development of New York when he founded the colony of Pavonia, now Hoboken, New Jersey. Perhaps it was Pauw's self-important gable that prompted a later occupant of **no. 166** to adorn his cornice gable with the pious motto *Solo Deo Gloria* (Glory to God Alone).

From Raadhuisstraat to Huidenstraat

This section rambles along in a muddle of styles, with some fine 18thC gable tops to be seen on the W side, notably **De Witte Lelie** (The White Lily) at no. 274, with its ornate Louis XIV style balustrade rising to a crested top.

From Huidenstraat to Leidsestraat

This beautiful stretch of Herengracht is best appreciated from the E side (where a few benches are provided). Philips Vingboons designed many of the houses on this bend, from the four dignified neck gables of the 1662 **Cromhouthuizen** at nos. 364–70, to the Classical pilastered facade at **no. 386**, which although built only one year later represents a decisive break with traditional gables and provides a foretaste of the dull styles of the 1660s and 1670s.

The ornate confectionery in French Renaissance style at **no. 380–82** – seen by puritanical Amsterdammers as the last word in bad taste – was built by A. Salm in 1889 for a rich client who wanted to emulate the chic mansions of New York's 5th Avenue. Twin houses seem to have been popular when this stretch of Herengracht was developed, and at **no. 396–98** and **no. 409–11** are two pairs of 17thC neck gables known respectively as the "twin brothers" and "twin sisters." Notice also the twin at **no. 390–92**, built about 1665 with sculpture in the neck gable depicting a man and a woman mysteriously stretching a cord between them.

From Leidsestraat to Vijzelstraat

The legendary Golden Bend, which occupies this short stretch, comes as a slight disappointment, though there are undoubtedly some magnificent houses — such as **no. 475**, which was built in the 1730s in a rich Louis XIV style. But other houses of the 1660s and 1670s present rather bleak exteriors, such as the **Andries de Graeff house** at no. 446, built for a prominent 17thC burgomaster; the **Huis van Deutz** at no. 450, designed by Philips Vingboons in 1663 for a banker; and the austere house by Adriaen Dortsman at **no. 462**, with its sculpture on the balustrade depicting the popular Dutch virtues of Welfare and Trade. **No. 476** was also built during the grim 1670s, but restyled in the 1740s to create one of the most elegant houses in Amsterdam.

From Vijzelstraat to the Amstel

The final stretch of Herengracht is somewhat less solemn and includes the four splendid neck gables at **nos. 504–10**, whose claw pieces are decorated with dogs, mermaids and dolphins. **Nos. 571–81** date from 1664, when four wealthy citizens reached the unprecedented decision to build four identical houses. The agreement did not apply to ornament, however, which is why the owner of **no. 579** was able to add the oversized figure of the Archangel Michael slaying a dragon, together with various other frivolous touches. The *Museum Willet-Holthuysen* is at no. 605.

Hollands Schouwburg

*Plantage Middenlaan 24 ☎ (020) 224308. Map **9**F8 ☷ Open Mon–Fri 10am–4pm, Sat, Sun, hols 11am–4pm. Tram 7, 9, 14 to Plantage Kerklaan.*

A deeply moving memorial to the Jewish victims of the war, located in the roofless shell of the former theater where many were confined before being deported.

Hortus Botanicus *(Botanical Garden)*

*Plantage Middenlaan 2 ☎ (020) 5222405. Map **9**F8 ☷ Open Mon–Fri 9am–4pm, Sat, Sun, hols 11am–4pm. Tram 9, 14 to Mr Visserplein, or metro to Waterlooplein.*

This tiny botanical garden on the E side of the city, close to Waterlooplein, was established in 1682 for the cultivation of medicinal herbs. Many exotic species were shipped back from the Dutch East Indies, largely on the initiative of the East India Company director Joan Huydecoper.

Highlights of this beautiful garden include the palm houses and the ornamental ponds. In Aug the colors are particularly vivid.

Informatiecentrum Dienst Ruimtelijke Ordening

*Keizersgracht 440 ☎ (020) 222962. Map **10**E3 ☷ Open Tues–Fri 12.30–4.30pm, also Thurs 6–9pm. Tram 1, 2, 5 to Keizersgracht.*

The information center of the department of town planning contains an extensive collection of maps, plans, photographs and models that illustrate Amsterdam's careful approach to urban planning.

Jewish Historical Museum   See *Joods Historisch Museum.*

Jodenbuurt
Map 12 6E. Tram 9, 14 to Mr Visserplein, or metro to Waterlooplein.
Until World War II, Amsterdam's Jewish quarter was located on the islands to the E of Oude Zijde. First to settle were the Portuguese and Spanish Sephardic Jews, who fled persecution in the late 16thC. They were followed in the 17thC by High German or Ashkenazi Jews, who were driven out of Poland and Germany. Drawn by Amsterdam's unique mixture of religious tolerance and economic opportunity, Jews played a profound role in the development of the city. The history of Jodenbuurt was brought to a terrible conclusion during the Nazi occupation, when some 70,000 Jews were deported from the city.

The entire area then fell into ruin and later became the scene of controversial developments such as the IJ tunnel access road, the metro and the Stadhuis/Muziektheater complex, which together have destroyed much of the character of the old Jodenbuurt. Only recently has the area begun to show signs of revival, largely due to the highly imaginative municipal housing by the architects Aldo van Eyck and Theo Bosch. This area now contains some of the finest postwar Dutch architecture, alongside the tragic remains of its Jewish past.

The main Jewish buildings to have survived are the synagogues overlooking J. D. Meijerplein. This square also contains the *Dokwerker* statue by Mari Andriessen, which commemorates the Feb 1941 dockers' strike held in protest at the persecution of the Jews. The N side of the square is dominated by the massive **Portuguese-Israelite Synagogue** (*open Mon–Fri 10am–12.30pm, 1–4pm, Sun 10am–1pm; closed Sat*), built by Elias Bouwman in 1671–75. On the S side of the square are the two High German synagogues, the **Grote Shul** on the right built in 1671 by Daniel Stalpaert, and the ornate **Neie Shul** built in 1752 in Louis XIV style. The *Joods Historisch Museum* now occupies these synagogues.

Jodenbreestraat and Sint Antoniesbreestraat, which connect Mr Visserplein with Nieuwmarkt, were devastated during the construction of the metro. The only relics of the old street are the twin neck gables at **Sint Antoniesbreestraat 64–72** (which are suspended from the modern buildings on either side), the splendid Classical **Pintohuis** built in 1651 for Isaac de Pinto at Sint Antoniesbreestraat 69, and the *Rembrandthuis*.

Joods Historisch Museum *(Jewish Historical Museum)*
J. D. Meijerplein 2–4 ☎ (020) 269945. Map 8F6 ▣ ৬ ▣ Open daily 11am–5pm. Tram 9, 14 to Mr Visserplein; metro to Waterlooplein.
The new Jewish Historical Museum, opened in 1987, provides an insight into Jewish faith, the Jewish community in the Netherlands and the horrors of the Holocaust. The museum occupies an attractive complex of four synagogues, which have been sensitively converted using techniques pioneered by the Amsterdam Historical Museum, such as overhead galleries offering unexpected views, and a street through the museum (formerly an alley with the Yiddish name Sjoelgass). The museum café, which occupies a small synagogue, offers kosher delicacies such as cheesecake.

Jordaan

Map 10. Tram 13, 14, 17 to Westermarkt.

This area was developed to the w of Prinsengracht at the same time as the *Grachtengordel*. Its role in the 1609 Plan was that of a humble industrial quarter and, to cut costs, the majestic geometry of the great canals was abandoned in favor of a dense grid pattern with narrow canals cut E to w along the course of existing drainage ditches. This gives the Jordaan a logic quite different from the rest of the city, and even native Amsterdammers become lost when they venture w of Prinsengracht. It helps a little to know that the streets running N to s are usually called *dwarsstraten* (cross-streets) and numbered E to w as 1ᵉ, 2ᵉ and 3ᵉ(sometimes written *Eerste, Tweede, Derde*), so that 1ᵉ Laurierdwarsstraat is the most easterly street to cross Lauriergracht.

The Jordaan is still an industrial quarter – there are over 900 small businesses registered within this compact area – but it is also a highly desirable residential area, which at first seems odd given the general air of shabby neglect and the fact that no fewer than seven of its eleven canals have been ignominiously filled in. What attracts people, especially students and artists, to the Jordaan is probably its vitality, with its innovative boutiques, galleries, restaurants and cafés. Perhaps this creative energy is a legacy of the 17thC, when numerous Huguenot refugees settled here after Louis XIV's revocation of the Edict of Nantes. There is even a theory that the name Jordaan is a corruption of the French word *jardin*, which seems particularly plausible given canals in the area with names such as Rozengracht (Roses Canal) and Lauriergracht (Laurel Canal).

The Jordaan is cut through the middle by the busy Rozengracht, where Rembrandt spent his final years. S of Rozengracht, the main shopping street is **Hazenstraat**, which is particularly good for unusual clothes. However, it is the area N of Rozengracht that is most lively, with the best shops on the cross-streets such as 1ᵉ Leliedwarsstraat and 1ᵉ Egelantiersdwarsstraat. There are also good brown cafés on almost every corner in this area.

Bloemgracht was once called the Herengracht of the Jordaan, but now has a somewhat neglected air, apart from the splendid trio of step gables at **nos. 87–91**, built at the rather late date of 1642 – long after the rest of Amsterdam had adopted Classical styles. The curious facade stones depict a man of the city, a man of the land and a man of the sea.

One of the special attractions of the Jordaan is its secretive *hofjes*, small almshouses founded by wealthy merchants in the 17thC. At Egelantiersgracht 105–141 is the intimate **St Andrieshofje**, which dates from 1615; its courtyard is generally open to the public. The nearby **Anslo's Hofje** at Egelantiersstraat 36–50 is a picturesque jumble of houses around three courtyards, reached through a small doorway on 2ᵉ Egelantiersdwarsstraat. Also open for visits is the much larger **Huiszitten-Weduwenhof** in Karthuizersstraat, built by city architect Daniel Stalpaert in 1650 as a home for impoverished widows.

Farther N at Lindengracht 149–63 is the **Suikerhofje**, established in 1670, with an inner courtyard open to visitors. Look out also for the witty facade stones nearby at **Lindengracht 53** (the Tangled Yarn) and **Lindengracht 55–57** (the Topsy-turvy World – this stone gives the date of construction upside down and the street name backwards).

Two more *hofjes* can be discovered in the quiet NW corner of the Jordaan at **Palmgracht 20–26** and **28–38**.

Keizersgracht

Maps **6**, **7**, **10**, **11**. *Tram 13, 14, 17 to Westermarkt; tram 1, 2, 4, 5, 16, 24, 25 to Keizersgracht.*

Keizersgracht is the central of the three great canals forming the 17thC *Grachtengordel*. The early 17thC part – from Brouwersgracht to Leidsegracht – matches *Herengracht* in grandeur, but the later section – from Leidsegracht to the *Amstel* – is less pleasing because many Herengracht houseowners bought up the adjoining lot on Keizersgracht to enlarge their gardens and perhaps put up coach houses. The best stretches of Keizersgracht to explore are Brouwersgracht to Raadhuisstraat and Runstraat to Leidsestraat.

From Brouwersgracht to Raadhuisstraat

The area from Brouwersgracht to Herenstraat contains mainly early 17thC buildings, including the lovely **Groenland Pakhuizen** (Greenland warehouses), at nos. 40–44, where whale oil was stored in enormous 10,000-liter (2,642 US gallon) tanks. Between Herenstraat and Leliegracht the 17thC architecture becomes rather more flamboyant. **Het Huis met de Hoofden** (The House with the Heads) at Keizersgracht 123 was built in 1622 by Hendrick de Keyser in a bustling Dutch Renaissance style, its six heads representing the Classical deities Apollo, Ceres, Mars, Pallas Athene, Bacchus and Diana.

Overlooking Leliegracht is a lofty Art Nouveau building designed by G. van Arkel in 1905 for an insurance company – the tile tableau at the top of the tower investing the insurance business with a rather far-fetched religious symbolism. Between Leliegracht and Raadhuisstraat is the **Coymans Huis** (*Keizersgracht 177*), a sober building in Dutch Classical style built a mere two years after the jaunty House with the Heads. Its reserved style found favor with the ruling élite and the architect, Jacob van Campen, later won the competition to design the Stadhuis (Town Hall, now the *Royal Palace*) on Dam.

From Raadhuisstraat to Leidsestraat

Between Raadhuisstraat and Reestraat, walk on the E side in order to admire the buildings opposite – especially **Keizersgracht 209**, with its statue of Hope holding a basket of fruit. From Reestraat to Berenstraat, don't overlook **Keizersgracht 244–46**, a matching pair of houses laden with lavish Louis XIV style cornices. The stretch from Berenstraat to Leidsestraat is particularly rich in architectural interest. The **Felix Meritis building** at Keizersgracht 324 was erected in 1786 by a group of high-minded businessmen fired with the idea of spreading art and scientific knowledge. The society's name – Felix Meritis (Deservedly Happy) – says it all. The building came into the hands of the Dutch Communist Party in 1946 and in the 1960s it became one of Amsterdam's first experimental theaters – renamed the Shaffy Theater after the actor Ramses Shaffy. **Keizersgracht 319** is a dignified elevated neck gable built in 1639 by Philips Vingboons, whose brand of Classicism kept alive the flamboyant tradition established by Hendrick de Keyser. The small portal at **Keizersgracht 384** was the entrance to the former Stadsschouwburg (city theater), which a fire destroyed in

1772. Anyone interested in urban planning in Amsterdam should visit the information center of the Amsterdam Planning Department, *Informatiecentrum Dienst Ruimtelijke Ordening*, at Keizersgracht 440. **The Gilded Star** at no. 387 is another perfect example of the elevated neck gable style, built almost at the end of the Golden Age in 1668. **Keizersgracht 446** is a splendidly ornate Louis XIV style dwelling from the 1720s, which was at one stage occupied by the art collector Adriaan van der Hoop, whose treasures included Rembrandt's *The Jewish Bride*.

Overlooking Leidsestraat is a ponderous late 19thC building erected for the New York Life Insurance Company and later taken over by the furniture shop Metz & Co. The Rietveld penthouse on the top floor provides a fascinating glimpse of the canal web from above. **Keizersgracht 508** is an appealing neo-Renaissance building with sculpture commemorating the 300th anniversary of the birth of the poet P. C. Hooft.

Between Leidsestraat and the Amstel
This stretch of Keizersgracht is essentially just a mews for the mansions on the "Golden Bend" of Herengracht. Examples of coach houses are at **Keizersgracht 481** and **485**. Any interesting buildings tend to be found on the w side – notably the splendid twins at **Keizersgracht 606–8** built in Louis XIV style in the 1730s. Also noteworthy are the twin houses by Adriaen Dortsman which form the *Van Loon* museum. Almost directly opposite is the **Fodor Museum**, a center for contemporary art exhibitions.

Koninklijk Paleis *(Royal Palace)* ★
Dam ☎ *(020) 248698. Map 11D4* ▨ ✗ *Open June–Aug 12.30–4pm; Sept–May by arrangement only. Tram 1, 2, 4, 5, 9, 13, 14, 16, 17, 24, 25 to Dam.*

The Town Hall of Amsterdam – now a royal palace – was built at the high point of the Golden Age, when the city was ablaze with civic pride. In 1648, some 13,656 wooden piles were driven into the ground to provide a stable foundation, and 17 years later the building – though still unfinished – was proudly opened, the tireless poet Vondel producing a 1,500-line ode to celebrate the occasion.

The Town Hall, one of the glories of European Baroque architecture, so outstripped any other building in Holland that the Emperor Louis Napoleon fitted it out in 1808 as his palace, forcing the city dignitaries to shuffle off to the Prinsenhof on Oude Zijds Voorburgwal. The building is still occasionally used by the Royal Family, but most of the year it stands sadly dark and empty.

Exterior
Amsterdam's Town Hall was designed in a severe Classical style by Jacob van Campen, whose use of sober yellow-gray Bentheim sandstone represents a decisive break with the bustling red brick and white stone facades of the early 17thC. To offset the stern appearance of Van Campen's Baroque box, the Antwerp-born sculptor Artus Quellien (or Quellinus) was appointed to decorate the building, and for 14 years he labored assiduously with a small army of assistants to create some of the most inventive sculpture of the 17thC.

The sculpture is highly moralistic in tone and includes the figure of Peace surveying Dam from the tip of the pediment. The motif of Peace recurs elsewhere as a reminder that the Town Hall was begun in the same hopeful year that the Treaty

of Münster was signed, bringing to an end the horrors of the
Eighty Years' War. The pediments are filled with magnificent
Baroque sculpture depicting the Oceans (facing Dam) and the
Continents (facing Raadhuisstraat) paying homage to the Maid
of Amsterdam. Quellien's painstaking decoration can only
properly be appreciated through binoculars, or by examining
the preliminary models displayed in the *Rijksmuseum* and
Amsterdams Historisch Museum.

"But where is the entrance?" admirers of the Town Hall
often ask. The main entrance to this magnificent building is
through a small concealed doorway at the right-hand side of
the arcaded *avant corps*. The reason for this uncharacteristic
modesty in an age dominated by pompous ceremony may have
been the sobering experience of the Anabaptist uprising in
1535, when a group of religious fanatics stormed the old Town
Hall.

Burgerzaal

The pinched entrance contrasts with the magnificent Baroque
drama of the lofty Burgerzaal at the top of the stairs. This vast
assembly hall rises through four floors to create the most
spacious interior in Amsterdam. The Maid of Amsterdam sits
primly at the E end of the Hall, flanked by the figures of
Strength and Wisdom, while above the entrance to the Council
Chamber (**Schepenzaal**) at the W end, the figure of Atlas
overlooks a sculptural group in which Justice, seated between
Death and Punishment, treads Avarice and Envy underfoot.

The Burgerzaal floor is inlaid with three maps – two
depicting the hemispheres and the third the heavens – across
which Amsterdam's ruling élite once proudly walked in their
black robes, deliberating policies with global repercussions.

Galleries

The council offices were located in the Galleries to the N and S
of the Burgerzaal, reached through arches decorated with
figures depicting the four elements: Earth, Water, Air and
Fire. The different council offices are identified by some of
Quellien's most imaginative work: Apollo, with his soothing
lyre, guards the Chamber of Petty Affairs; Diana, goddess of
hunting, unloads her booty at the entrance to the Treasury;
Venus (who looks as if she is about to hurl an apple at Mars, the
god of war) indicates the room in which marriages were
registered; festoons hung with ink pots, wax seals and other
symbols of bureaucracy flank the door into the City Secretary's
Office; and a depiction of the Fall of Icarus once chastened
debtors as they entered the Bankruptcy Court. It is worth
poring over the fantastic wealth of erudite sculpture, which
conceals delightful touches, such as the playful cherubs that
adorn the two mantelpiece friezes in the Schepenzaal.

The paintings commissioned for the new Town Hall display
a plodding moralizing tone, with none of the wit and
imagination of Quellien's sculpture. Govert Flinck's *Solomon's
Prayer for Wisdom* and Erasmus Quellien's *Amsterdam
Glorified* in the Schepenzaal are heavily influenced by the
surging Baroque of Rubens. The city magistrates' bias towards
didactic bombast led to their rejection of Rembrandt's
Conspiracy of Claudius Civilis, which failed to exploit the full
political potential of the revolt of the Batavians against the
Romans.

As a souvenir of King Louis Napoleon's residence here in
the early 19thC, the Royal Palace boasts an extensive collection
of Empire-style furniture.

Leidseplein

Vierschaar

The heavily fortified ground-floor rooms are occupied by
prison cells, the city bank vaults and the Vierschaar (Hall of
Justice), where the death sentence was pronounced. This
involved an elaborate baroque ceremony in which the
condemned prisoner was brought before the city magistrates,
who were seated on the long bench beneath the statues of four
voluptuous Caryatids representing women in various states of
remorse and anguish. The panels between the Caryatids are
decorated with reliefs showing judicial incidents from the
Bible and Classical mythology, while the frieze above bears
grisly reminders of death. After the prisoner had been led into
this exquisite tomb, the bronze doors, decorated with
thunderbolts, skulls and a curling serpent, were closed and the
death sentence solemnly pronounced.

Leidseplein

Map 6F3 Tram 1, 2, 5, 6, 7, 10 to Leidseplein.
Once the site of a gate at the sw edge of the 17thC city,
Leidseplein first began to assume a cultural role in the 18thC
when the **Stadsschouwburg** (Municipal Theater) was rebuilt
here. This was replaced in 1894 by a bustling Renaissance
confection by J. L. Springer.

Leidseplein received a further boost with the completion in
1902 of the elegant Art Nouveau **American Hotel**, designed
by W. Kromhout. Café society began to develop in the grand
Café Américain and in less pretentious locations such as
Eijlders and **Reijnders** (see *Cafés*). In the 1950s Leidseplein
became the territory of the "Pleiners" (who modeled
themselves on English "Mods"), while the "Dijkers"
(equivalent of the "Rockers") hung out around the
Nieuwendijk.

Numerous cinemas are found around Leidseplein, along
with several alternative centers for the arts including the
famous, if somewhat jaded, **Melkweg** (the Milky Way). There
are also restaurants of every nationality, including an explosion
of pizzerias and trattorias, which give the streets off
Leidsestraat a distinctly Mediterranean ambience. Nor does
Leidseplein ever go to sleep: after the cafés have closed, there
is still plenty of action in the discos, nightclubs and piano bars.

Madame Tussaud

*Kalverstraat 156 ☎(020) 229949. Map 11E4 ◪ ✳ Open
10am–6pm. Tram 4, 9, 14, 16, 24, 25 to Spui.*
Modeled on the famous London waxworks museum,
Amsterdam's Madame Tussaud contains lifelike effigies of
historical figures, world leaders and pop stars. Highlights
include Anne Frank in hiding, Rembrandt in his atelier and an
Amsterdam brown café.

Maritime Museum   See *Nederlands Scheepvaart Museum* .

Nederlands Scheepvaart Museum *(Dutch Maritime Museum)* ★

*Kattenburgerplein 1 ☎(020) 262255 ◪ ▬ ✳ Open Tues–Sat
10am–5pm. Sun, hols 1–5pm. Bus 22, 28 from Centraal
Station to Kadijksplein.*
The Dutch maritime museum is a must for anyone who loves
ships, models of ships, figureheads, globes, maps, charts, sea

battles or portraits of admirals. If you finally tire of room after room of rigged ships and stormy seas, you can gaze through the arched warehouse doors to the busy harbor where gray warships slide slowly past brightly painted houseboats, and the spires of Amsterdam look not unlike a 17thC painting.

In 1973 the museum moved to its present location in the former arsenal of the Amsterdam Admiralty. This stern Classical block designed by Daniel Stalpaert in 1656 stands in splendid isolation on the edge of the Oosterdok. It was here that Amsterdam's warships were fitted with rigging and sails, and equipped with weapons, clothes and provisions for the long voyages to the East and West Indies. The gleaming brass pumps used to supply ships with drinking water can be seen in the courtyard, along with various war-damaged cannons.

The museum contains 30 packed rooms covering every aspect of navigation in the Netherlands from Roman trade on the Rhine to surfboarding. For those who find their interest flagging after 14 rooms, an escape route is helpfully signposted to the restaurant. The museum has also taken pains to provide a highly informative illustrated booklet in English.

One of the most interesting exhibits is the beautiful bottle-green and gold *trekschuit* (rm 5), a type of horsedrawn passenger boat used on the Dutch canal network from the 17th to the 19thC. The *trekschuit* offered a reliable but – as almost every traveler complained – agonizingly slow method of transport. Travelers from Rotterdam to Amsterdam, for example, would spend 11 hours in the cramped and smoky cabin watching the flat Dutch fields slowly glide by.

Also worth seeing are the curious Japanese paintings of the 17thC Dutch trading post in the Bay of Nagasaki (rm 11), the tea clipper model (rm 15) and, in the same room, the melodramatic mementoes relating to the national hero Van Speyk (1802–31), who in the Belgian revolt of 1831 blew up his ship rather than allow it to fall into the hands of the rebels. Attractions that might interest children include the submarine periscope (rm 24), which gives a 360° view of the city. Finally, three restored ships are moored outside the museum: a herring drifter, a steam-powered icebreaker and a lifeboat.

The seldom-visited area around the Scheepvaart Museum is rich in maritime interest, with the imposing 1642 warehouses of the West India Company overlooking Oude Schans at 's Gravenhekje, the early 17thC East India Company warehouses at Prins Hendrikkade 176, Admiral de Ruyter's house at Prins Hendrikkade 131 and a splendid row of 84 18thC warehouses lined up along the Entrepôtdok (reached through the monumental gate on Kadijksplein). It is also possible to walk along the Entrepôtdok to reach the **Werf 't Kromhout**, where a number of boats in various states of repair can be visited.

Nederlands Theater Instituut(Dutch Theater Institute)
Herengracht 168 ☎(020) 235104. Map **11C4** 🖃 ▣Open Tues–Sun 11am–5pm. Tram 1, 2, 5, 13, 14, 17 to Dam.
Philips Vingboons' first neck gable house, located at Herengracht 168, is one of five handsome canal houses that comprise the Dutch Theater Institute. Vingboons' 1638 house, built for the founder of the West India Company, Michiel Pauw, now contains a delightful theater museum. This organizes temporary exhibitions on theater, dance, mime,

cabaret, film and television in the Netherlands, drawing on its fascinating collection of costumes, props, models, posters, recordings and videos. Background information is generally provided in English.

The interior, refurbished in Louis XIV style in the 1730s, is well worth a glance. It includes lavish stucco decoration in the hall by the sculptor Jan van Logteren, a fine spiral staircase, and two rooms decorated by the landscape artist Isaac de Moucheron with scenes from the life of Jephthah, an Israelite judge who sacrificed his daughter in fulfilment of a vow.

Nieuwe Kerk ★

Dam ☎(020) 268168. Map 11D4 ▨ & ▪Open Mon–Sat 11am–4pm, Sun 12–3pm. Tram 1, 2, 4, 5, 9, 13, 14, 16, 17, 24, 25 to Dam.

The Nieuwe Kerk on Dam is one of the few churches in the Netherlands open to the public – not as a church but as a lively social and cultural center, which includes a small bookshop and a brown café. At various times of the year, this huge whitewashed Protestant church is also used for exhibitions of paintings, photographs and antiques.

The Nieuwe Kerk has had an eventful history following its foundation in the 15thC as Amsterdam's second parish church. It burned down in 1421, 1452 and again in 1645, when it was accidentally set alight by a workman on the roof. After rebuilding the church to its former Gothic glory, the city council was browbeaten by the strict Calvinist burgomaster, Willem Backer, into building a tower at the w end to ensure that the church was not upstaged by the new Town Hall. "God's wrath must surely fall on a city that spends such treasure on the outward appearance of a worldly building," Backer darkly warned; but after his death and the outbreak of the First Anglo-Dutch War, the plan was quietly abandoned, leaving only the stump of the tower standing on N. Z. Voorburgwal. When the Town Hall was converted to a royal palace in the 19thC, the Nieuwe Kerk was elevated to the national church of the Netherlands. Since then Dutch monarchs have been crowned here, including the current monarch, Queen Beatrix, in 1980.

The oldest part of the church is the choir, built of rough stone around 1400, while the nave was added in the 1430s in a "streaky bacon" style of alternating rows of brick and stone. A number of small shops have been built onto the side of the church, while on Gravenstraat there is an imposing Classical building of 1642, where poor relief was distributed.

The main feature of the interior is the magnificent organ, built in 1645. Jacob van Campen, the architect of the town hall, designed the casing to look almost like a Classical neck gable facade. Artus Quellien, who produced the town hall's sculpture, festooned the organ base with cherubs and musical instruments, while Jan Gerritsz. van Bronkhorst decorated the organ shutters with scenes from the life of David. The church also boasts a remarkable pulpit built by Albert Jansz. Vinckenbrinck in 1645–64 in a rich Mannerist style. The pulpit is illustrated with works of charity, while its large tester is adorned with a remarkably flamboyant tower.

On the former site of the high altar, the sculptor Rombout Verhulst erected a bombastic tomb to Admiral Michiel de Ruyter, who died while fighting the French at the Battle of Messina in 1676. A somewhat less pompous tomb by Verhulst

for Admiral Jan van Galen, who died during the Battle of
Leghorn, is to be seen on the N wall.

Nieuwe Zijde *(New Side)*
Maps **11**, **12**. *Tram 1, 2, 5, 13, 17 to Dam.*
This area, "the new side," which extends W from Damrak and
Rokin to *Singel*, mirrors the canal pattern of *Oude Zijde*
almost exactly. But its character is completely different due to
the filling in of its canals in the 19thC, which lends a rather
melancholy atmosphere. It is also very much more crowded,
especially along Kalverstraat – Amsterdam's principal
shopping street – which follows the course of the 13thC dike
along the W side of the Amstel. Less claustrophobic streets
with interesting shops include St Luciensteeg, just N of the
Amsterdams Historisch Museum, and Gravenstraat, which
bends around the back of the *Nieuwe Kerk*. There is a stamp
market on N.Z. Voorburgwal just S of Dam and a cluster of
bookshops between Spui and Dam, both of which add to the
variety of Nieuwe Zijde.

The area around Dam is particularly animated, though the
dignity of the *Royal Palace* is somewhat marred by the
Neo-Gothic pile of the **Postkantoor** (post office) at N.Z.
Voorburgwal 182, whose turreted skyline led to its being
ridiculed in a 19thC cartoon as "the pear mountain – an
experiment in fruit architecture." N of Dam, notice the
attractive group of houses at the **Blaeu Erf** (Blaeu's Yard)
(*N.Z. Voorburgwal 87–99*), named after the printing works of
the 17thC map-maker Jan Blaeu which stood here. The
picturesque 1633 Renaissance house at N.Z. Voorburgwal 75
is the **Makelaarsgildehuis** (realtors' guild house), adorned
with the stubborn motto "Freedom is not for sale at any
price." Farther N at N.Z. Kolk 28 is the 1620
Korenmetershuisje (corn exchange).

S of Dam, N.Z. Voorburgwal passes the *Amsterdams
Historisch Museum* and leads to Spui, a particularly attractive
square where the two canals of Nieuwe Zijde once converged.
The *Begijnhof* occupies the N side, while to the S is the 1787
Maagdenhuis, formerly a girls' orphanage. To the right is the
1633 **Old Lutheran Church**. The statue of a cute street
urchin, **Het Amsterdamse Lieverdje**, was donated by a
cigarette company and provided a popular target for Provo
demonstrations in the 1960s.

Voetboogstraat, which contains some unusual shops, leads S
to the dramatic gateway of the **Rasphuis** at Heiligeweg 19, a
model house of correction, set up in 1596, where men were put
to work shaving a hard type of Brazilian wood used for dyeing.
The portal, probably built by Hendrick de Keyser in 1603,
shows the Maid of Amsterdam punishing two criminals above
a rumination by Seneca: "It is virtuous to tame that which
everyone fears."

Nieuwmarkt
Map **12**D6. *Metro to Nieuwmarkt.*
One of the most fascinating areas of Amsterdam, Nieuwmarkt
is particularly rich in sights associated with the Dutch painter
Rembrandt van Rijn. To the S of the square, Nieuwmarkt,
lies the university, and to the E a particularly beautiful area of
silent, forgotten canals. The fringes of the red light district
impinge slightly on the W and N sides of Nieuwmarkt, but the
seediness can easily be avoided.

The dominant feature of Nieuwmarkt is the dusky medieval hulk of the **Waag**, formerly a turreted city gate on the E edge of the city. When the city expanded outwards in the 17thC, the moat around the gate was filled and the building converted to a weigh house. Various local guilds met in the upstairs rooms, which were reached by separate staircases in the different towers. The ornate 17thC entrances still survive: the guild of artists used the door decorated with the figure of St Luke, while the masons' entrance is distinguished by a mason's head and tools. Notice the tower with its curious trial windows, which were painstakingly built by apprentices in order that they might qualify as master masons. The guild of surgeons, which used the door inscribed *Theatrum Anatomicum*, commissioned Rembrandt's famous early work *The Anatomy Lesson of Dr Tulp*, now hanging in the Mauritshuis in Den Haag (see *Excursions*).

Another relic of the medieval city wall is the Schreierstoren (Tower of Tears) at the N end of Geldersekade, which takes its name from the legend that women would climb this tower to watch their husbands' ships depart.

Something of the former splendor of Kloveniersburgwal, which runs S from Nieuwmarkt to the Amstel, can be seen in the **Trippenhuis** at Kloveniersburgwal 29. This splendid Classical palace modeled on the Amsterdam **Stadhuis** was built by Justus Vingboons in 1660–64 for the brothers Louis and Hendrick Trip, who achieved unprecedented domestic grandeur by concealing their separated dwellings behind a single facade. The most remarkable feature of the house is its two chimneys, modeled on cannons. Other military emblems can be discerned in the fresco – a reminder that the Trip family was one of Europe's largest and most unscrupulous arms manufacturers, with no qualms about supplying both the Roundheads and Cavaliers during the English Civil War. In 1815 the separate dwellings were joined to house the *Rijksmuseum*.

Amsterdammers are fond of pointing out the exceptionally narrow house at Kloveniersburgwal 26 known as the **Kleine-Trippenhuis**, which was supposedly built in 1696 for a family servant, using stone left over from the Trippenhuis.

The W side of Kloveniersburgwal is dominated by drab 19thC university buildings, but there are one or two hidden delights to be found down the side streets, such as the 1633 wine merchants' guild house (**Wijnkopersgildehuis**) at Koestraat 10–12, and the former offices of the Dutch East India Company at Oude Hoogstraat 24. This almost forgotten relic of Amsterdam's trading past contains a courtyard worth entering to view the exceptionally ornate 1606 Mannerist scrolled gable, built some four years after the foundation of the East India Company.

Continuing S on Kloveniersburgwal, you come to **no. 62**, with its rich sea imagery, and the stately **Poppenhuis** at no. 95, built by Philips Vingboons in 1642. Directly opposite is the E gate of the **Oudemanhuis**, once a home for old men, with sculpture by Anthonie Ziesenis added in 1786.

The **Doelen Hotel** overlooking the S end of Kloveniersburgwal is decorated with the two principal figures from Rembrandt's *Night Watch*, a reminder that this was the site of the tower in which the company of civil guards met. Furthermore, the Syndics of the Cloth Guild, whom Rembrandt painted in 1662, met in the **Lakenhal** on the nearby Groenburgwal. A last relic of the once flourishing linen trade on this island is the **Saaihal**, at Staalstraat 7, which was built by Pieter de Keyser in 1641.

To reach the tranquil area E of Nieuwmarkt from here, continue N along the quiet Groenburgwal, turn right along Raamgracht, then turn left and follow the canal Zwanenburgwal N to the picturesque lock, the **St Antoniessluis**.

Straight ahead is the Oude Schans, a canal that obtains a certain grandeur from the **Montelbaanstoren**, a defensive tower on the E edge of the 16thC city which in 1606 was given an ornate spire by Hendrick de Keyser. On the corner of Oude Schans and Prins Hendrikkade are the imposing warehouses built in 1642 for the Dutch West India Company, whose main trading interests were sugar and furs.

Head W along Binnenkant to reach the magnificent **Scheepvaarthuis**, built for seven shipping companies in 1912 by the Amsterdam School architects Johan van der Mey, Michel de Klerk and P. L. Kramer. Notice the fantastic maritime details decorating the outside of the building, such as whales, ships, navigators' heads, mermaids, ocean deities and even rippling iron railings.

Walk around the outside of the Scheepvaarthuis and turn right down the enticingly rural Buiten Bantammerstraat, then cross a rather medieval Amsterdam School-style bridge and turn left to reach Lastageweg. This leads to the narrow canal Rechtboomsloot, where a right turn leads to Kromboomsloot, a dark, silent and forgotten canal, where at **no. 22** Amsterdam's Armenian community built a Rococo church in 1714.

NINT Technisch Museum

Tolstraat 129 ☎ (020) 646021. Map 8J7 ⬛ ♿ ▣ ✱ Open Mon–Fri 10am–4pm, Sat, Sun 1–5pm. Tram 4 to Lutmastraat.

Located in a former diamond-cutting factory in the 19thC district of Amsterdam Zuid, the technology museum NINT is particularly geared towards schoolchildren. The aim is to make science fun and there are countless push-button machines and models to demonstrate how things such as magnets, electricity, cars and telephones work. The explanatory notes are in Dutch, but this need not be a deterrent since most children are quite content to dash from one working model to the next, leaving their parents to puzzle over the theory.

Oude Kerk ★

Oudekerksplein 23 ☎ (020) 249183. Map 11D5 ⬛ ✗ compulsory for tower ◁≣ Church open Mon–Sat noon–4pm; tower open June to mid-Sept Mon and Thurs 2–5pm, Tues and Wed 11am–2pm. Tram 4, 9, 16, 24, 25 to Dam, then 10min walk.

Begun around 1200, burned to the ground in 1274 by the troops of Count Floris V, rebuilt as a hall church and then converted to a basilica around 1500, the Oude Kerk is Amsterdam's oldest and most fascinating church. Of particular interest are the massive wooden vaulted roofs, the frescoed columns, the delightful misericords illustrating various traditional proverbs, the ornate gravestones of eminent Amsterdammers, and the 16thC stained-glass windows in one of the choirs, known as the *Nieuwe Vrouwenkoor*, depicting the life of the Virgin.

Dedicated to St Nicholas, patron saint of sailors, the Oude Kerk echoes Amsterdam's seafaring past in features such as the Hamburgerkapel, which was built in the early 16thC by Hamburg merchants living in Amsterdam. Ships appear everywhere: on the vaulted roof, on the various monuments to Dutch admirals who died in battle, on the small organ, and even crudely carved on the back of the wooden choir screen. Rembrandt's wife Saskia, who died in 1642, is buried in a grave numbered 29K, near the small choir organ.

The Oude Kerk's famous large organ was built during 1738–42 by Johannes Caspar Müller; the small choir organ was recently replaced, although the decorative casing dates from the 17thC.

The Oude Kerk also boasts a 17thC carillon built by bell-maker François Hemony, which is played every Sat from 4–5pm as Amsterdammers rush to finish their shopping.

The gracious Late-Gothic spire, which was built by Joost Jansz. Bilhamer in 1565, can be climbed to obtain a view of the old city.

Oude Zijde (Old Side)
Map 11. Tram 4, 9, 14, 16, 24, 25 to Spui.

The "Old Side" runs E from Damrak and Rokin to Kloveniersburgwal, which marks the limit of the medieval city. This quarter consists of Warmoesstraat, formerly a dike along the *Amstel*, and the two canals O.Z. Voorburgwal and O.Z. Achterburgwal, whose names literally mean before and behind the city wall.

As its name suggests, Oude Zijde is the oldest area of the city, and is packed with historic interest. Unfortunately, some of its finest buildings are buried in the red light district, which lies to the N of the line formed by Damstraat, Oude Doelenstraat and Oude Hoogstraat. But venture only a few steps S of this demarcation line to discover the most tranquil and beautiful area of the city, with numerous old gateways richly adorned with symbolic sculpture and verse.

To see Oude Zijde at its best, turn off Rokin down the narrow Langebrugsteeg to reach Grimburgwal, turn left down O.Z. Voorburgwal and walk to Oude Hoogstraat, then turn right and right again to return by O.Z. Achterburgwal.

Grimburgwal is a particularly pleasing corner of the medieval city at the convergence of three canals. Many of the narrow streets in this part of town provide reminders of former convents and monasteries in names such as Gebed Zonder End (Prayer Without End), a narrow lane that once divided two convents.

The view E of Grimburgwal is terminated by the **House on the Three Canals** at O.Z. Voorburgwal 249, an early 17thC step-gabled house built of rosy red brick trimmed with whitened sandstone.

Turning left down O.Z. Voorburgwal you can see the former **St Agnietenkapel** behind a jaunty 16thC Mannerist portal at O.Z. Voorburgwal 231. This 15thC chapel belonged to the convent of St Agnes, which, like many in medieval Amsterdam, adopted the rather relaxed rules of the Third Order of St Francis of Assisi. The building now houses the historical collection of the University of Amsterdam.

The S end of O.Z. Voorburgwal was dubbed "the velvet canal" in the 18thC because of the numerous rich merchants who settled here, putting up ornate facades such as **O.Z.**

Voorburgwal 237 and **no. 217**, with their exceptionally fine
Louis XIV tops. At no. 197 is a former **stadhuis** (town hall),
built in Amsterdam School style during the 1920s and
incorporating on the S side of the courtyard the Classical
Admiraliteitsgebouw (Admiralty Office), built in the 1660s.
The city council moved here in 1808 when Louis Napoleon
established his Royal Palace in the Stadhuis on Dam.

At O.Z. Voorburgwal 300 is the **Stadsbank van Lening**,
the municipal bank, which was established here in a rugged
warehouse built by Hendrick de Keyser in 1616. The famous
Dutch poet Joost van den Vondel (1587–1679) worked in the
bank as a bookkeeper until he was 81. Notice in the alley to the
right of the building the doorway with a relief by Hendrick de
Keyser depicting a woman pawning her property at the bank.
The bank building to the left of the warehouses, which was
added in 1669, has a lengthy edifying poem above the entrance
explaining the virtues of pawn banks.

The curious Mannerist gate to the right of the alley Enge
Lombardsteeg formerly led to an inn whose name De Brakke
Grond (The Brackish Ground) tells something of the terrain
on which Amsterdam was built. Other revealing names near
here are **Slijkstraat** (Slime Street) and **Rusland** (Rushes
Land).

Amsterdam's involvement in the slave trade is recalled by
the sculpture decorating the 1663 facade at **O.Z.
Voorburgwal 187**, which depicts Black slaves and American
Indians on tobacco bales.

To reach the *Oude Kerk* and the *Museum Amstelkring*, you
must venture N of Oude Doelenstraat into the fringes of the red
light district. Above the door of **O.Z. Voorburgwal 136** is a
bust of Admiral Tromp and a scene from the Third Anglo-
Dutch War of 1673.

Returning S on **O.Z. Achterburgwal**, you pass the
attractive square, Walenplein, overlooked by the **Waalse
Kerk** at O.Z. Achterburgwal 157. This chapel formerly
belonged to a monastery and was given to the Walloon
community in 1587. These French-speaking Protestants who
had fled from the Spanish-occupied Southern Netherlands
added a Mannerist gateway on Oude Hoogstraat and in 1647 a
Classical entrance facing Walenplein.

At O.Z. Achterburgwal 185 is a dignified Classical building
built in 1645 that houses the **Spinhuis**, a house of correction
where women were made to spin wool as a form of therapy.
Notice the ornate Ionic portal in Spinhuissteeg, which bears a
moralistic motto by the poet P. C. Hooft telling visitors not to
be alarmed by the punishments because their motivation is
love and not revenge.

At the S end of O.Z. Achterburgwal are two more gateways,
the **Oudemanhuispoort** and the **Gasthuispoort**.

Piggy bank Museum   See *Spaarpotten Museum*.

Prinsengracht
*Map 6, 7, 8, 10, 11. Tram 13, 14, 17 to Westermarkt; tram 1, 2,
4, 5, 16, 24, 25 to Prinsengracht.*

"The Princes' Canal" is the outermost canal of the 17thC
Grachtengordel. Earmarked in the 1609 Plan for warehouses,
workshops, churches, shops and artisan dwellings, the canal
lacks the architectural splendors of *Herengracht* and
Keizersgracht, but offers instead a bustling blend of brown

cafés, boutiques, art galleries and houseboats. It is rather tiring to walk the entire 3km (2 miles) of Prinsengracht, so limit yourself to short stretches, such as that from Brouwersgracht to Rozengracht or from Reguliersgracht to the *Amstel*.

From Brouwersgracht to Nieuwe Spiegelstraat
The intersection of Prinsengracht and Brouwersgracht offers fine views in every direction, which can be enjoyed from the traditional brown café **Papeneiland** or the newer, but just as brown, **'t Smackzeyl**. Proceeding S, one reaches **Noordermarkt**, a small square tinged with the shabby charm characteristic of the Jordaan, which lies just to the w. The unusual octagonal **Noorderkerk** was built as a Protestant church in 1620–23, probably by Hendrick de Keyser. Some curious little shops and cafés have taken root around the church; and at Prinsengracht 85–113 is the **Starhofje**, built in a rather utilitarian early 19thC style.

A much lovelier *hofje* is found between Noordermarkt and Westermarkt: **Zon's hofje** at Prinsengracht 159–71, built in 1765. The secluded courtyard is generally open to the public. Notice inside the impressive gateway with its facade stone showing Noah's Ark surrounded by a curious collection of animals. Beyond, the E side of the canal is dominated by 18thC warehouses, while the w side has numerous houses with 18thC shop fronts. Prinsengracht is not entirely mundane, however, and the frothy Rococo sculpture decorating the top of **Prinsengracht 126** is as lavish as anything on the more prestigious canals. Visit the brown café **De Prins** to enjoy the fine view down Leliegracht, and glance into the window of **Oey's Etalage** at Prinsengracht 128, where art of a somewhat surreal tendency is exhibited.

The *Anne Frank Huis* is located at Prinsengracht 263, while nearby is the *Westerkerk*. The French philosopher René Descartes spent the summer of 1634 living in a French schoolteacher at Westermarkt 6.

Between Westermarkt and Nieuwe Spiegelstraat, Prinsengracht assumes an amiable, although somewhat undistinguished character. The **Pulitzer Hotel** at Prinsengracht 315–31 made a unique contribution to architectural conservation when it restored 24 gable houses to create a 250-room hotel. The **Pulitzer Art Gallery** is located within the complex. Other art galleries and chic restaurants have sprung up nearby, particularly in Reestraat.

From Nieuwe Spiegelstraat to the Amstel
The stretch of Prinsengracht between Nieuwe Spiegelstraat and Reguliersgracht is a touch more distinguished, and on the w side blends into the tranquil **Weteringbuurt**. At no.855–99 is the **Deutzenhof**, an alms house established in 1695 by Agnes Deutz who, according to the inscription above the entrance, "exercised her love and faith as a comfort for the poor and an example to the rich." *(Closed to the public.)*

Overlooking Reguliersgracht is the wooden Amstelkerk, which looks decidedly out of place in its urban setting. This church was erected in 1670 as a temporary Protestant church that was intended to be replaced eventually by a much larger church on the Amstelveld. The plan was abandoned, however, leaving Amstelveld with a rather sad appearance, enlivened only by the plant market held here every Mon. Opposite is a rare 19thC Neoclassical church **De Duif**.

The final stretch of Prinsengracht is a picturesque confusion of houseboats and gable houses drenched in wisteria.

Het Rembrandthuis Museum *(Rembrandt House)*
Jodenbreestraat 6 ☎ *(020) 249486. Map* **126E** 🚹 *Open
Mon–Sat 10am–5pm, Sun, hols 1–5pm. Tram 9, 14 or metro
to Waterlooplein.*

Rembrandt was only 33 years old when he bought this
distinguished red-shuttered Classical house on the principal
street of the *Jodenbuurt*. He lived here from 1639–58 when
financial difficulties forced him to move to a more modest
house in the *Jordaan*.

The main attraction of the museum is its extensive collection
of some 250 etchings and drawings by Rembrandt. Some of
these illustrate biblical themes, while others show the gentle
landscape of the river Amstel which Rembrandt visited
frequently after his wife Saskia's death. Perhaps the most
delightful etchings, however, are those in the mezzanine room
showing Rembrandt's compassionate eye for beggars, street
musicians, organ-grinders, rat-catchers and other 17thC
figures. The museum also contains an informative exhibition
on etching techniques.

Royal Palace See *Koninklijk Paleis.*

Rijksmuseum ★
Stadhouderskade 42 ☎ *(020) 732121. Map* **6G3** 🚹 🚻 ≈
*Open Tues–Sat 10am–5pm, Sun, hols 1–5pm. A visiting card
for admission to the Six Collection can be obtained at the
information desk in the museum shop on production of a
passport. Tram 6, 7, 10 to Spiegelgracht; tram 1, 2, 5 to
Leidseplein.*

The national museum of the Netherlands houses a diverse
range of collections, of which its 17thC Dutch paintings are by
far the most important. Established by King Louis Napoleon
in 1808 along the lines of the Louvre in Paris, the
Rijksmuseum collection was initially housed in the Royal
Palace on the Dam, but later moved to the Trippenhuis on
Kloveniersburgwal. Eventually the collection outgrew this
canal house, and P. J. H. Cuypers was commissioned to build a
new Rijksmuseum in the fashionable area of the 19thC ring
near the Vondelpark. The intention was to have a building in
Dutch Renaissance style, but Cuypers – a fervent Catholic –
could not suppress his Gothic tendencies, and the building is
imbued with an unmistakable medieval flavor with its
Burgundian roofs and exuberant decoration. King William III
was so upset at what he called "the monastery" that he refused
to set foot in the building.

Exterior

The bustling architectural detail is best appreciated from the
formal 18thC garden on Hobbemastraat, where tile tableaux
depict famous Dutch and Flemish artists, a relief shows
Rembrandt at work on his *Staalmeesters* (above the tunnel
entrance), and curious sculptures on the roof show masons at
work on the building.

The building, completed in 1885, soon proved too small for
the ever-growing collection. In 1915 the **Drucker Extension**
was added to house 18th–19thC paintings and Asiatic art. The
outside walls of the extension are laden with a fascinating
collection of old architectural fragments rescued from
demolished buildings. These include several medieval and
Renaissance gateways from different Dutch cities; the most
impressive is the Waterpoort from Gorinchem, which has been

built into the structure of the Rijksmuseum. There is also an ornate 18thC gateway from one of the many vanished country houses on the Amstel. Notice too the small Rococo pavilion at the back of the museum.

The collections

If you have only a short time to spare, concentrate on the works of Rembrandt, Vermeer, De Hoogh and the other Dutch Masters. A useful introduction to the 17thC painting is the slide show (with English, French and German commentary), shown every 20min in the Film Theater.

If time allows, set off to explore the neglected departments of the Rijksmuseum – Medieval Painting, Sculpture and Applied Art, Dutch History, 18th–19thC Dutch Painting and Asiatic Art – all of which offer delightful surprises. One of the best ways to begin is to select one of the *Viewfinder* leaflets in English at the desk in the museum shop. These offer various different routes through selected rooms of the museum, each route describing 10–12 objects that illustrate a particular theme such as townscapes, decorative glass, interior decoration, Dutch landscape painting from the 17th–19thC, hidden meanings in Dutch art or technical virtuosity. Some of these routes might appeal to children, such as the one entitled "How many hairs are there on a dog (in a painting)?", which deals with Realism in art. There is also a route that explains the riot of decoration on the exterior of the museum. Each route can be covered in about 30min, although it is easy to lose the way or find a particular route closed – in which case ask a guard for assistance.

17thC painting

The glory of the Rijksmuseum is its collection of 17thC Dutch paintings (rms 208–36) and in particular its Rembrandts (rms 221, 224, 229–30). Pride of place is given to *The Company of Frans Banning Cocq and Lieutenant van Rutenburch*, which hangs in a room, purpose-built in 1906, at the end of the Gallery of Honour. This large painting was commissioned in 1642 by a company of the civil guards to hang in their meeting hall at the end of Kloveniersburgwal. Later it became so covered with grime that it was mistaken for a night scene, thus acquiring the totally unjustified name *The Night Watch*. Now that the painting has been thoroughly cleaned it is possible to see the masterful way in which Rembrandt picks out details of expression and costume as the guards emerge dramatically from the building into a pool of sunlight.

The Rijksmuseum has a total of 18 Rembrandts spanning his working life, from an exquisite *Self Portrait* at the age of 22, before he moved from Leiden, to a troubled *Self Portrait as the Apostle Paul*, painted in 1661 after he had been forced to move out of his house on Jodenbreestraat because of financial difficulties. His mastery of *chiaroscuro* (the Italian technique of mixing light and shade) is seen in the tender *Holy Family*, in which Rembrandt sets the Nativity in the dark cellar of a Dutch house. Other portraits show his wife Saskia, his son Titus dressed in a monk's habit, and presumably his mother as *The Prophetess Anna*. Rembrandt produced some of his most tender work towards the end of his life, such as his portrait of *The Wardens of the Amsterdam Drapers' Guild* and the haunting *Portrait of a Couple* (better known as *The Jewish Bride*), painted when he was 61.

Another highlight of the Rijksmuseum is its collection of paintings by the Delft School (rm 222). Johannes Vermeer used strong light and bold colors to give an almost religious significance to quiet domestic scenes such as *The Kitchen Maid* and *Woman Reading a Letter*, and captured the warmth of Delft brick houses in *The Little Street*, which he painted from the window of his house looking across to the old people's home opposite. Pieter de Hoogh also painted tranquil domestic interiors such as *Maternal Duty*, which is bathed in a mellow golden light, and *Interior with Women beside a Linen Chest*, and was particularly fond of the *doorkijk* – a view through several rooms to the outside.

The other paintings in the 17thC collection are arranged rather haphazardly. Saenredam's methodical studies of church interiors in Assendelft, Haarlem and Utrecht possess an almost mystical stillness, while his view of the old town hall of Amsterdam conveys its shabby charm. The merry domestic scenes of Jan Steen such as *The Feast of St Nicholas* and the boisterous peasants of Adriaen van Ostade's *The Skaters* might seem to belong to a more carefree world than Rembrandt, but the paintings had a deep moral purpose – for example, the eggshells casually strewn across the floor warn of the dangers of reckless indulgence. Even the still lifes of Heda and Claesz. contained hidden meanings, such as a fallen glass that symbolized death.

Frans Hals was less inclined to turn a painting into a sermon, and his *Wedding Portrait of Isaac Abrahamsz Massa and Beatrix van der Laen* is full of good humor, while the almost impressionistic *Merry Drinker* reflects the epicurean mood of Haarlem in the Golden Age. Amsterdam was a very serious and sober city by comparison, to judge from Werner van den Valckert's group portraits of the Governors and Governesses of the Amsterdam Leper Asylum. Even the figures in Bartholomeus van der Helst's *The Celebration of the Peace of Münster in the Headquarters of the St George's Guard, Amsterdam* do not seem to be enjoying themselves particularly. The feast is taking place in the guild's meeting hall on *Singel*, where the university library now stands. Notice also Van der Helst's unflattering portrait of Gerard Bicker.

The greatest landscape artist of the Golden Age was Jacob van Ruisdael, whose compellingly romantic *The Mill near Wijk bij Duurstede* shows a heavily overcast sky threatening the small figures in the foreground. His uncle, Salomon van Ruysdael, favored a more placid landscape (*River Landscape with Cattle Ferry*), while Jan van Goyen's scenes were as shabby as Adriaen van Ostade's interiors. Least Dutch in character are the landscapes of Aelbert Cuyp, whose *River Landscape with Riders* is bathed in an Italianate golden hue.

Medieval painting

The small medieval art collection (rms 201–4) contains several fine works by 15thC Northern Netherlandish artists, notably Geertgen tot Sint Jans and the Master of the Virgo inter Virgines (named after his most famous work). The subject matter is invariably religious, though the artists do not hesitate to dress the figures in sumptuous 15thC garments and include views of blue-roofed Burgundian cities in the background. The most appealing work is the Master of Alkmaar's *Seven Works of Charity*, a painting that has had more than its fair share of misfortune: the monks' faces were vandalized during the Iconoclasm and damp later caused further damage. Notice the modest figure of Christ in each of the scenes.

The arrival of the Renaissance in the Netherlands is marked

by Jan van Scorel's *Mary Magdalene* (rm 205). His pupil
Maerten van Heemskerck's *Erythraean Sibyl* is interesting for
the hazy view of Delft in the background.

The excesses of Flemish Mannerism are illustrated by
Joachim Bueckelaar's irreverent *Jesus with Martha and Mary*,
while Joos de Momper's *River Landscape with Boar Hunt*
conveys a breathtaking sense of space.

Sculpture and applied art

The Rijksmuseum's vast collection of sculpture and applied art
is spread over the three floors of the w wing. The collection is
arranged in chronological order: Medieval, Renaissance and
Classical works on the first floor; 18thC works in Louis XIV
and XV style on the ground floor; and finally Louis XVI,
Empire and Art Nouveau pieces in the basement. If interested
in a particular subject, check whether it is covered by one of
the *Viewfinders*.

Among the medieval works (rms 238–48), the most
important are the exquisite late 15thC sculptures by Adriaen
van Wesel, who is regarded as the greatest Dutch sculptor of
the middle ages (rms 241–42). The Flemish art of
miniaturization is demonstrated by the incredible "*devotional
nut* " (rm 241) carved by Adam Dirksz, which was carried on
pilgrimages in a copper case inside a velvet bag. The
melancholy sculpture of Northern Germany (rm 245) and the
painfully honest Realism of the Southern Netherlands
(rm 246) contrast with the rather placid vision of Dutch
sculptors such as the Master of Koudewater.

The tormented Mannerism of the late 16thC is mainly
represented by tapestries and furniture (rm 250), while the
solemn temper of mid-17thC Dutch Classicism is illustrated
by the beautiful furnished room from a Dordrecht house
(rm 252), the room of sculptures by Artus Quellien (rm 258),
and the furniture designed by Philips Vingboons for the
Huydecoper mansion on Singel (rm 258a). The remarkable
Chinese room from Leeuwarden illustrates the Dutch
fascination with Oriental art in the 17thC (rm 261).

Descend to the ground floor for the highly popular
dollhouses (rm 162), made in the 18thC with painstaking
attention to detail.

The development of Dutch interior design from the early
18thC to the early 20thC can be followed in the furnished
rooms: Louis XIV style emerging under William III
(rms 164–65 and 167–69), the more delicate Rococo or Louis
XV style appearing in the mid-18thC (rms 173–76, including
the dollhouse in rm 175), and the cool and formal Louis XVI
style developing towards the end of the century (rm 179 and
basement rms 25, 27 and 29). The gilded luxury of the Empire
style was introduced during the French Occupation (rm 33),
and a beautiful room in Art Nouveau style rewards those who
manage to penetrate to the remotest corner of the museum
(rm 34).

18th–19thC painting

After the Golden Age, Dutch painting took a tumble into
whimsy. The pleasant little scenes of Cornelis Troost seem
weak in comparison with the softly sensual pastels of the 18thC
Swiss painter Jean-Etienne Liotard (rm 139), and perhaps the
finest Dutch work of the period is Jan Kels' *The Writer*
(rm 142), with its unmistakable hint of Vermeer.

Early 19thC painting (rms 143–44) was highly Romantic in
flavor, as in the landscapes of Koekoek and Nuijen and the

highly atmospheric view of Amsterdam's *Raampoortje* by
W. J. Troostwijk.

A new sensibility entered Dutch painting in the second half
of the 19thC when the artists of the Hague School, inspired by
the French Schools, turned their attention to the dune and sea
landscape of the Dutch coast (rms 145–48), producing placid
scenes such as Anton Mauve's *Morning Ride on the Beach*. The
Amsterdam Impressionists preferred to capture action and
excitement in their work, as expressed in Breitner's
thunderous *Horse Artillery*, or his *Bridge over the Singel at
Paleisstraat, Amsterdam*, which reflects the feverish activity of
late-19thC Amsterdam.

Asiatic art

The peaceful department of Asiatic Art (rms 11–23) contains
some highly expressive examples of Indonesian art, such as the
ferocious *Head of a Kala* and the exquisite *Head of Jatayu,
King of the Birds*. Japanese art is represented by the miniature
perfection of a birdcage, a smoking cabinet and a casket in the
shape of a crane. Note also the whimsical painting of a *Fox in
Festive Attire*. The more monumental character of Chinese art is
illustrated by the 12thC wooden statue of *Avalokiteshvara*,
while the 12thC Indian bronze of *Shiva, Lord of the Dance* is
particularly impressive. Finally, look for the superb set of 12
Chinese cups from the Kangxi period, in which the months of
the year are illustrated by a different plant or flower.

Dutch history

This is the least enticing section of the museum, despite a
facelift in 1971. The medieval section (rm 101) fails to come to
terms with a potentially fascinating period, the most
interesting exhibit being the set of panels of *The St Elizabeth's
Day Flood*, showing the aftermath of the disastrous flood of
1421 which created the vast inlet s of Dordrecht known as the
Hollands Diep. At the exit of the room is the bookchest that
Hugo Grotius purportedly hid in to escape from Loevestein
Castle. The religious quarrels that led to Grotius' banishment
are the subject of the nearby painting by A. van de Venne,
entitled *Fishing for Souls*.

The center of attention is the spacious 17thC square, which
fills the former E courtyard of the building. The extent of
Dutch trading interests is illustrated by the series of six
paintings of East India Company settlements, which originally
hung in the company's Amsterdam head office on Oude
Hoogstraat. Also of interest is the painting of *The Battle of the
Haarlemmermeer* (1573) in which the Spanish fleet, based in
pro-Catholic Amsterdam, defeated the Dutch rebels and
captured Haarlem. The inland sea on which the battle
occurred was drained in the 19thC and was later to become the
site of Amsterdam's Schiphol airport.

The rooms that follow have an air of neglect, indicating
perhaps Dutch historians' lack of interest in the periods
following the Golden Age. The most interesting room is
devoted to Dutch trading links with China and Japan, and
includes an intriguing Japanese painting showing scenes from
the Dutch settlement on Nagasaki. Foreigners were forbidden
to enter the city, so that the Dutch were confined to a small
fan-shaped island in the bay of Nagasaki.

Print rooms

Interesting temporary exhibitions of prints from the
Rijksmuseum's vast collection are found in the rooms just
beyond the restaurant (rms 128–33).

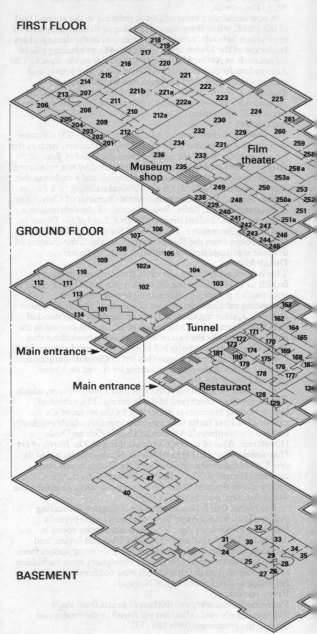

RIJKSMUSEUM FLOOR PLAN

FIRST FLOOR

218 219
217
216 220
215 221
214
213 207 221b 221a 222
206 208 211 222a 223 225
205 204 209 210 212a 224 261
203 202 201 212 230 260 259 258
236 234 232 229 231 258a
Museum 235 233 Film 253a
shop theater 250 253
249 250a 252
238 248 251
239 240 247 251a
241 242 243 244 245 246

GROUND FLOOR

107 106
108
109 105
110 102a
112 111 102 104
113 103
114
101
163
162
Tunnel 164
171 165
172 170
Main entrance → 173 174 169
181 180 175 168
179 176 167
178 177
Main entrance → Restaurant 13
128
129

BASEMENT

47
40
32
31 30 33
24 34 35
25 29 28
27 26

FIRST FLOOR
Painting 15th–17th Century
201 Geertgen tot Sint Jans
204 Lucas van Leyden
206 Mannerists
209–210 Frans Hals
211 Rembrandt
214 Ruisdael
216 Jan Steen
222 Vermeer
224 Night Watch
225 Foreign Schools
229–230 Rembrandt

Sculpture & Applied Art 1
15th–17th Century
238–247 Middle Ages
248 Italy
249 Acquisitions
250 Renaissance
251a Treasure room
253 Glass & Silver
253a Colonial art
254 Vianen & Lutma
255–257 Delftware
258 17th Century Sculpture

GROUND FLOOR
Dutch history
101 Middle Ages & Revolt
102 Republic, East & West Indies, Ship models
102a Everyday life
103–104 Sea battles against England
105 William III of Orange
107 Deshima, Sri Lanka
110 Battle of Waterloo
114 World War II

Print Room
128–133 Prints & drawings

Painting 18th–19th Century
136–137 Cornelis Troost
139 Pastels
140 Miniatures
144–145 Romanticism
146–148 The Hague School
149 Amsterdam School

Sculpture & Applied art II
138 Islamic art
162 Dolls' houses
166 Lace
170–171 Meissen
177 Silver

BASEMENT
Asiatic art
12 Indonesia
13–14 Japan
15–16 China
17–18 India
19–23 China

Study collections
40 Tiles
47 Painting

Sculpture & Applied art III
24 Glass
28 European porcelain
30 Textiles
32 Dutch porcelain
33 Empire
34 Art Nouveau

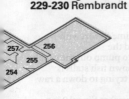

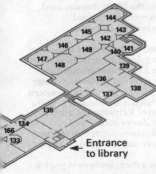

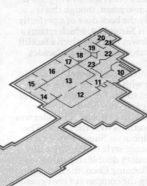

Singel

Maps 6, 10, 11. Tram to Centraal Station, Dam, Spui or Muntplein.

This canal marks the transition from the compact medieval city with its narrow streets, to the spacious and elegant 17thC canal web. From 1487 to 1585 it formed a moat on the w side of the city – Singel means literally a girdle – and the buildings on the inside of the canal therefore tend to be older and somewhat lower in height than those opposite. Nothing now remains of the medieval wall on Singel except for the brick base of the Munttoren.

Measuring slightly more than 1.6km (1 mile), Singel is one of the most pleasant canals for walking and offers an interesting range of architectural styles.

N end of Singel to Raadhuisstraat

This end of the canal has a breezy, maritime flavor, with seagulls swooping and screeching around the Haarlemmersluis, one of the locks used to pump out the canals each night. One of Amsterdam's best-known fish stalls is located on the bridge – if the prospect of trying to down a raw herring tempts.

Het Spaanse Huis (The Spanish House) at Singel 2 is a ruggedly utilitarian step gable from the 1600s that was used both as a warehouse and home by a merchant named Cruywagen; the facade stone showing a wheelbarrow (*kruiwagen*) is a play on his name.

The view s is beautifully accented by the circular **Lutheran Church**, a grand Classical building designed in Doric style by Adriaen Dortsman in the 1670s on a somewhat cramped site. The church now serves as a rather splendid conference center for the Sonesta Hotel, and on Sun mornings is used for concerts.

Several houses near the former harbor are adorned with sea imagery. The beautiful Rococo top of **Vriesland** at Singel 24 shows an 18thC sailing ship, while **Zeevrucht** (Fruit of the Sea) at Singel 36 boasts a superb Rococo centerpiece adorned with foamy waves. A refuge for stray cats is located on a barge moored at this spot on Singel.

Singel 7, which is no wider than a door, features in guided tours as the narrowest house in Amsterdam, though this is something of a myth as it is merely the back door of a perfectly normal house. Another curiosity is **Singel 64**, which retains a 17thC step-gabled top while the lower part was given a facelift in the 18thC; this illustrates the casual way in which facades and parts of facades are replaced.

Between Blauwburgwal and Torensteeg, **Singel 116** was affectionately dubbed "the house with the noses" after some friends of the 18thC owner offered to pay for the decoration of the claw pieces flanking the neck gable, provided that these included portraits of the owner and his two sons. The offer was taken up and these unflattering portraits were the result. The handsome De Dolphijn (The Dolphin) at Singel 140–42 was designed in a flamboyant Renaissance style by Hendrick de Keyser in the early 17thC. This jaunty double step gable was later the home of Captain Frans Banning Cocq, the dashing character with the red sash leading the company of civil guards in Rembrandt's *Night Watch*.

One of Amsterdam's most sensitive modern buildings is Theo Bosch's **Faculteit der Letteren** (Literature Faculty) which fills almost an entire block, between Torensteeg and Raadhuisstraat. Those interested in architecture can enter the building to experience the structure's marvelous transparency.

From Raadhuisstraat to Muntplein

Singel, from Raadhuisstraat to Heisteeg, has a pleasing human
scale, and the narrow alleys to the E are inviting to explore.
Here you find antiquarian booksellers, wizened stamp dealers
and old-fashioned tobacconists in cramped interiors that retain
a medieval character. The most splendid house on this stretch
is **Singel 288**, which ruffles its Rococo plumage like some
exotic bird. The austere Art Deco **Bungehuis**, a 1930s office
building now used by the university, looks on with stern
disapproval. The beautiful facade stone *In de Vergulde
Haringbuys* (In the Gilded Herring Boat) adorns Singel 358,
where Rembrandt's son Titus lived for a time with his family.
Also worth a glance is **Singel 390**, with reclining figures on the
cornice and a highly ornate doorway. The Adam and Eve
facade stone at **Singel 367** wittily recalls the apple market that
formerly occupied this stretch of canal.

The final stretch of Singel between Heisteeg and Muntplein
features several bold buildings, such as the soaring church **De
Krijtberg** at Singel 446, which was built during the
neo-Gothic fever of the 19thC to replace a clandestine Jesuit
church. The 1633 **Old Lutheran Church** opposite looks
quite dainty by comparison. The row **Singel 421–25** now
accommodates the university library. The middle building,
known as the **Bushuis** (Arsenal), is a manic Mannerist
invention of 1606 which originally housed the armory of the
guild of crossbow archers. The new library building to the
right stands on the site of the meeting hall of this guild, whose
group portrait by Bartholomeus van der Helst hangs in the
Rijksmuseum. The **Odeon** theater at Singel 460 occupies an
attractive neck gable built by Philips Vingboons in 1662.

The final stretch of Singel is enlivened on one side by the
Flower Market, which is overlooked by the ornate spire of
the **Munttoren**, erected on the brick stump of a medieval
tower by Hendrick de Keyser.

Six Collection

*Amstel 218 ☎ (020) 255468. Map 8F6 ⊡ ✗ compulsory.
Open May–Oct Mon–Fri 10am–noon, 2–4pm; Nov–Apr
Mon–Fri 10am–noon. To view the Collection, a visiting card
must be obtained in advance at the Rijksmuseum information
desk (passport required). As the guided tour lasts about 1hr it
is advisable to arrive by 11am or 3pm. Ring bell at door
marked "Art Promotion Amsterdam" for admittance. Tram 4,
9, 14 to Rembrandtsplein; tram 6, 7, 10 from Rijksmuseum to
Oosteinde.*

The formal introduction required in order to view the Six
Collection makes a visit to this beautiful 18thC house on the
Amstel a unique experience. On arrival you are treated to a
fascinating guided tour of the house, which is crammed with
mementos of the Six family, who first moved to Amsterdam as
Huguenot refugees in the early 17thC.

The principal treasure of the collection is Rembrandt's
deeply tender portrait of his friend Jan Six in a somewhat
pensive mood, with a marvelous glint of sunlight striking the
collar of his cloak.

The Six Collection also boasts two miniatures by Lucas van
Leyden, a portrait by Frans Hals of Dr Tulp (who married a
stepdaughter of Jan Six) and a view of the Buurkerk in Utrecht
by Pieter Saenredam.

Spaarndammerbuurt
Bus 22 from Centraal Station to Zaanstraat; tram 3 to Haarlemmerplein.

In three separate housing units in NW Amsterdam dating from World War I, the Amsterdam School architect Michel de Klerk displays his full range of talents. On the w side of Spaarndammerplantsoen, a small square, is a 1914 row of houses with parabolic arches punctuating the skyline, while opposite is the more dashing row built for the Eigen Haard housing association in 1916 in which the familiar parabolas are combined with brick sculpture and vibrant colors. But it is the triangular block further w on Zaanstraat, built in 1917 and nicknamed "The Ship," that shows the full force of De Klerk's creative gusto, with its surreal towers and billowy brick walls mixed with more traditional motifs of North Holland building style. Walk around it once to take in the wealth of detail, such as the distinctive chunky lettering and dramatic doorways, then peer into the courtyard to discover the small community hall, which has the air of a village church.

The Zaanhof, just w of The Ship, was built in 1918 by H. J. M. Walenkamp. Its vaguely medieval towers and pointed gables create the protective mood of a village, harking back to the semi-enclosed Begijnhofs. Just N is another quiet square, the Zaandammerplein, designed by K. P. C. de Bazel in his distinctive geometrical style and built in 1916–23.

Spaarpotten Museum
Raadhuisstraat 20 ☎ (020) 221066. Map 11D4 ⛪ ✸ Open Mon–Fri 1–4pm. Tram 1, 2, 5, 13, 14, 17 to Dam.
An eccentric collection of some 12,000 piggy banks and money boxes from all over the world, ranging from beautiful terracotta models to horrendous modern kitsch.

Stedelijk Museum ★
Paulus Potterstraat 13 ☎ (020) 5732911. Map 6H2 ⛪ ⬧ ═ Open 11am–5pm. Tram 2, 3, 5, 12 to Van Baerlestraat.
Amsterdam's municipal (*stedelijk*) museum of modern art looks decidedly old-fashioned from the outside, although the interior is ultra-modern. It was built in 1895 in a bustling neo-Renaissance style that was perhaps intended to counteract P. J. H. Cuyper's neo-Gothic *Rijksmuseum* at the opposite end of Museumplein. Under its energetic postwar director Willem Sandberg the interior was whitewashed, while his successor Eddy de Wilde was even more ruthless and disposed of the reputedly hideous collection of period furniture bequeathed to the museum by its founder Sophia Augusta Lopez-Suasso. These sweeping measures, though somewhat unfair to Mrs Lopez-Suasso, have turned this old building into one of the most striking modern art galleries in Europe.

This dynamic approach means that nothing remains in the same place for very long in the Stedelijk. The best way therefore to approach the museum is to look first at the noticeboard in the hall (rm 1) to find out about temporary exhibitions and events. Then pick up the free plan and monthly bulletin from the information desk (rm 15) to find out where the various collections are located. Photography is usually shown in rm 13, applied art and graphic design in rm 14, video art in the small sunken theater in rm 14, prints on the mezzanine floor (rm 114) and exhibitions of local art organizations in the new wing (rms 30, 130).

The permanent collection begins with a modest selection of late 19th and early 20thC paintings, with works by Cézanne, Monet, Chagall, Kandinsky and Matisse (including his large cut-paper work *La Perruche et la Sirène* in rm 225a). But the main strength of the Stedelijk is its depth of coverage of more recent modern artists such as Appel, Dubuffet, De Kooning and Schoonhoven. The Stedelijk's aim – to show the development of a particular artist's style – is most effective in the case of its large Kasimir Malevitch collection, since Malevitch himself selected this series of paintings to show his development from Realism to Suprematism. His earliest paintings, dating from 1910, are splashed with bright colors in impressionistic style; figures become more metallic in 1912 (*Taking in the Rye*); colorless abstraction appears in 1912–13 (*Head of a Peasant Girl*); Cubism in 1913 (*Desk and Room*); and finally in 1915 Suprematism emerges triumphant.

Another important cluster of works covers the Dutch *De Stijl* group, who were clearly influenced by Malevitch. Both the painter Piet Mondrian and the architect Gerrit Rietveld strove to impose a framework of order on the freely-floating forms of Suprematism.

The Stedelijk's **postwar collection** begins with the COBRA group, whose first exhibition was held in the Stedelijk in 1959. Willem Sandberg was so taken with COBRA that he commissioned Karel Appel to decorate the walls of the original museum coffee shop (off rm 15).

Under Eddy de Wilde, the Stedelijk turned towards American trends of the 1960s such as Color Field Painting and Pop Art. A chilling note is struck by Edward Kienholz's *Beanery* (rm 12), a sleazy American bar into which you can walk and stand among disconcerting waxwork dummies with clocks as faces.

The Stedelijk also owns a magnificent mechanical dance-hall organ, built in Antwerp in 1924 and restored and presented to the Stedelijk by the Amsterdam publishing house De Bezige Bij (The Busy Bee). As well as playing traditional tunes, **The Busy Drone** (as it was renamed) is used for performances of jazz, classical and contemporary music, including specially commissioned pieces by contemporary Dutch composers. Concerts are given Tues 12.30–1.30pm in the *Aula* (rm 15a).

The restaurant, a popular meeting place for artists, overlooks an attractive sculpture garden that includes an eccentric invention by Tinguely.

Technology Museum   See *NINT Technisch Museum*.

Theater Institute   See *Nederlands Theater Instituut*.

Town Planning Information Center   See *Informatiecentrum Dienst Ruimtelijke Ordening*.

Tropenmuseum *(Tropical Museum)*
Linnaeusstraat 2 ☎ (020) 5688200. Map 9G9 ⬛ 💺 🚹 Open Mon–Fri 10am–5pm, Sat, Sun, hols noon–5pm. Tram 9, 10 to Mauritskade.
Devoted to the developing world and its problems, this museum is located on the E side of the 17thC moat, facing the grim Muiderpoort built 1769–71. The building was constructed in 1916–26 to house the Dutch Colonial Institute

Tuschinski

and betrays an entrenched traditionalism in its anachronistic
blend of Renaissance pear-shaped towers and Gothic beaver-
tailed roofs. The lofty main hall with its cool arcades and
colorful majolica friezes of plants brings a certain tropical
allure to bland E Amsterdam, and the occasional Indonesian
gamelan or Andean flute concert adds an exotic flavor to a
rainy Sun afternoon.

The bias of the former Colonial Institute is evident in the
sculpture depicting episodes from Dutch colonial history, and
in an attempt to produce a more balanced view of the Third
World, the building was purged of all derogatory exhibits in
the 1970s and renamed the Tropenmuseum. Not everyone
approved of the new look, however, and an irate
Amsterdammer scrawled in the Visitors' Book: "It's a
nightmare. All the lovely old objects have gone."

The museum is divided by continent, with Asia and Oceania
on the first floor, and Africa, Latin America and the Middle
East on the second floor.

Although the labels are all in Dutch, the museum is worth a
visit simply to enjoy the visual delight of wandering through
reconstructed streets from different Third World countries,
and to peer into the dark, dusty interiors. Much of the
audiovisual material is also in Dutch, but the tape recordings
of musical instruments are interesting.

The museum is constantly buzzing with exhibitions and
activities, many of them aimed at children. The basement
theater, **Soeterijn** (☎ *(020) 5688500)*, specializes in films
and plays relating to the Third World, while interesting
programs of non-Western dance and music feature in the main
hall.

Tuschinski
*Reguliersbreestraat 26 ☎ (020) 262633. Map **7**F5 ▣ Open
2–10pm. Tram 4, 9, 14, 16, 24, 25 to Muntplein.*
This cinema looks as if it might have been abandoned after the
filming of some early 20thC Hollywood epic. Its remarkable
towers in particular seem to have been lifted straight out of
D. W. Griffith's *Intolerance* and planted in this narrow
Amsterdam street, while the interior, with its luxurious
peacock carpets and dazzling decor, seems the perfect setting
for a romantic scene between Gloria Swanson and Rudolf
Valentino.

This lavish 1921 Art Deco cinema was the dream of Abram
Tuschinski, a Jewish emigré from Poland who later died in a
concentration camp. The Cannon group now own the six-
screen complex and have carefully preserved the original style.
Although the main lobby is accessible to the general public,
only holders of film tickets will be admitted to the rest of the
building.

If visiting Tuschinski 1 – the most opulent of the interiors –
it is worth paying the extra for a balcony seat to enjoy the full
impact of the glamorous setting.

Van Gogh Museum ★
*Paulus Potterstraat 7 ☎ (020) 764881. Map **6**H3 ▣ ♿ ☲
Open Tues–Sat 10am–5pm, Sun, hols 1–5pm. Tram 2, 3, 5,
12 to Van Baerlestraat.*
The museum was opened in 1973 to house the superb
collection of some 200 paintings and 500 drawings bequeathed
by Van Gogh's brother Theo to his son Vincent. The building,

an uncompromising modern design by the Dutch *De Stijl* architect Gerrit Rietveld, is set in the small park between the *Rijksmuseum* and the *Stedelijk*. The spacious interior is particularly impressive.

The ground floor covers the years 1880–87. This includes the bleak paintings from the two years Van Gogh spent in the small Brabant town of Nuenen, culminating in his compassionate painting of *The Potato Eaters*. There are also a few hesitant Impressionist works from his Paris period.

The first floor covers the final three years of his life, from 1887-90 – a period of astonishing creativity. The paintings are arranged chronologically, following the dramatic changes that occurred after his move to Arles in Provence in early 1888. The spring blossom was one of the first things to catch Van Gogh's eye, then the beach at Les Saintes-Maries in the summer, the harvest at La Crau and the plowed fields in Sept. But his finest works were painted after his admission to a sanatorium near St-Rémy (following the well-known episode in which he cut off his ear): *Branch of Almond Tree in Blossom* and *Still Life: Vase with Irises*. A hint of the gloomy colors of Holland seems to creep back in *The Garden of the St Paul's Hospital in St-Rémy* and *Undergrowth*. Finally, there are the tormented landscapes painted during the last three months of his life while staying at Auvers-sur-Oise, including the bleak *Crows over the Wheatfield*.

The second floor of the museum is devoted to Van Gogh's collection of 19thC Japanese prints, mainly of actors and courtesans, whose tormented expressions perhaps influenced his later landscapes. The third floor contains further works by Van Gogh and a small collection of paintings by contemporaries such as Emile Bernard and Toulouse-Lautrec.

Van Loon, Museum

*Keizersgracht 672 ☎(020) 245255. Map **7**G5 ▨ Open Mon 10am–noon, 1–5pm; ring bell to enter. Tram 16, 24, 25 to Keizersgracht.*

The museum provides a rare opportunity to penetrate behind the facade of a stately canal house and savor something of the everyday life of its inhabitants. The building and its twin at Keizersgracht 674, were built by Adriaen Dortsman shortly after the completion of this section of the *Grachtengordel* and illustrate the dry Classical style of the 1670s. The only touches of decoration are the four Classical deities on the balustrade, representing Minerva, Mars, Vulcan and Ceres.

One of the earliest occupants of no. 672 was Rembrandt's pupil Ferdinand Bol, who lived here until 1680. In 1884 the house was bought by the Van Loon family, who still own it. For those who enjoy piecing together family trees, the museum boasts some 50 portraits of family members, ranging from 17thC oil paintings of heroic Dutch rebels to sepia photographs from the 1920s, by which time the Van Loons had become solid pillars of respectability.

Previous generations have left their mark in other ways too, such as the initials of Abraham van Hagen and Catharina Trip that are worked into the staircase balustrade, and the monogram of Hendrik Sander in the master bedroom. The dilapidated Rococo moldings and chairs too frail to sit upon add to the mood of faded grandeur.

Perhaps the most splendid feature of the house is its formal garden, leading to a coach house disguised as a Neoclassical temple. Notice too the adjoining coach house, with its reclining statues and pretty clock tower buried behind the foliage.

Vondelpark

Stadhouderskade. Map 6G1 👓 💷 *Tram 1, 2, 5, 6, 7, 10 to Leidseplein.*

Named after the prolific 17thC Amsterdam poet Joost van den Vondel, the park is an extensive area of woods and lakes in the 19thC ring between *Leidseplein* and the *Rijksmuseum*.

The park was designed in 1865 by the Dutch landscape architects J. D. and L. P. Zocher, who abandoned the coldly formal French garden style popular in 18thC Holland, and introduced the more Romantic and irregular English style.

In the 1960s and 1970s the Vondelpark became a famous hippie camping ground. Although such spontaneity is no longer tolerated, the Vondelpark still attracts large numbers of musicians, fire eaters, jugglers and the like, and in the summer regular performances of music, theater and poetry are given in the open-air theater in the middle of the park. As a result the Vondelpark has lost its quiet English escapism, and has become more like Central Park in New York.

In the summer months tea is served by the lakeside in the **Ronde Blauwe Theehuis** (Round Blue Tea House), a daring modern building of 1937 now looking a touch dilapidated. The café terrace of the **Filmmuseum** is particularly enchanting on balmy summer evenings.

Westerkerk

Prinsengracht 281 ☎ *(020) 247766. Map 10C3* 👣 *Church open May–Sept 10am–4pm; tower open June to mid-Sept Tues, Wed, Fri, Sat 2–5pm. Tram 13, 14, 17 to Westermarkt.*

When Hendrick de Keyser was commissioned in 1620 to build a new Protestant church on the w side of the *Grachtengordel*, he showed his lingering loyalty to lofty Gothic proportions, although he had mastered all the details of the Italian Renaissance. So there is a certain tension in the building, especially in the six gables on the exterior.

De Keyser died in 1621, however, and the tower was completed by his son Pieter in a more strictly Classical style. Although Amsterdam had by then broken with its Hapsburg past, it chose to top the tower with the imperial crown granted to the city by Maximilian I in 1489.

The tower features in several sketches by Rembrandt, who spent the last years of his life in a house on the Rozengracht, and is buried in the church. The tower, still the tallest in Amsterdam, can be ascended.

Listen for the carillon on Tues between noon–2pm.

Willet-Holthuysen, Museum

Herengracht 605 ☎ *(020) 264290. Map 8F6* 🚤 *Open Tues–Sat 10am–5pm, Sun, hols 1–5pm. Tram 4, 9, 14 to Rembrandtsplein.*

This museum offers a rare opportunity to enter a handsome 18thC *Herengracht* residence, albeit via the tradesmen's entrance. The first room encountered is therefore the kitchen, which conveys a convivial glow with its bright copper utensils and gleaming tiles decorated with exotic caged birds.

The upstairs rooms come as something of an anticlimax, with their sad gray and insipid green walls, limpid Louis XVI decoration and timid chiming clocks. Only the magnificent blue room at the front conveys any deep impression. The 18thC portraits, too, possess a pallid character, as if all the energy had drained out of Amsterdam, and these descendants of bold merchants and mariners had crept to this quiet stretch of Herengracht to fade away undisturbed.

The house and its collection of Delftware, glass and paintings were bequeathed to the city in the 19thC by Abraham Willet and his wife Louise Holthuysen, who died childless. The first curator of the museum was callous enough to write a sensational novel about the couple's unhappy life and the wife's lonely death from cancer in a house filled with cats.

Looking from the upstairs windows of the house to the tree-lined canal below, the genius of the Plan of the Three Canals, which gave each house an almost rural setting, can be appreciated. The rear garden, in the formal French style of Daniel Marot, confirms one man's caustic observation that Dutch gardens are "scrawled and flourished in patterns like the embroidery of an old maid's work bag."

Zandhoek
*Map **4**C3. Tram 3 to Zoutkeetsgracht.*

To escape the crowds head for the three remote and almost traffic-free islands to the NW of Centraal Station, **Bickerseiland, Prinseneiland** and **Realeneiland.** With their quaint wooden bridges, wharves and tangle of ships' rigging, these islands preserve a 17thC seafaring flavor.

The Zandhoek, located on the most northerly, Realeneiland, contains a delightful row of 17thC merchants' houses. Further charm is added by the row of traditional sailing boats moored along the harbor front, recalling 19thC photographs by Jacob Olie, who lived at Zandhoek 10.

South of here is Bickerseiland, once the property of the 17thC merchant Jan Bickers, which retains the atmosphere of a small village despite the redevelopment on the Westerdok side. Although most of the buildings on Bickerseiland are modern, they manage to suggest a 17thC scale, and the creation of a small urban farm along the harbor front has turned this into one of the most attractive corners of the city.

West of here lies Prinseneiland, which was given over in the 17thC to vast warehouses. Some of these hulks now lie empty and crumbling, while others have been given a new lease of life as apartments. At the SW tip of the island, overlooking Nieuwe Teertuinen, is a small artist's studio that once belonged to the 19thC Impressionist George Breitner.

Zoo See *Artis*.

Zuiderkerk
*Zandstraat. Map **12**E6 ⊠ X compulsory ◁≡ Church closed. Tower open June to mid-Oct Wed 2–5pm, Thurs–Sat 11am–2pm. Metro to Nieuwmarkt.*

Completed in 1611 by Hendrick de Keyser, this was the Netherland's first Protestant church. Although laden with Renaissance ornament, the design is still largely Gothic, as is seen in the octagonal tower with its pear-shaped top.

The church is now closed to the public, but the tower can be climbed for a panoramic view of the renovated *Nieuwmarkt*.

Siena's famous main square inspired the layout of the **Zuiderkerkplein**, which provides a pleasant spot to listen to the carillon concerts, given Thurs noon–1pm.

Where to stay

"You see it all below the level of the water, soppy, hideous, and artificial," complained Matthew Arnold on a visit to Holland in 1859, "and because it exists against nature, nobody can exist there except at a frightful expense, which is very well for the natives, who may be thankful to live on any terms, but disagreeable for foreigners, who do not like to pay twice as much as elsewhere for being half as comfortable." While this remark probably says more about Matthew Arnold as a traveler than Holland as a destination, there is a grain of truth in the accusation. Dutch hotels are generally expensive for what they offer, although there are some comforting exceptions in each price category, such as, in Amsterdam, the **Amstel Inter-Continental**, **Pulitzer**, **Ambassade**, and **Wijnnobel**.

Reservations

At busy times of the year, most hotels in Amsterdam are fully booked, except for the very expensive luxury hotels and the very basic youth hotels. Good, modestly priced hotels are few and far between, so try if possible to book several weeks in advance. (A letter written in English should be acceptable.) Busy times of the year include Easter, Ascension, Whitsun and All Saints Day (Nov 1). If a last-minute booking is unavoidable, try the hotel booking services of the VVV (tourist office) at Schiphol airport or Centraal Station, although the standard of accommodations offered can be minimal. At Centraal Station, expect to line up for about 1hr in the high season.

Price

The price categories quoted for each hotel in this book are intended as a rough guide to what you can expect to pay. There are five categories: cheap, inexpensive, moderate, expensive and very expensive. (See *How to use this book* for the approximate prices to which these refer.)

Meals

Dutch hotel breakfasts generally consist of cold meats, a boiled egg, Gouda cheese and various types of bread. Breakfast is usually included in the price, especially in less expensive hotels. If not, however, it sometimes makes a pleasant change to slip out to a café for breakfast (see *Cafés* for suggestions) or to sample Sun brunch Dutch-style at the *Amstel Hotel*.

Choosing a hotel

Apart from price, a convenient location is usually the most important factor in choosing a hotel, so it is best to decide on where you want to stay first and then to pick the most suitable hotel in the area (see *Hotels classified by location*).

In Amsterdam, the most popular location is the museum quarter, close to the *Rijksmuseum*, *Van Gogh Museum*, *Stedelijk Museum*, *Concertgebouw* and *Leidseplein*. The *Vondelpark* is also nearby for those who like to start the day with a brisk run. Hotels in this area are often situated in 19thC mansions in quiet streets with relatively easy parking.

For many people, however, a visit to Amsterdam would not be complete without staying in a historic house on one of the canals. Here, the main drawbacks are smallish rooms, steep staircases and impossible parking, but intrepid travelers are

Hotels

prepared to put up with these minor inconveniences for the
pleasure of an oak-beamed roof over their heads and a view of a
canal to wake up to. There are, however, very few hotels on the
main canals, and reservations are essential.

Another area worth considering is the historic center, which
is convenient for reaching the main sights, while being close to
Centraal Station if you intend to make any excursions outside
Amsterdam. A good hotel in this area does not come cheap and
parking is again virtually impossible, although many larger
hotels have their own parking lots.

Hotels in Amsterdam Zuid are popular with businessmen
visiting the World Trade Center or RAI exhibition center, and
are also close to suburban railway stations with frequent
services to Schiphol airport, Leiden, Den Haag, Delft and
Rotterdam. The main drawback of the area is that it is rather
far from the principal sights, and it is necessary to rely on taxis
or trams.

The selection of hotels in this guide has been made not only
to give a wide choice of price and location, but also with
various other priorities in mind: atmosphere, hospitality,
relative quiet, space and views.

Hotels classified by location
Historic center

Amsterdam Ascot ▥▥▥
Capitool ▥▥
Doelen Crest ▥▥▥
Europe ▥▥▥
Grand Hotel Krasnapolsky ▥▥▥
Roode Leeuw ▯▯
Schiller ▥▥▥
Amsterdam Sonesta ▥▥▥
Canal ring
Agora ▯▯
Ambassade ▯▯
Canal House ▯▯
Estheréa ▯▯
Pulitzer ▯▯ to ▥▥▥
Wiechmann ▯▯
Museum quarter
Acca ▥▥ to ▥▥▥

Acro ▢ to ▯▢
American ▥▥▥
Arthur Frommer ▯▢ to ▥▥
Barbizon Centre ▥▥ to ▥▥▥
Engeland ▯▢
Holland ▯▢
Museum ▯▢
Owl ▢
Terdam ▯▢
Toro ▯▢
Trianon ▯▢
Wijnnobel ▢
Amsterdam Zuid
Amstel Inter-Continental ▥▥▥
Okura ▥▥▥
Plantage
Olszewski ▢

Acca
Van de Veldestraat 3A
☎(020) 625262 ☎10840. Map
6H3 ▥▥ to ▥▥ 25 rms ▭ 25
ᴀᴇ ⊙ ⊙ ᴠɪsᴀ Tram 2, 3, 5, 12 to
Van Baerlestraat.
*Location: In a quiet street 5mins'
walk from the Van Gogh Museum.*
Businessmen who are fed up with
anonymous concrete hotels
planted in the middle of suburbs
might enjoy the stylish ambience
and intimacy of this recently
opened hotel in an elegant 19thC
quarter of Amsterdam. Although
small, the Acca boasts a beautiful
atrium lobby, a sauna and tasteful,
well-equipped rooms. It is ideally
situated for visiting the major art
galleries, shopping on P. C.
Hooftstraat and enjoying the
nightlife on *Leidseplein*.
▨ ‡ ▢ ▱ ☞ ☎ ♨

Acro ✿
Jan Luykenstraat 44
☎(020) 620526 ☎10415. Map
6G3 ▢ to ▯▢ 46 rms ▭ 40 ⇌
Tram 2, 3, 5, 12 to Van
Baerlestraat.
*Location: In a quiet street, 5mins'
walk from the Rijksmuseum.* Most
budget hotels in Amsterdam are
best left well alone, but the Acro is
one that can be recommended
wholeheartedly. It is located in an
elegant 19thC street close to the
major art museums, with good
tram connections to the rest of the
city. The lobby is modern and
tasteful, there is a small bar serving
espresso coffee and drinks, and the
bedrooms are bright and spacious,
with attractive modern furniture,
sparkling bathrooms (all with
showers) and double glazing. The
prices are slightly above the rock-

87

bottom rate, but it is well worth paying those few extra guilders to stay in a hotel that is comfortable and hospitable.
✉ ✦

Agora
Singel 462 ☎ *(020) 272200. Map* **7F4** ▯ *14 rms* ▭ *11. Tram 1, 2, 5 to Koningsplein.*
Location: On a canal near the flower market. A cheerful hotel with a tasteful breakfast room and pleasant, bright bedrooms furnished with a few antiques. The front rooms (slightly more expensive) overlook a lively assortment of university buildings on the *Singel* canal.
✦ ✉

Ambassade ♣
Herengracht 341
☎ *(020) 262333* ⚫ *10158. Map* **11E4** ▯ *42 rms* AE VISA *Tram 1, 2, 5 to Spui.*
Location: On an elegant canal, 5mins' walk from the Begijnhof.
Those who rank romance and ambience above practical details such as direct-dial telephones and minibars should try for a room here. The fact that it is almost impossible to get one at short notice indicates that this hotel, located in a row of 17th and 18thC merchants' houses on Amsterdam's most elegant canal, has something special to offer. What you will enjoy here – as in no other Amsterdam hotel – is the pleasure of residing in a traditional canal house, furnished with a splendid collection of antique clocks, chairs and paintings. Service is polite and efficient, and special features such as the comfortable lounge and exquisite breakfast room make this one of Holland's great small hotels.
▯ ✉ ◁

American
Leidsekade 97
☎ *(020) 245322*
⚫ *11379. Map* **6F2** ▥ *185 rms* ▭ *185* ═ AE ⚫ ⚫ VISA *Tram 1, 2, 5, 6, 7, 10 to Leidseplein.*
Location: On Leidseplein, surrounded by cultural attractions. This is the hotel for those who enjoy the bustle and action of the city. It is located in one of Amsterdam's most glorious Art Nouveau buildings, built in 1902 by Willem Kromhout. The hotel has recently been modernized to keep abreast of the times, but the furnishings have been tastefully

chosen to mirror the Art Nouveau élan of the architecture. The location is ideal for enjoying the cinemas, theaters and cafés around *Leidseplein*. Amsterdam's nightlife can also be experienced in the hotel's elegant **Café Américain** (see *Cafés*).
✦ ▯ ✉ ═

Amstel Inter-Continental
Professor Tulpplein 1
☎ *(020) 226060* ⚫ *11004. Map* **8G7** ▥ *111 rms* ▭ *111* ═ AE ⚫ ⚫ VISA *Tram 6, 7, 10 to Oosteinde; or metro to Weesperplein.*
Location: On the River Amstel, 10mins' walk from Waterlooplein. This grand palace hotel, built in 1867 by the dynamic entrepreneur Samuel Sarphati, is by far the most splendid hotel in the city, with its magnificent entrance hall, impeccable service and beautiful floral displays. It is true that the rooms are a little smaller than you might expect, and the views not always ravishing, but this does not seem to put off the kings and queens, film stars and pop singers who frequent this hotel. Perhaps the best occasion to savor the full grandeur of the Amstel is at its Sun champagne brunch, which is served in the glittering **Spiegelzaal** (▯ *reservation essential, dress informal, Sun 11.30am–3pm; no admittance after noon*). The genteel service, live piano music and abundance of beautifully prepared dishes (salads, cold meats, fish mousses, soups, scrambled eggs, pâtés, breads and desserts) make this the perfect escape from the Sabbatarian gloom of a Dutch Sunday.

A more intimate atmosphere is found in the Amstel Hotel's restaurant **La Rive**.
✉ ✦ ♿ ▯ ✉ ◁ ♣

Amsterdam Ascot
Damrak 95–98
☎ *(020) 260066*
⚫ *16620. Map* **11C5** ▥ *110 rms* ▭ *110* ═ AE ⚫ ⚫ VISA *Tram 4, 9, 16, 24, 25 to Dam.*
Location: On the Dam, 5mins' walk from Centraal Station.
Businessmen who once checked into large hotels on the outskirts of Amsterdam are now recognizing the advantages of inner-city locations, and several new hotels have recently opened in the center of the city to fill the gap. One of the best situated is the Swiss-owned

Ascot, which is just around the corner from the *Royal Palace*, and close to shops, restaurants, cafés and cinemas. Getting around town is effortless, as most trams stop near the hotel, while excursions can easily be made from Centraal Station, a 5min walk away. Rooms are stylish and well-equipped, and although the hotel does not have parking there is a 24hr parking garage at the nearby **Grand Hotel Krasnapolsky**.

🛦 ☐ ◻ ⌂ ♨

Arthur Frommer ♣

Noorderstraat 46
☎(020) 220328
📺14047. Map **7G5** ▥ to ▦
90 rms ➟ 90 ➟ ➟ ⊕
⊙ 𝚅𝙸𝚂𝙰 Tram 16, 24, 25 to *Prinsengracht.*

Location: In a quiet street of the Weteringbuurt, 5mins from the Rijksmuseum. This pleasant, comfortable hotel is situated in a tranquil corner of the city settled by Huguenot refugees in the late 17thC. It is the brainchild of Arthur Frommer, indefatigable author of *Europe on $5 a Day,* and offers, he says, "a straightforward no-frills honesty." Like many American-owned hotels in Amsterdam, it is furnished in a style that attempts to recapture the glow of the Dutch Golden Age, although the addition of Colonial America trappings such as rocking chairs and reproduction oil lamps somewhat confuses the effect.

⌂ 🛦 ⌂

Barbizon Centre

Stadhouderskade 7
☎(020) 851351 📺 12601.
Map **6G2** ▥ to ▦ 242 rms ➟ 242 ➟ ➟ ⚿ ⊕ ⊙ 𝚅𝙸𝚂𝙰 Tram 1, 2, 5, 6, 7, 10 to Leidseplein.

Location: Overlooking Leidseplein. Art lovers who associate the name Barbizon with muddy brown and drab green landscape paintings may be wary about booking into the Barbizon Centre. However, the interior of this building – built in 1929 to accommodate Olympic athletes – has been expertly modernized in a style that bears little relation to the 19thC paintings of the Barbizon School. The bedrooms are well-equipped and tastefully furnished, and those at the front enjoy a view of the bright lights of *Leidseplein.* For athletic guests, there is a fully-equipped health center, which includes a sauna, Turkish bath, gym and lounge.

🛦 ♿ ☐ ⌂ ♨ 🎿 ♨

Canal House

Keizersgracht 148
☎(020) 225182 📺10412. Map **10D3** ▥ 19 rms ➟ 19 ⚿ ⊕ ⊙
𝚅𝙸𝚂𝙰 Tram 13, 14, 17 to *Westermarkt.*

Location: On a quiet 17thC canal 5mins' walk from the Westerkerk. This small, friendly hotel situated in two historic canal houses is owned by an American couple who have furnished it throughout with antiques to recreate the mood of the Golden Age. Perhaps some would say they have gone too far, for even telephones and televisions are excluded from the bedrooms, but for those who appreciate silence (the hotel is probably the quietest on the canals) and a good night's sleep in a comfortable bed, the Canal House is ideal. Special features include a Victorian-style bar – where you are offered a welcome drink on arrival – and an opulent breakfast room, once an insurance company's office. Rooms on the front, including a few attic hideaways, offer fine views, while those at the back overlook a peaceful garden, which is illuminated at night.

⌂ ⌂

Capitool

Nieuwe Zijds Voorburgwal 67
☎(020) 275900 📺 14494. Map **11D4** ▥ 148 rms ➟ 148 ⚿ ⊕
⊙ 𝚅𝙸𝚂𝙰 Tram 1, 2, 5, 13, 17 to Dam.

Location: Just w of the Dam. One of several new hotels that have sprung up in the historic center of the city, the Capitool is discreetly concealed behind the facade of a former printing works (dating from 1904). The furnishings are tasteful without being overly luxurious, and a sauna takes some of the misery out of winter tourism. Its location is ideal for sightseeing, although if you have a car, it could prove a disadvantage to be so centrally situated.

🛦 ♿ ☐ ⌂ 🎿 ♨

Doelen Crest

Nieuwe Doelenstraat 24
☎(020) 220722 📺14399.
Map **11E5** ▥ 86 rms ➟ 86 ➟
⚿ ⊕ ⊙ 𝚅𝙸𝚂𝙰 Tram 4, 9, 14, 16, 24, 25 to Muntplein.

Location: On the river Amstel, 2mins' walk from Muntplein and ideally situated for the opera house. It would be hard to find a better hotel from which to explore Rembrandt's Amsterdam, for this elegant 19thC Neoclassical building stands on the site of the medieval tower where Rembrandt painted the *Night Watch*. The event is recalled by the figures of Frans Banning Cocq and Lieutenant van Rutenburch high on the E wall and, in the depths of the building, by a fragment of wall (now a protected monument) on which the painting originally hung. Even the dark browns and golds of the furnishings evoke the mellow mood of a Rembrandt, while the attractive suite (*rm 515* **▥**) offers a superb view down the canal Kloveniersburgwal to the *Waag*, the former weigh house, where the *Anatomy Lesson of Dr Tulp* was painted.

🛉 ☐ ♞

Engeland

Roemer Visscherstraat 30a
☎ *(020) 180862. Map* **6G2** **▯**
28 rms **AE** *Tram 1, 2, 5, 6, 7, 10 to Leidseplein.*
Location: In a quiet street of distinctive 19thC buildings, 5mins' walk from the Rijksmuseum. A cheerful, inexpensive hotel decorated with vases of bright flowers, and offering breakfast in a pleasant room overlooking the back garden. The hotel occupies two of seven highly unusual 19thC houses built in distinctive European architectural styles.

▱

Estheréa

Singel 303–307
☎ *(020) 245146* ☎ *14019. Map* **11E4** **▯** *72 rms* **AE** ⊕
⊕ **VISA** *Tram 1, 2, 5 to Spui.*
Location: On a 17thC canal 5mins' walk from the Begijnhof. This very friendly hotel is conveniently located to explore the most beautiful area of the old city, and there is a frequent tram service that will take you to the main art museums. The rooms are well-equipped but small, and those at the front enjoy an attractive view of the *Singel* canal.

🛉 ▱

Europe

Nieuwe Doelenstraat 2–8
☎ *(020) 234836* ☎ *12081. Map*
11E5 **▥** *100 rms* **▭** *100* ⇄ **AE**
⊕ ⊕ **VISA** *Tram 4, 9, 14, 16, 24, 25 to Muntplein.*
Location: Situated in the heart of Amsterdam on the site of a medieval bastion. Primarily geared toward business travelers, the Hotel Europe pampers its guests with every modern luxury, including the only hotel swimming pool in

the city. From the outside, it is a merry bustle of late 19thC Renaissance details, but inside an elegant Neoclassical tone prevails, with pale yellow walls and Empire furnishings. Most of the rooms overlook the river Amstel and the prettiest view is probably towards the Munttoren, a tower that is illuminated at night.

🛉 ♿ ☐ ▱ ♥ ☎ ≈

Grand Hotel Krasnapolsky

Dam 9 ☎ *(020) 5549111*
☎ *12262. Map* **11D4** **▥** *370 rms*
▭ *370* **▭** ⇄ **AE** ⊕ ⊕ **VISA** *Tram 4, 9, 16, 24, 25 to Dam.*
Location: On the Dam, 5mins' walk from Centraal Station. Named after the Polish emigré who built the hotel in 1883, the Krasnapolsky is a huge, bustling hotel on Amsterdam's main square, boasting a splendid 19thC Winter Garden where breakfasts are served. More recently, the hotel has added three other gardens, including a Japanese and a roof garden, which add a touch of relief to the seemingly endless corridors. The rooms are comfortable and modern, although the views can be drab.

🛉 ♿ ☐ ▱ ♞

Holland

P. C. Hooftstraat 162
☎ *(020) 764253, (020) 831811 for reservations.* ☎ *14275. Map*
6H2 **▯** *67 rms* **AE** ⊕ ⊕
VISA *Tram 2, 3, 5, 12 to Van Baerlestraat.*
Location: In a quiet street close to the Vondelpark. Like other hotels run by the AMS group (the **Trianon, Museum** and **Terdam**), the Holland is an inexpensive but comfortable hotel, set in a quiet, yet convenient location.

▱ 🛉

Museum

P. C. Hooftstraat 2 ☎ *(020) 621402, (020) 831811 for reservations*
☎ *14275. Map* **6G3** **▯** *120 rms*
▭ *120* ⇄ **AE** ⊕ ⊕ **VISA** *Tram 6, 7, 10 to Spiegelgracht.*
Location: Next to the Rijksmuseum. A comfortable hotel recently modernized by the AMS group. Request a room overlooking the *Rijksmuseum* to savor the delights of Cuypers' neo-Gothic style. (See also **Holland, Terdam** and **Trianon** hotels.)

🛉 ▱

Okura Amsterdam

Ferdinand Bolstraat 333
☎ *(020) 787111* ☏ *16182. Map*
7H4 ▥▥▥ *400 rms* ▭ *400* 🚗 ▭
▭ AE ◉ ◉ VISA *Tram 12, 25 to*
Cornelis Troostplein.

*Location: Midway between RAI
and the Rijksmuseum.* Situated in
Amsterdam's 20thC ring close to
RAI and the beltway, this 23-story
Japanese-owned hotel is ideal for
business travelers who prefer not
to get tangled up in the narrow
inner-city streets. Not that you feel
isolated in the Okura, for the city is
spread out below, with some rooms
overlooking the modern
architecture of Amsterdam Zuid
while others look N to the spires of
the *Rijksmuseum* and the cranes of
the harbor. Another appealing
feature of the Okura is its slightly
Japanese flavor, from the shop in
the basement selling *sake* to the
beautiful **Yamazato** restaurant,
which overlooks a miniature
Japanese garden. But there are
Western features as well, including
the French cuisine of the **Ciel
Bleu** restaurant on the top floor
and the typically Dutch products
that are on sale in the hotel's
souvenir shop.
⌂ ≛ ▢ ⌷ ≪ ⛟

Olszewski

Plantage Muidergracht 89
☎ *(020) 236241. Map* **9F8** ▢
*20 rms. Closed Dec to Mid–Jan.
Tram 7 to Nieuwe Keizersgracht or
tram 9, 14 to Plantage Kerklaan.*
*Location: E of Waterlooplein,
5mins' walk from the
Tropenmuseum.* A friendly hotel
run by a Polish couple, in a quiet
street close to the zoo. The rooms
are spacious and bright, and the
furniture, although 20yrs out of
date, still remains in perfect
condition.

Owl

Roemer Visscherstraat 1
☎ *(020) 189484* ☏ *13360. Map*
6G2 ▢ *34 rms* ▭ *34* AE ◉ VISA
*Tram 1, 2, 5, 6, 7, 10 to
Leidseplein.*
*Location: In a quiet street, 5mins'
walk from Leidseplein.* This quiet,
recently modernized hotel set in an
elegant 19thC quarter is
conveniently placed for visiting
Amsterdam's major sights.
  The bedrooms are pleasant,
although small, and the breakfast
room has a bright and cheerful
atmosphere.
≛ ⌷

Pulitzer ✿

Prinsengracht 323
☎ *(020) 228333* ☏ *16508. Map*
10C3 ▥▤ *to* ▥▥▥ *250 rms* ▭ *250*
▭ AE ◉ ◉ VISA *Tram 13, 14, 17
to Westermarkt.*

*Location: A canalside hotel, 5mins
from the Westerkerk.* No other hotel
in Amsterdam manages to combine
the romantic attractions of a canal
residence with the modern
facilities of a business hotel. The
Pulitzer is situated in a block of
twenty-four 17th and 18thC
merchants' houses and warehouses
that retain many picturesque
details such as brick walls, oak
beams and mezzanine floors. It is
part of the Pulitzer's policy to
allocate guests their favorite
rooms; to enjoy the graceful urban
setting, it is worth asking for a
room on *Keizersgracht*; or if you
wish to listen to the birdsong and
the gentle chimes of the nearby
Westerkerk, request a room that
overlooks the rambling gardens.
As befits a hotel owned by the
founder of the Pulitzer Prize, the
Pulitzer has a highly cultured
ambience, and guests can enjoy
modern art exhibitions in the
beautiful Pulitzer Art Gallery or
occasional open-air concerts in the
hotel gardens. But the event all of
Amsterdam flocks to is the extraordinary concert given at the end of
Aug by a small musical ensemble,
performed on a flotilla of barges
moored alongside the hotel.
⌂ ≛ ▢ ⌷ ≪ ⛟

Roode Leeuw

Damrak 93–94 ☎ *(020) 240396.
Map* **11D5** ▥▢ *85 rms* AE VISA *Tram
4, 9, 16, 24, 25 to Dam.*
Location: Just off the Dam. This is
a well-kept, old-fashioned hotel in
a convenient and bustling location.
The rooms at the front are
particularly bright and well-
proportioned, but suffer slightly
from the throb of traffic. An airy
breakfast room, small lounge and
lively café terrace add to its charm.
≛ ⌷

Schiller

Rembrandtsplein 26
☎ *(020) 231660* ☏ *14058.
Map* **7F5** ▥▥▥ *97 rms* ▭ *97* ▭ AE
◉ ◉ VISA *Tram 4, 9, 14 to
Rembrandtsplein.*
*Location: Overlooking
Rembrandtsplein.* The Schiller was
a favorite meeting place of Dutch
artists in prewar years, and it still

retains an artistic mood due to its remarkable collection of 700 paintings by the former owner Frits Schiller. One of the prime virtues of this hotel, now run by the UK Crest group, is its friendly desk staff. However, the bedrooms, crowded with standard Crest gadgets such as a trouser press and tea-making equipment, are somewhat characterless, though comfortable enough. Rooms at the front enjoy a pleasing view of Rembrandtsplein, though they can sometimes be noisy.
‡ ☐ ⟋

Sonesta

Kattengat 1 ☎ (020) 212223 ⊕ 17149. Map **11C5** ▮▮▮ 425 rms ⊟ 425 ⇌ ▱ ⇛ AE ⟨⟩ ⟨⟩ VISA Tram 1, 2, 5, 13, 17 to Martelaarsgracht.

Location: At the N end of Singel, 5mins' walk from Centraal Station. A luxury hotel situated in a historic quarter of the old city close to the harbor. The main feature that distinguishes the Sonesta from other large hotels in Amsterdam is its splendid collection of about 1,000 modern paintings and sculptures, including attractive works by the Dutch COBRA artists.

These works decorate the lobbies, bars, the **Rib Room** restaurant and the bedrooms of the Sonesta, so that a stay here can be a painless way to keep in touch with contemporary artistic trends. Other attractions in the hotel include the **Splash Sonesta Fitness Club** (see *Sports and activities*) and concerts in the **Sonesta Koepelzaal** (see *Nightlife and the arts*).
‡ ♿ ⟋ ⚐ ⚑

Terdam ✿

Tesselschadestraat 23–29 ☎ (020) 126876, (020) 831811 for reservations ⊕ 14275. Map **6G2** ▮ 54 rms ⊟ 54 AE ⟨⟩ ⟨⟩ VISA Tram 1, 2, 5, 6, 7, 10 to Leidseplein.

Location: In a quiet street, 5mins from Leidseplein. The most distinctive of the AMS-group hotels, with a lobby and bar decorated in a style reminiscent of the Vienna Secessionists of the early 20thC. The bedrooms, however, are furnished in the standard style of the AMS group, which also owns the nearby **Holland, Museum** and **Trianon** hotels.
⌂ ‡ ⟋

Toro ✿

Koningslaan 64 ☎ (020) 737223. Map **6H1** ▮ 12 rms AE ⟨⟩ ⟨⟩ VISA Tram 2 to Valeriusplein.

Location: In a quiet street on the S side of the Vondelpark, a short tram-ride from Leidseplein. This bright, elegant 19thC villa filled with plants and flowers exudes an English air. The bedrooms are spacious and comfortable (some with views of the Vondelpark), and the attractive breakfast room is furnished with antiques and family portraits. This is an ideal hotel for families, and parking in the area is relatively easy.
⌂ ⟋

Trianon ✿

J. W. Brouwersstraat 3–7 ☎ (020) 732073, (020) 831811 for reservations ⊕ 14275. Map **6I2** ▮ 53 rms ⊟ 53 ⟨⟩ ⟨⟩ Tram 3, 5, 12, 16 to Museumplein.

Location: Next to the Concertgebouw. A conveniently located hotel furnished in the comfortable, no-fuss style of the AMS group. (See also **Holland, Museum** and **Terdam** hotels.)
⌂ ‡ ⟋

Wiechmann

Prinsengracht 328–330 ☎ (020) 263321. Map **6F3** ▮ 33 rms. Tram 1, 2, 5 to Prinsengracht.

Location: N of Leidseplein on the edge of the Jordaan. A well-situated hotel with simple, modern rooms at a range of prices, some enjoying a canal view. The lobby and breakfast room are furnished with antiques, and an impressive suit of armor stands sentinel at the entrance.

Wijnnobel ✿

Vossiusstraat 9 ☎ (020) 622298. Map **6G2** ☐ 12 rms. Tram 1, 2, 5, 6, 7, 10 to Leidseplein.

Location: In a quiet street overlooking the Vondelpark, 5mins from the Rijksmuseum. This friendly, family-run hotel is ideally suited for young people or families on a limited budget. The rooms are bright, clean and spacious; those at the front enjoy a view of the Vondelpark and the golden glow of the floodlit **American Hotel** at night. The only drawbacks are the hotel's lack of a breakfast room or private bathrooms, but for those who can dispense with such luxuries, this is one of the most pleasant cheap hotels in the city.

Eating in Holland

Dutch cuisine, not renowned for creative flair, relies on solid staples such as Gouda cheese, meat and vegetables. Specialties such as *erwtensoep* (thick pea soup) and *hutspot* (stew) may be sustaining on winter days, but are hardly the stuff of gourmets' dreams. Probably the most succulent food in Holland is yielded by the seas, estuaries and lakes, including *maatjes haring* (cured raw herring), *gerookte IJsselmeer paling* (smoked IJsselmeer eel) and *Zeeuwse mosselen* (Zeeland mussels).

There are also a few specialties based on exotic herbs and spices brought back by the Dutch East India Company's ships in the 17thC, such as the distinguished *Friese nagelkaas* (Frisian clove cheese).

Dutch pancakes (*pannekoeken*) are also worth sampling, particularly the mini-pancakes called *poffertjes* sold at gaudy fairground stands set up permanently on main squares such as the Dam and Westermarkt in Amsterdam, and the Neude in Utrecht.

Another legacy of Holland's Far Eastern trade is the large number of Indonesian, Chinese, Japanese and Thai restaurants, which offer exotic and spicy alternatives to traditional Dutch food. Holland is particularly famous for Indonesian restaurants, which lay on spectacular *rijsttafels* (rice tables). These consist of a huge spread of dishes – sometimes requiring additional tables to hold them all – that include a large bowl of white rice (*nasi*), prawn crackers (*kroepoek*), a cooked vegetable salad (*gado-gado*), several types of spicy meats, peanuts, coconut, fruit and various hot sauces. The *rijsttafel*, generally accompanied by tea, beer or water, forms a complete meal, and it is neither customary nor wise to order starters or desserts.

The main types of Indonesian cuisine are Javanese (fairly mild), Balinese (hot) and Sumatran (almost unbearably hot). It is prudent to sample a small amount of each dish to avoid unpleasant shocks, and to extinguish hot tastes with rice, *kroepoek* or vegetables. Many of Holland's best Indonesian restaurants are found in Den Haag, where a large number of ex-colonials settled after Indonesian independence, but Amsterdam also offers some interesting restaurants, such as the grand **Indonesia** and the convivial **Speciaal**. For those whose palates are not accustomed to such spicy dishes, Holland also boasts numerous Chinese and Japanese restaurants.

Since the early 18thC, Holland has looked towards France for much of its culinary inspiration. This is reflected today in the growing number of elegant (and often expensive) restaurants offering French-style *nouvelle cuisine*. At its best, this involves delightful and imaginative dishes presented with flair, although sometimes it seems to be merely an excuse to charge inflated prices for deflated portions. The acknowledged masters of *nouvelle cuisine* in Holland are the Fagels, a family of chefs who at the last count were running no fewer than ten restaurants in Holland, each with a quite different character. In Amsterdam, you can choose between John Fagel's **Tout Court** and Marcel Fagel's **Blue Berry Hills**.

Amsterdam's Utopian zeal has led to the establishment of numerous vegetarian restaurants in recent years. Unfortunately, they tend to seem rather off-putting to those who wish to combine gastronomic joys with moral scruples or dietary requirements, since there is generally no alcohol available and kitchens tend to close early. Generally, gourmet vegetarians do

93

better to choose an ordinary restaurant offering a vegetarian menu, such as **La Rive** or **Sancerre**, or simply order the vegetarian dish (*vegetarische schotel*) in a café such as **Het Molenpad**.

Probably the most horrifying experience a food-lover will ever encounter is a Dutch Sunday, when most restaurants (especially in the provinces) are closed and often the only place to obtain food is a slot machine at the railway station. Fortunately, Amsterdam is not afflicted by this Protestant curse, but it is wise not to venture into remote areas without first ascertaining that there is somewhere open from which to obtain food. The best bet is usually an Indonesian or Chinese restaurant, or a pancake house in the country. Otherwise, take your cue from the Dutch and never embark on a journey without a supply of cheese sandwiches.

Choosing a restaurant in Amsterdam

Amsterdam offers a wide choice of restaurants to suit every taste or gastronomic whim. Dutch people tend to eat their main meal in the evening, and have light lunches of cheese or ham rolls (*broodje kaas/ham*), or bread with eggs and cheese or ham (*uitsmijter kaas/ham*).

Most cafés serve *broodjes* and *uitsmijters*, and excellent kosher sandwiches can be obtained at **Sal Meijer** (*Scheldestraat 45 ☎ (020) 731313; tram 12, 25 to Scheldestraat*). Try also **Betty's Coffeeshop** (*Rijnstraat 75 ☎ (020) 445896; tram 4, 12, 25 to Victorieplein; closed Fri, Sat, Sun lunch*) for delicious non-kosher Jewish pastrami sandwiches or blintzes, or **Caffè Panini** (*Vijzelgracht 3-5 ☎ (020) 264939; tram 16, 24, 25 to Prinsengracht*) a modern Italian-style café offering *focaccia* (Tuscan bread) and *panini* (rolls) filled with Italian cheese or Parma ham.

Those accustomed to a more substantial midday meal may find the choice is somewhat limited. In the neighborhood of the art museums, try **Sama Sebo** for an Indonesian lunch, **Fong Lie** for Chinese dishes or **Mirafiori** for Italian cuisine. On Leidseplein, **Het Swarte Schaep** offers excellent French cuisine and **Manchurian** serves delicious Oriental dishes. Near the Dam, **Die Port van Cleve** provides sustaining Dutch food, and **Treasure** offers unusual Peking *dim sum* lunches. The **La Ruche** restaurant at De Bijenkorf (see *Shopping*) also offers a wide range of dishes at moderate prices.

Travelers on a limited budget tend to head instinctively towards the sprawl of inexpensive Italian, Greek and Spanish restaurants s of Leidseplein. However, it is often just as cheap and sometimes more convivial to eat in cafés that offer meals (known as *eetcafés*). The menus are usually written on blackboards and the dishes are traditional and sustaining. The *dagschotel* (dish of the day) is usually inexpensive and nourishing. The main drawbacks of café eating are the noise and smoke, but for some this is part of the charm of such places. **Het Molenpad** has a friendly atmosphere, **Oblomow** is more sophisticated, and **Van Puffelen** consistently attains gastronomic heights (see *Cafés* for all three).

Outstanding in their respective price categories are the following restaurants: **Dynasty** (Chinese ◼◼); **Het Stuivertje** (Dutch ◻); **Blue Berry Hills** (French ◻ to ◼); **Het Swarte Schaep** (French ◻ to ◼◼◼); **Valentijn** (French ◼◼◼); **Sama Sebo** (Indonesian ◻ to ◼); and **Van Puffelen** (see *Cafés* ◼).

Restaurants classified by type of cuisine

American
Rib Room 🔳🔳
The World According to Garp 🔲 to 🔲

Chinese
Dynasty 🔳🔳
Fong Lie 🔳
Manchurian 🔳🔳
Treasure 🔳

Danish
Kopenhagen 🔳🔳

Dutch
Keijzer 🔳🔳
De Knijp 🔳
Die Port van Cleve 🔲 to 🔳
Sluizer 🔳
De Smoeshaan 🔳🔳
Het Stuivertje 🔳
Warstein 🔳

Fish
Bols Taverne 🔳🔳
Lucius 🔳
Sluizer 🔳

French
Blue Berry Hills 🔲 to 🔳
Ciel Bleu 🔳🔳 to 🔳🔳
L'Entrecôte 🔲 to 🔳

De Prinsenkelder 🔳🔳 to 🔳🔳
La Rive 🔳🔳
Sancerre 🔳🔳 to 🔳🔳
Het Swarte Schaep 🔳🔳 to 🔳🔳
Tout Court 🔳🔳 to 🔳🔳
De Trechter 🔳🔳
Valentijn 🔳🔳

Indonesian
Cilubang 🔲
Indonesia 🔳
Sama Sebo 🔲 to 🔳
Speciaal 🔳
Tempo Doeloe 🔳

Italian
Mirafiori 🔲 to 🔳
Tartufo 🔲 to 🔳

Japanese
Umeno 🔲 to 🔳
Yamazato 🔳🔳 to 🔳🔳

Cafés (see *Cafés* for descriptions)
Blincker 🔲
De Engelbewaarder 🔲
Frascati 🔲
Het Land van Walem 🔲
Het Molenpad 🔲
Oblomow 🔲
Van Puffelen 🔳

Blue Berry Hills
Kerkstraat 138 ☎ *(020) 220689.
Map 6F3* 🔲 to 🔳 AE 🔘 CB VISA
*Last orders 11pm. Tram 1, 2, 5 to
Keizersgracht, or tram 6, 7, 10 to
Spiegelgracht.*
For pauper gourmets who find most *nouvelle cuisine* restaurants expensive or off-putting, Marcel Fagel's Blue Berry Hills is the answer. Its location – on the ground floor of a noisy student hotel – may seem a touch eccentric, but the interior is ornate and comfortable, and the cuisine (which is what really matters) is exquisite. The menu, though small, is delightful, and always includes one main course costing no more than a café's "dish of the day." Blue Berry Hills also offers a combined dinner-and-theater arrangement for ART (American Repertory Theater) performances (see *Nightlife and the arts*).

Bols Taverne
Rozengracht 106
☎ *(020) 245752. Map 10D2* 🔳🔳
AE CB VISA *Closed Sun. Tram 13, 14, 17 to Westermarkt.*
Situated in a beautifully restored 17thC step gable house, this restaurant is named after the Pieter Bols distillery, established near here in 1649. The restaurant is warm and convivial, with traditional wooden furniture and

romantic 19thC marine paintings. Fish features prominently on the menu, and there are tempting combinations of unusual types such as poached monkfish, deep-fried salmon trout and crayfish served in dill sauce, or three filets of salmon trout prepared in different ways and served with Norwegian lobster sauce. Portions are enormous, presentation careful, and the meal is brought to a delightful conclusion by the chocolate beans and small glass of Bols *crème de cacao* liqueur that accompany the coffee. The restaurant maintains a fleet of eight sleek black cars, and on request will ferry you to and from the restaurant. Its sister restaurant **Warstein** offers the same service.

Ciel Bleu
Okura Hotel, Ferdinand Bolstraat 333 ☎ *(020) 787111. Map 7H4*
🔳🔳 to 🔳🔳 ➡ 🍴 AE 🔘 CB VISA *Last orders midnight. Closed lunch. Tram 12, 25 to Cornelis Troostplein.*
This French restaurant situated on the top floor of a 23-story Japanese hotel offers the twin attraction of a romantic view and delicate *nouvelle cuisine*. The set menus are well thought out and *flambéd* dishes are particularly well presented. The name "Ciel Bleu" should not be taken too literally: Dutch skies are

seldom blue, and their fascination, as 17thC landscape painters discovered, lies in dramatic cloud formations and sudden rainstorms. To enjoy the full spectacle, choose a bright, changeable day, and book a window table. But don't arrive too early in the summer, for the service here is so efficient that you may find yourself at the end of the meal long before the sun has set.

Cilubang ✿
Runstraat 10 ☎ *(020) 269755. Map* **10***E3* □ AE © VISA *Last orders 11pm. Closed lunch, Mon. Tram 1, 2, 5 to Spui.*
A short walk from *Spui*, this tastefully decorated Indonesian restaurant offers a modest and inexpensive *rijsttafel*. Popular with young people.

Dynasty
Reguliersdwarsstraat 30 ☎ *(020) 268400. Map* **7***F4* □□ AE © VISA *Last orders 11pm. Closed lunch, Tues, and mid-Dec to mid-Jan. Tram 1, 2, 5 to Koningsplein, or tram 4, 9, 14, 16, 24, 25 to Muntplein.*
Situated amid a bevy of chic restaurants, Dynasty outshines them all with its sublime Thai and Cantonese cuisine, delighting the palate with rare herbs and unusual spices. Décor is equally exotic, with silk wall hangings and a curious arrangement of upturned parasols suspended from the ceiling. In summer, there is the added attraction of a garden terrace. The menu is crammed with tempting dishes, such as *The Sixth Happiness* (duck, jellyfish, and century-old egg), *Phoenix and the Dragon* (duck and lobster on a bed of watercress with stir-fried mushrooms) and *Yunnan lamb* (lamb seasoned with Szechuan peppercorns and garlic). Perhaps the best option for the perplexed diner is *The Offering of the Emperor*, a combination dish of four exotic starters. Always crowded, early reservation is essential. It is sometimes easier to get a table at its sister restaurant **Manchurian** on Leidseplein.

L'Entrecôte ✿
P. C. Hooftstraat 70 ☎ *(020) 737776. Map* **6***H2* □ *to* □□ *Closed Sun, Mon and July. Tram 2, 3, 5, 12 to Van Baerlestraat.*
Following a simple formula that has proved highly successful in France, this glamorous Art Deco

restaurant offers diners a straightforward choice of veal or steak, served in the Belgian manner with salad and French fries, and accompanied by red Côtes du Rhône or white Burgundy house wine. This simple menu results in rapid service, making L'Entrecôte an ideal place to dine before going on to a concert at the nearby Concertgebouw (10mins' walk). If you decide to linger, however, you can choose from an extensive selection of imaginative desserts.

Fong Lie
P. C. Hooftstraat 80 ☎ *(020) 716404. Map* **6***H2* □□ AE © *Closed Mon, last three weeks in July. Tram 2, 3, 5, 12 to Van Baerlestraat.*
An intimate Chinese restaurant offering delicate cuisine in a friendly atmosphere. The menu is small but tempting, and the dishes are brought to the table in the twinkling of an eye, making this ideally suited for a quick lunch between art museums or a light supper before a concert at the nearby Concertgebouw. Specialty: *Tsjha Sioe Mai* (fried "butterflies").

Indonesia ✿
Singel 550 ☎ *(020) 232035. Map* **11***F4* □□ AE © VISA *Last orders 10pm. Tram 4, 9, 14, 16, 24, 25 to Muntplein.*
The illuminated tower on Muntplein provides a romantic backdrop to this first-floor Indonesian restaurant, which combines friendly, attentive service with traditional costumes and an opulent Neoclassical interior. *Rijsttafels* (including one for vegetarians) are well-balanced and not too hot (apart from a few ferocious Balinese specialties).

Keijzer
Van Baerlestraat 96 ☎ *(020) 711441. Map* **6***I2* □□ AE © *Closed Sun. Tram 3, 5, 12, 16 to Museumplein.*
A conservative Dutch restaurant dating from 1903 and patronized by musicians performing at the Concertgebouw. The house specialty is *sole à la meunière*, but you can also sample local delicacies such as Texel lamb and smoked IJsselmeer eel. The restaurant is tucked away at the back of a bustling café, which ensures a pleasant level of animation even when the restaurant is quiet.

De Knijp
Van Baerlestraat 134
☎ *(020) 714248. Map 6I2* 🚋 🅿
🔵 *Last orders midnight. Closed
Sat lunch and Sun lunch. Tram 3,
5, 12, 16 to Museumplein.*
While conductors and pianists
performing at the Concertgebouw
traditionally dine at **Keijzer**, the
rest of the orchestra seems to
prefer the more casual ambience of
De Knijp. The interior has a slight
fin de siècle mood, and the cuisine
combines Dutch heartiness with a
touch of traditional French flair.
This is a useful restaurant to know
about if you are staying in a hotel
that is in Amsterdam's museum
quarter.

Kopenhagen
Rokin 84 ☎ *(020) 249376. Map
11E4* 🚋 🅰🅴 🔵 🔵 *Last
orders 10pm. Closed Sun. Tram 4,
9, 14, 16, 24, 25 to Spui.*
A popular Danish restaurant,
5mins' walk from the Dam,
decorated in a jovial nautical style
that one either loves or hates.
Kopenhagen's fish specialties are
delicious.

Lucius
Spuistraat 247 ☎ *(020) 241831.
Map 11E4* 🚋 🅰🅴 🔵 🔵 🆅🅸🆂🅰 *Last
orders 11pm. Closed lunch. Tram
1, 2, 5 to Spui.*
This chic seafood restaurant on
Spuistraat offers a wide choice of
maritime delights, including
salmon, oysters and mussels from
northern waters and fresh bass and
John Dory from the
Mediterranean. The restaurant
interior is fashionably frugal, with
long wooden benches, and the
menus are written up on large
blackboards. Service is friendly
and attentive.

Manchurian
Leidseplein 10a ☎ *(020) 231330.
Map 6F3* 🚋 🅰🅴 🔵 🔵 🆅🅸🆂🅰 *Last
orders 10.30pm. Closed mid-Dec
to mid-Jan. Tram 1, 2, 5, 6, 7, 10
to Leidseplein.*
An Oriental restaurant decorated
in delicate pastel colors and
offering a range of exquisite dishes
from the kitchens of Canton,
Peking, Mongolia, Thailand and
Indonesia. The crispy starters
such as Cantonese *dim sum* and
Golden Triangle (a spicy spring
roll) are worth sampling.
Manchurian is under the same
management as its sister
restaurant **Dynasty** on the
Reguliersdwarsstraat.

Mirafiori ✿
Hobbemastraat 2
☎ *(020) 623013. Map 6H3* 🚋 *to*
🚋 🅰🅴 🔵 *Last orders 11pm.
Closed Tues. Tram 1, 2, 5, 6, 7, 10
to Leidseplein.*
This staunchly traditional Italian
restaurant is marvelously
anachronistic with its marble
stairway, thick linen tablecloths
and signed black-and-white
photographs of Italian celebrities
of the 1960s. Italophiles will
appreciate the traditional Italian
cuisine, the patriotic wine list
and the brisk *buon giorno* with
which the manager greets his
guests.

Die Port van Cleve
Nieuwe Zijds Voorburgwal 178
☎ *(020) 240047. Map 11D4* 🚋
to 🚋 *Tram 1, 2, 5, 13, 14, 17 to
Dam.*
This cavernous dining hall is
something of an Amsterdam
institution. It was opened in 1870
behind the *Royal Palace* and soon
became famous for its steaks: so
famous that it has been serving
steaks ever since. For those who
might hesitate at the door, the
restaurant plays on one's gambling
instincts by numbering each steak
and presenting a bottle of wine
whenever the number ends in
three noughts. At the time of
writing, the lucky customer who
ordered steak no. 5,549,000 was
not far away. The cuisine here,
though substantial, is presented
with a touch of flair, and there is
nothing quite like the thick
erwtensoep (pea soup) to fortify
you for a brisk walk along the
canals. The *bodega* on the left-
hand side as you walk in is a more
intimate, Dutch-style room in
which to have a light lunch or a
sherry.

De Prinsenkelder
Prinsengracht 438
☎ *(020) 267721. Map 6F3* 🚋 *to*
🚋 🅰🅴 🔵 🔵 🆅🅸🆂🅰 *Last orders
10pm. Closed lunch, Mon. Tram
1, 2, 5, 6, 7, 10 to Leidseplein.*
This low, oak-beamed 17thC
warehouse cellar with its gleaming
Delft tiles and shining brass pots
calls to mind a Dutch Master
painting of the Golden Age. The
menu, however, is firmly based on
French *nouvelle cuisine* and uses
fine ingredients from the
delicatessen on the corner of
Leidsestraat. Both the restaurant
and the delicatessen are owned by
the Dikker en Thijs group.

Rib Room

Sonesta Hotel, Kattegat 1
☎ *(020) 212223. Map 11C5* 🍴🍷
🍷 🆎 💳 🔳 *VISA Tram 1, 2, 5, 13,*
17 to Martelaarsgracht.

The **Sonesta** (see *Hotels*) is
famous for its collection of modern
paintings, and its Rib Room
restaurant is enlivened with
colorful abstract works by Dutch
COBRA artists such as Appel and
Corneille. The cuisine has a
distinctive American vigor and the
specialty is all-you-can-eat prime
rib of beef, flown in from the
States and aged until it reaches a
peak of tenderness. Imported
Canadian lobster is also available,
while on Sun American-style
brunch is served.

La Rive

Amstel Hotel, Professor Tulpplein
1 ☎ *(020) 226060. Map 8G7*
🍴🍷 🍷 🆎 💳 *VISA Last orders*
10.30pm. Closed lunch. Tram 6, 7,
10 to Oosteinde.

Tucked away on the ground floor
of the **Amstel** (see *Hotels*) is the
small La Rive restaurant, which
was opened in 1955 to replace the
grand but slightly outdated
Spiegelzaal. The name may be
French, but the atmosphere in La
Rive is that of an English private
club, with tables concealed in small
alcoves to create a measure of
privacy. Despite this heavy
traditionalism, the French-style
cuisine prepared by chef Paul van
der Meij is decidedly creative and
at times even eccentric,
particularly his set menus based on
single themes. On fine summer
evenings, the restaurant moves out
onto the riverside terrace, and is
quickly fully booked. Its warm
furnishings and excellent pianist
make it attractive on cold winter
nights as well. As might be
expected, men are required to wear
a jacket and tie.

Sama Sebo ✿

P. C. Hooftstraat 27
☎ *(020) 628146. Map 6G3* 🔲 *to*
🍴🍷 🆎 💳 💳 *Closed Sun, hols,*
mid-July for two weeks. Tram 1,
2, 5 to Leidseplein, or tram 6, 7, 10
to Spiegelgracht.

A convivial Indonesian restaurant
with batik tablecloths, Indonesian
masks and soporific background
music. Sebo's *rijsttafel* may not be
the biggest in town, but it is one of
the most fragrant and refined, with
sauces that are dark and full-
bodied, but never too spicy.
Dinner reservations should be

made well in advance, though it is
easier to squeeze in at lunchtime to
sample inexpensive mini-*rijsttafels*
based on rice (*Nasi goreng*) or
noodles (*Bami goreng*).

Sancerre

Reestraat 28 ☎ *(020) 278794.*
Map 10D3 🍴 *to* 🍴🍷 🆎 💳 *VISA*
Last orders 10.30pm. Closed Sat
lunch and Sun lunch. Tram 13, 14,
17 to Westermarkt.

Three elegant 18thC shops have
been run together to create this
tasteful two-floor restaurant with
bright pink tablecloths and
contemporary paintings on the
walls. Four set menus are offered,
including a vegetarian one, and the
cuisine is delicate and French. As
might be anticipated, the wine list
is strong on Sancerres, with a
choice of ten whites, two reds and a
rosé.

Sluizer

Utrechtsestraat 43–45
☎ *(020) 226376 (Dutch*
restaurant); (020) 263557 (fish
restaurant). Map 7F5 🍴 🆎 💳
Last orders midnight. Tram 4 to
Keizersgracht.

The two Sluizer restaurants – one
offering Dutch food while the
other specializes in fish – combine
the conviviality of a brown café
with upscale cuisine. The Art
Deco fish restaurant is the more
adventurous of the two, and offers
a huge choice of fish (poached,
fried or grilled), *coquilles Saint-*
Jacques, *waterzooi* (a Belgian fish
stew) and crab casserole. The
service at Sluizer is friendly and
the menu invites customers who
find the salmon too dry to send it
back to the kitchen.

De Smoeshaan

Leidsekade 90 ☎ *(020) 276966.*
Map 6F2 🍴 *Last orders*
10.30pm. Closed lunch. Tram 1, 2,
5, 6, 7, 10 to Leidseplein.

Attached to a small theater, De
Smoeshaan preserves something of
the artistic ambience of a brown
café, while offering cuisine that is a
shade more sophisticated.
Specialties include *eendeborst met*
bosbessensaus (duck's breast in
bilberry sauce), and *gevulde*
gerookte zeetongrolletjes (filets of
sole rolled and stuffed with
smoked salmon). The restaurant
serves generous portions and the
set menu offered is excellent value.
A simpler lunch menu is offered
downstairs in the café **De**
Smoeshaan (see *Cafés*).

Speciaal ♦
Nieuwe Leliestraat 142
☎(020) 249706. *Map* **10C3** ☐
*Last orders 11pm. Tram 13, 14, 17
to Westermarkt.*
The Speciaal is situated in a rather
dingy street in the baffling
Jordaan. From the outside, the
restaurant looks no larger than a
boutique, but it opens out
miraculously at the back into an
attractive bamboo-lined room with
slowly revolving ceiling fans. A
tropical heat builds up as the
restaurant fills, and ziggurats of
rijsttafel dishes are piled
precariously onto the plate-
warmers. As well as a choice of two
rijsttafels, the menu offers an
interesting selection of Indonesian
meat, chicken and fish dishes.
Although beer is the usual
accompaniment to an Indonesian
meal – helping to extinguish any
unexpected explosions of spices on
the palate – the Speciaal also offers
a small selection of well-chosen
wines for those who prefer wine
with their meal.

Het Stuivertje ♦
Hazenstraat 58 ☎(020) 231349.
Map **10E2** ☐ AE ⊕ ⊙ VISA *Last
orders 11.30pm. Closed lunch,
Mon. Tram 13, 14, 17 to
Westermarkt.*
This friendly restaurant named
after the Dutch 5ct coin is
decorated in the style of a
traditional brown café, while the
accent is on cuisine with a slight
French flavor. The clientele is
unusually diverse and the
restaurant is always bursting at the
seams, so that a reservation is
essential. The excellent steaks are
particularly popular, but there is
also a *dagschotel* (dish of the day)
for the more adventurous. The
hearty portions of vegetables and
salads at Het Stuivertje are
legendary, and the wine list is
thoroughly researched.

Het Swarte Schaep ♦
Korte Leidsedwarsstraat 24
☎(020) 223021. *Map* **6F3** ☐ *to*
☐ ≥ AE ⊕ ⊙ VISA *Last orders
11pm. Tram 1, 2, 5, 6, 7, 10 to
Leidseplein.*
Until a few years ago there were
several excellent French
restaurants around Leidseplein,
but one by one they have packed
up and moved to the suburbs,
leaving only one – the
appropriately named "Black
Sheep" – as a lonely outpost of
good cuisine. The building dates

from 1687, and is richly furnished
with heavy dark wood and polished
brass utensils. The cuisine
combines the traditional virtues of
the French kitchen with the best
features of *nouvelle cuisine*, and
offers superb steaks, duck and
game, accompanied by vegetables
cooked to perfection. The old-
world courtesy of the waiters, the
wide choice of set menus and the
thick leather-bound wine list
illustrate Het Swarte Schaep's
serious commitment to good dining.

Tartufo
Singel 449 ☎(020) 277175. *Map*
11F4 ☐ *to* ☐ AE ⊙ VISA *Last
orders 11pm. Closed Sat lunch
and Sun lunch. Tram 1, 2, 5 to
Koningsplein; or tram 4, 9, 14, 16,
24, 25 to Muntplein.*
A friendly restaurant specializing
in inventive pasta dishes such as
tagliatelli with fresh salmon and
chives in a cream sauce. Lunch is
served in a cool, tiled kitchen with
curious Post Modern triangular
tables; dinners are eaten in the
more formal upstairs dining area.
The choice of either large or small
portions at lunch is a welcome
innovation.

Tempo Doeloe
Utrechtsestraat 75
☎(020) 256718. *Map* **8F5** ☐
AE *Last orders 11pm. Closed
late Jan–early Feb. Tram 4 to
Keizersgracht.*
Don't let the refined décor and
elegant porcelain in this small
Indonesian restaurant deceive you
into expecting delicate cuisine.
The Javanese, Balinese and
Sumatran dishes prepared by Don
Ao from the island of Celebes
make no concessions to the
Western palate, and when a dish is
described as *pedis* (sharp) it means
just what it says. But for those
attracted by hot spicy dishes,
Tempo Doeloe is a must. The
restaurant's specialties include the
chili-strewn *Nasi Koening*, the
rijsttafel Istemewa, the vegetarian
dish and, to bring the meal to a
soothing conclusion, traditional
Indonesian *spekkoek* (layered spice
cake).

Tout Court
Runstraat 13 ☎(020) 258637.
Map **10E3** ☐ *to* ☐ *Last orders
11.30pm. Closed lunch, Mon.*
Situated on a delightful street, this
small, popular and bustling
restaurant run by John Fagel offers
exquisite French provincial cuisine

Restaurants

tinged with elements of *nouvelle cuisine.*

This is not a restaurant for the conservative palate: the specialties are kidney, liver and brains, and the sauces tend to be rich. Portions are just right, service is impeccable, and the set menus cater to every need from a light pre- or post-theater *souper* to a gastronomic extravaganza. Tout Court is one of Amsterdam's best restaurants, so it is advisable to reserve several days in advance to avoid disappointment.

Treasure
Nieuwe Zijds Voorburgwal 115
☎(020) 234061. Map **11D4** ▮▯
AE ◉ ◉ VISA *Last orders 10pm. Tram 1, 2, 5, 9, 13, 14, 16, 17, 24, 25 to Dam.*

The extensive menu of this friendly Chinese restaurant on Nieuwe Zijds Voorburgwal includes curiosities such as squirrel fish, Charlie Chaplin duck and a certain dish known as *Pun Fan Pei*, which the menu tantalizingly claims is "a mysterious Chinese dish indescribable in Western terms." The vast ten-course Peking or Szechuan banquets are particularly good value, but for more modest appetites Treasure offers a rare opportunity to sample Peking-style *dim sum* lunches. Very strongly recommended are the *Sze Pao Hsia*, which are shrimp pouches wrapped in a crispy pancake.

De Trechter
Hobbemakade 63
☎(020) 711263. Map **6I3** ▮▮▮▮
AE ◉ ◉ *Last orders 10pm. Closed lunch, Sun, Mon and mid-July to early Aug. Tram 16 to Ruysdaelstraat.*

De Trechter (called "The Funnel" because of its unusual shape) offers *nouvelle cuisine* at its most refined in an intimate interior that suggests the mood of a private dinner party. The service is friendly and attentive, and the exquisite dishes created by Jan de Wit are presented on attractive plates that harmonize with the cuisine.

Delightful *amuse-gueules* appear at unexpected moments when interest might be flagging. Its consistent excellence ensures that this tiny restaurant is always fully booked, and it is advisable to reserve well in advance in order to be sure of getting a table.

Umeno
Agamemnonstraat 27
☎(020) 766089. □ to ▮□
Closed Wed. Tram 24 to Olympiaplein.

This small, traditional Japanese restaurant near Olympiaplein offers fragrant, colorful dishes presented with consummate delicacy. Its businessmen's lunch, which is served at a breathtaking pace, is eagerly devoured by Japanese executives attending trade fairs at the RAI exhibition center, which is not far from here.

Valentijn
Kloveniersburgwal 6
☎(020) 242028. Map **11E5** ▮▮▮▮
AE ◉ ◉ VISA *Closed lunch, Mon, Tues. Metro to Nieuwmarkt.*

This exquisitely furnished restaurant on Kloveniersburgwal offers superb *nouvelle cuisine* in a friendly, relaxed setting that appeals to young, artistic Amsterdammers. The *verrassingsmenu* (surprise menu) is a delightful introduction to this versatile restaurant, and the *zomermenu* (summer menu) features fresh seasonal specialties. The restaurant's location on the edge of the red-light district is slightly incongruous: diners who are not keen to encounter the sex shops and brothels are advised to head up Kloveniersburgwal from Muntplein. Specialties of the restaurant include *gebakken zeeduivel in bladerdeeg* (fried monkfish in puff pastry) and *three sorbets Valentijn.*

Warstein ✿
Spuistraat 266 ☎(020) 229609.
Map **11E4** ▮□ AE ◉ VISA *Last orders 10pm. Closed Mon. Tram 1, 2, 5 to Spui.*

Owned by the same dynamic duo as **Bols Taverne** on Rozengracht, Warstein is a restaurant with considerable vitality and culinary flair, and although it may make an occasional slight mistake, this is quickly forgiven. The restaurant's two-tier modern interior has the atmosphere of a Spanish hacienda, with flowers just about everywhere. Warstein offers a simple choice of five excellent 3-course menus, with particularly interesting fish dishes. Portions are enormous.

The meal ends with a complimentary cup of coffee, which is served with a glass of water and a glass of Bols liqueur.

The World According to Garp
Reguliersdwarsstraat 49 ☎ *(020)*
279988. Map 7F4 ☐ *to* ▮▮ AE
⊕ CB VISA *Closed Sun. Tram 1, 2,*
5 to Koningsplein or tram 4, 9, 14,
16, 24, 25 to Muntplein.

A relaxed restaurant in modern
Dutch style, including the
obligatory ferns without which no
restaurant on the fashionable
Reguliersdwarsstraat is complete.
Wholesome North American
cuisine dominates the menu,
including inexpensive jumbo-sized
hamburgers, San Francisco trout,
Maryland turkey, cheesecake,
apple pie and fine California wine.
There is a pleasant bar downstairs
where you can sip inexpensive
cocktails while listening to
mournful blues music.

Yamazato
Okura Hotel, Ferdinand Bolstraat
333 ☎ *(020) 787111. Map 7H4*
▮▮▮▮ *to* ▮▮▮▮ ⟵ AE ⊕ CB VISA *Last*
orders 10pm. Tram 12, 25 to
Cornelis Troostplein.

Yamazato is situated in
Amsterdam's only Japanese hotel,
the **Okura** on Ferdinand Bolstraat
(see *Hotels*). The restaurant offers
a wide range of traditional
Japanese dishes such as *sashimi*
(raw fish), *tempura* (deep-fried
delicacies) and seaweed soup. The
restaurant is tastefully furnished
and overlooks a miniature
Japanese garden. The hotel also
offers a sushi bar and a *teppan-yaki*
steak house, where steaks are
grilled on large hot plates that are
set into the tables.

Cafés

Amsterdam's cafés combine the homey comforts of London
pubs with the bohemian spirit of Paris cafés; they are quiet
places where you can linger over a coffee, read the newspaper,
sample an exotic beer or ruminate on films and fashions.

Traditional brown cafés

Amsterdam's brown cafés take their name from their dark
wood interiors and traditional furnishings; the atmosphere is
enhanced by bare wooden floorboards that creak like the deck
of a boat, wooden wainscoting, mustard-colored walls and a
rather haphazard selection of tables and chairs. Many of these
cafés have been in business since the 17thC, and their dark,
candlelit interiors retain something of the atmosphere of a
Golden Age painting. Occasionally, there is a hint of former
splendor in an ornate lamp, coat hook or calligraphic detail,
but the overwhelming mood is one of gentle decline. The
nostalgic atmosphere is often rounded off by a group of men
with oversized mustaches reminiscing about the good old days,
which in Amsterdam can mean anything from the 1920s back
to the 1640s.

The best brown cafés serve as a home away from home for
Amsterdammers, many of whom live in cramped, dark
apartments. They are places to linger over a beer (*pils*), coffee
(*koffie*) or soda water (*spa*) without feeling rushed. In all but
the most brusque establishments, you can spend a long rainy
afternoon reading a book from beginning to end without being
disturbed. Some cafés even provide Dutch and foreign
newspapers and a well-lit reading table. Most cafés will offer
filled rolls (*belegde broodjes*), *uitsmijter* (a Dutch specialty of
bread and ham or cheese, topped with fried eggs) and apple
cake (*appelgebak*), as well as traditional Dutch snacks such as
bitterballen (meatballs) and various types of *worst* (sausage).
Unless you only have one drink, it is customary to keep a
running bill and pay for everything at the end.

The friendliest cafés in Amsterdam are often the simply
furnished places in the city center. Beyond *Singelgracht* (the
outer limit of the 17thC city) the cafés tend to become

smothered in fussy domestic details such as frilly lace curtains and thick Persian carpets on the tables to protect them from beer stains.

Proeflokalen

An entirely different Amsterdam drinking institution is the *proeflokaal*, or tasting house. Originally these were attached to *jenever* (Dutch gin) distilleries and allowed customers to sample the product before purchasing a bottle. Although licensing laws now prohibit them from selling *jenever* in bottles, the *proeflokaal* still retains the atmosphere of a shop rather than a café. These are ideal spots for an apéritif – most being situated in attractive 18thC buildings in the old part of the city. One generally samples *jenever* – *oude* (old) or *jonge* (young) – served in tulip-shaped glasses filled to the brim.

Other tempting specialties are *bessen jenever* (flavored with berries), *citroen jenever* (flavored with lemon), *taainagel* (a seamen's *jenever*, which translates as "tough as nails"), *korenwijn* (a strong malt liquor distilled with juniper berries), *brandewijn* (brandy wine) and *Beerenburg* (a herbal bitter invented by the Amsterdam spice merchant Hendric van Beerenburg). There are also numerous specialties traditionally associated with festive occasions such as *kandeel* (an egg punch served to a mother and guests after childbirth) and *Bruidstranen* ("bride's tears," served at weddings). *Boerenjongen* (farmer boy) and *boerenmeisje* (farmer girl) contain respectively raisins and apricots in *brandewijn*, and are traditionally given to children.

Sherry and wine bars

Amsterdam also has a number of specialized sherry bars, such as the friendly and informed **Continental Bodega** (*Lijnbaansgracht 246*). For a good selection of wines, try **Mulliner's Wijnlokaal** (*Lijnbaangracht 267*).

Modern cafés

In the 1980s, young Amsterdammers made a decisive break with tradition when they began to frequent bright white architect-designed cafés with zinc tables, walls of mirrors and Post Modern architectural details. Although in the beginning these ultramodern cafés sent a shiver of dismay through the old brown cafés, they now seem to have settled into the fabric of the city and some – such as **De Blincker** – have even begun to acquire an endearing scruffiness.

Undoubtedly the most exciting new café in Amsterdam is found on the sixth floor of the department store **Metz & Co.** (see *Shopping*). Reached via the tiny elevators or, for the energetic, by the ornate staircase, this spacious café offers a splendid bird's-eye view of the city.

Eetcafés

An increasing number of cafés, particularly student brown cafés and modern cafés, have begun to offer complete meals at reasonable prices. The menu – usually chalked on a blackboard – often includes a dish of the day (*dagschotel*) and a vegetarian dish (*vegetarische schotel*). The cuisine usually consists of solid Dutch fare, although a few *eetcafés* such as **Van Puffelen** and **Het Molenpad** offer a hint of *nouvelle cuisine* at prices just slightly above the norm. Food is generally ordered at the bar and tipping is not expected.

Specialized cafés

Another recent trend is the emergence of specialized cafés. These include chess cafés such as **Het Hok** (*Lange Leidsedwarsstraat 134*), theater cafés, and jazz cafés (see *Nightlife and the arts*), women-only cafés such as **Saarein** (*Elandsstraat 119*), specialized beer cafés such as **Gollem** (*Raamsteg 4*), drugs cafés (which display a marijuana leaf on the window), punk cafés, gay cafés such as **April** (*Reguliersdwarsstraat 37*) and even a Belgian café, **De Brakke Grond**.

Pâtisseries

The austerity of Dutch Protestantism does not permit the guiltless consumption of cakes and pastries that goes on in neighboring Germany and Belgium but there are a handful of small cafés in Amsterdam where those with a sweet tooth can indulge their cravings. **Banketbakkerij Lanskroon** (*Singel 385*) is an austere but friendly place to ingest a few hundred calories, whereas **Berkhoff** (*Leidsestraat 46*) strives, with its house pianist, to create a more elegant ambience. (See also **Pâtisserie Pompadour** under *Food and drink* in *Shopping*.)

De Admiraal
Herengracht 319
☎ *(020) 254334. Map* **11***D4.*
Open Mon–Fri noon–midnight,
Sat 5pm–midnight, closed Sun .
☲ *open noon–3pm, 5–10.30pm.*
Tram 1, 2, 5, 13, 14, 17 to Dam.
This unexpectedly spacious *proeflokaal* in a curiously stunted 19thC neo-Renaissance building is stacked to the ceiling with *jenever* kegs big enough to conceal a cow. It is the only *proeflokaal* in Amsterdam that invites one to linger, with its sofas constructed from *jenever* kegs, candlelit alcoves hung with tapestries, and extravagant arrangements of flowers. Ranged along the bar are picturesque liqueurs produced by Amsterdam's last surviving independent distillery – **De Ooievaar** in the Jordaan – with intriguing names such as *Bruidstranen* ("bride's tears," a drink with tiny gold and silver leaves traditionally reserved for weddings), *Roosje zonder doornen* ("rose without thorns," containing petals of four types of roses) and *Papagaaiensoep* ("parrot soup," containing various types of nut).

Américain
Leidseplein 28 ☎ *(020) 245322.*
Map **6***F3. Open Sun–Wed*
11am–midnight, Thurs–Sat
11am–1am ☲ *Tram 1, 2, 5, 6, 7,*
10 to Leidseplein.
The **American Hotel** (see *Hotels*) was designed by Willem Kromhout in 1902, combining elements of Venetian Gothic and Art Nouveau. The hotel café overlooking *Leidseplein* brought a new grandeur to Amsterdam with its vaulted ceilings, languid murals and exotic lampshades. Although service can be brusque and the prices steep, it is difficult not to be enchanted by the opulent interior of the Américain, with its softly evocative golden light.

De Blincker
St Barberenstraat 7
☎ *(020) 271938. Map* **11***E5.*
Open 10am–1am ☲. *Open*
5–9pm. Tram 4, 9, 14, 16, 24, 25
to Spui.
The dazzling two-tier interior of the Blincker looks like a cross between an oil refinery and a greenhouse. The café is attached to the **Frascati Theater** (see *Nightlife and the arts*) and tends to fill with avant-garde theater goers as the evening wears on. The masks and plaster noses attached to the wall provide a nice touch of whimsicality and the Frascati theater's well-designed posters contribute lively touches of color.

De Brakke Grond
Nes 43 ☎ *(020) 260044. Map*
11*D5. Open 10am–1am* ☲ *Tram*
4, 9, 16, 24, 25 to Dam.
This quiet café is attached to the **Vlaams Cultureel Centrum** (Flemish Cultural Center), which exists to promote the culture of Dutch-speaking Belgium. The café's contribution is to offer a range of potent Belgian beers in a rather formal modern Belgian setting. Try the creamy-topped *Grimbergen* from the tap; or one of

the bottled beers, each meticulously poured into its proper glass. *Duvel* and *Wittekop* are pleasant light beers, while *Geuze Lambiek* from the Brussels area is a darker and sweeter brew. The upstairs restaurant offers a taste of the culinary culture of Belgium, featuring several unusual dishes prepared in beer, as well as *waterzooi* – the traditional fish stew.

De Doffer
Runstraat 12 ☎ (020) 226686. Map 10E3. Open noon–1am. Tram 1, 2, 5 to Spui.
A popular student café whose candles flicker invitingly into the early hours.

De Drie Fleschjes
Gravenstraat 16 ☎ (020) 248443. Map 11D5. Open Mon–Sat noon–8pm, closed Sun. Tram 1, 2, 4, 5, 9, 13, 14, 16, 17, 24, 25 to Dam.
A convivial *proeflokaal* dating from 1650, De Drie Fleschjes (The Three Jars) is located in a bell gabled house behind the *Nieuwe Kerk*. The green and cream wooden interior is softly lit by lamps in old brass fittings, and a solitary candle flickers romantically on top of the beer tap. Occasionally, the bartender will ascend a stepladder to replenish a glass from one of 43 padlocked casks, each marked with the name of a local business. De Drie Fleschjes' regulars range from organizations with their own private casks – such as the Rabobank and the Air Force's 32nd Tactical Fighter Squadron – to boisterous locals and students.

De Engelbewaarder
Kloveniersburgwal 59 ☎ (020) 253772. Map 11E5. Open 11am–1am ⟹ Tram 4, 9, 14, 16, 24, 25 to Spui.
A gloomy brown café on the E side of town with monstrous Amsterdam School-style iron lamps casting pools of soft light. De Engelbewaarder (The Guardian Angel) maintains its reputation as a literary café with regular readings and exhibitions. On Sat afternoons, particularly peaceful in this part of town, one can quietly read the newspaper as the affable house cat slumbers on top of the pinball machine; on Sun, however, jazz sessions draw considerable crowds. Good café food and a tempting range of beers

make this one of Amsterdam's finest brown cafés.

Eijlders
Korte Leidsedwarsstraat 47 ☎ (020) 242704. Map 6F3. Open noon–1am. Tram 1, 2, 5, 6, 7, 10 to Leidseplein.
A cozy brown café just off *Leidseplein* that hits exactly the right note as far as most Amsterdammers are concerned. Bartenders in long aprons provide a touch of sophistication, but locals ensure the elegance does not get out of hand by piling their coats and scarves on the wrought-iron lampstands. Once the haunt of artists and poets, Eijlders is still the place for frequent excellent exhibitions of modern paintings.

Frascati
Nes 59 ☎ (020) 241324. Map 11E5. Open Mon–Sat 10am–1am, Sun 5pm–1am ⟹ Open 5–11pm. Tram 4, 9, 14, 16, 24, 25 to Spui.
The dark and dingy Nes, tucked away behind Rokin, is an unlikely setting for a café as smart as Frascati, with its burgundy-red walls and gleaming brass fittings. The café belongs to the **Frascati Theater** (see *Nightlife and the arts*) – as does the astonishing **De Blincker** around the corner – and a rather arty crowd gathers here to read *Volkskrant* theater reviews, fill in applications for grant money and gorge on enormous slices of *appelgebak*. Frascati serves food until midnight.

Het Hooghoudt Proeflokaal
Reguliersgracht 11 ☎ (020) 255030. Map 7F5. Open noon–8pm, closed Sun ⟹ Tram 4, 9, 14 to Rembrandtsplein.
A dark 17thC warehouse cellar with walls lined with casks, and *jenever* distilling equipment dangling from the ceiling beams. Although it calls itself a *proeflokaal*, Hooghoudt is closer to a traditional brown café, and offers such comforts as a reading table and a simple menu. During the day, it is popular with bankers from nearby offices on *Herengracht*, while after dark it is a favorite stopping point for tours of the red-light district.

Hoppe
Spui 20 ☎ (020) 237849. Map 11E4. Open 11am–1am. Tram 1, 2, 5 to Spui.
In most civilized cities Hoppe

would probably be deemed a dive, but in nostalgia-prone Amsterdam it is a cherished memento of the Golden Age. Into Hoppe's smoke-choked sawdust-strewn interior pile a curious bundle of people, from professors of literature to unemployed seamen. The décor resembles a down-at-heel doctor's waiting room, and above the bar is a vast oil painting. The crush is almost always suffocating, although on sunny days it eases slightly as the hordes of drinkers spill out into the street, conversing in anything up to six languages.

Jacquet
Raadhuisstraat 6
☎*(020) 278500. Map 11D4* 💳
💳 ═ *Open Mon–Wed 10am–9pm, Thurs–Sat 10am–10pm, closed Sun. Tram 1, 2, 5, 13, 14, 17 to Dam.*
An elegant café-brasserie on a bustling corner, furnished in the currently chic colonial style, with tiled floor, rampant palms and not a trace of brown to be seen. Popular with a broad cross section of Amsterdammers, many of whom are as beautiful as the Hollywood stars whose photographs adorn the walls. Jacquet occupies a dazzling Art Nouveau corner building from 1901 known as the **White House.**

Karpershoek
Martelaarsgracht 2
☎*(020) 247886. Map 11C5. Open 7am–1am. Tram 1, 2, 5, 13, 17 to Martelaarsgracht.*
Amsterdammers are deeply fond of the scruffy, nostalgic Karpershoek, which has stood on the old harbor front since 1629. The café is conveniently close to Centraal Station, and its clock is set five minutes fast to ensure that regulars don't miss the last train to Purmerend or Paris.

De Koningshut
Spuistraat 269 ☎*(020) 264276. Map 11E4 Open 2.30pm–1am. Tram 1, 2, 5 to Spui.*
A jovial Brueghelian interior with antique beer tankards, jawbones and other curious paraphernalia dangling from the roof beams.

Het Land van Walem
Keizersgracht 449
☎*(020) 253544. Map 6F3. Open 9am–1am.* ═ *Tram 1, 2, 5 to Keizersgracht.*
You have to be up with the lark to get a seat in this furiously

fashionable café with the busiest espresso machine in town. Walem's unshakable success is the result of its quietly modern interior design, excellent food and coffee, wide stock of international newspapers and periodicals, friendly service, and rear garden complete with a classical teahouse. By noon the chances of finding an unoccupied seat are somewhat slim.

Het Molenpad
Prinsengracht 653
☎*(020) 259680. Map 6F3. Open noon–1am* ═ *Open noon–3pm, 6–8pm. Tram 1, 2, 5 to Prinsengracht.*
A quiet brown café on *Prinsengracht*, where you can sit and read a book undisturbed, offering excellent café cuisine in friendly surroundings. The mill path (*molenpad*) that ran just s of here until it was swallowed up by the Fourth Expansion of 1609 is depicted in a painting by the window. The Molenpad puts on temporary exhibitions of contemporary art. Its minuscule terrace becomes impossibly crowded on sunny afternoons.

Morlang
Keizersgracht 451
☎*(020) 252681. Map 6F3. Open Mon–Sat 9am–1am, Sun 10am–1am* ═ *Tram 1, 2, 5 to Keizersgracht.*
The ground floor and basement of this 18thC canal house have been attractively furnished in Post Modern style. With its fine views and creative menu, Morlang is a pleasant alternative to the overcrowded **Het Land van Walem** next door.

Oblomow
Reguliersdwarsstraat 40
☎*(020) 241074. Map 7F4. Open 11am–1am* ═ 💳 💳 💳 *Tram 1, 2, 5 to Koningsplein.*
A chic modern café named after the slothful antihero of Goncharov's novel and located on a street that epitomizes the new ethic of shabby elegance. The dazzling white interior designed by architects Peter Sas and Onno de Vries in a former coach house caused a considerable stir when it was opened in 1981, breaking every rule of traditional brown café style. The front is decidedly colonial, with palms gently swaying in the breeze of the ceiling fans, while the middle part mixes

Cafés

Moorish-Spanish and 1950s elements. Visit Oblomow in the early afternoon to enjoy its mood of dreamy lethargy, or come in the evening to join the fashionable set. The Oblomow's restaurant is attractively located in an 18thC room overlooking the garden and offers reasonably priced food, including tasty salads.

Papeneiland
Prinsengracht 2 ☎ *(020) 241989. Map 11B4. Open 11am–1am, closed Sun. Tram 3 to Haarlemmerplein.*

A friendly brown café on the edge of the *Jordaan*, occupying a 17thC step gable house blessed with a picturesque view of Brouwersgracht and *Prinsengracht*. The café's name is inscribed in ornate calligraphy on the exceptionally tall windows, while the interior is evocative of a Dutch Old Master, with Delft tiles and antique brass hanging lamps. The view from the front window was captured by Breitner on a cold winter's day in 1901 in a painting that now hangs in the *Amsterdams Historisch Museum*.

Pieper
Prinsengracht 424 ☎ *(020) 264775. Map 6F3. Open noon–1am. Tram 1, 2, 5 to Prinsengracht.*

A snug old brown café on Prinsengracht possessing that nonchalant shabbiness that Amsterdammers assiduously cultivate in their cafés, dogs, bicycles and streets. The photographs and press cuttings on the wall remind one that this unassuming wooden interior is one of Amsterdam's most venerable institutions and the soft light that falls through the stained-glass windows invokes an ache of mellow nostalgia in the most hardened of citizens. The steep descent to the restrooms is quite giddying after a tot or two of Bols.

Pilserij
Gravenstraat 10 ☎ *(020) 250014. Map 11D5. Open noon–1am. Tram 1, 2, 4, 5, 9, 13, 14, 16, 17, 24, 25 to Dam.*

An exquisite recreation of a *fin de siècle* interior in what was until recently a stationery store. The scratchy jazz recordings add to the outré mood, and the elegant room at the back seems designed for romantic assignations beneath the wispy hanging ferns.

De Prins
Prinsengracht 124 ☎ *(020) 249382. Map 10D3. Open 11am–1am* ☎ *Open 11am–2pm, 6–10pm. Tram 13, 14, 17 to Westermarkt.*

Beautifully located in one of a series of 18thC gable houses at the w end of Leliegracht, De Prins' tall sash windows overlook a picturesque muddle of typical Amsterdam details. De Prins looks deceptively old, but is in fact a newcomer to the café scene. Its décor is somewhat bizarre. The breakfast of toast, egg, ham, cheese, *ontbijtkoek* (a gingerbread specialty), pumpernickel and currant bread makes a pleasant prelude to a Sun morning stroll through the *Jordaan*.

Henri Prouvin
Gravenstraat 20 ☎ *(020) 239333. Map 11D5. Open Mon–Fri noon–8.30pm, Sat 2–8.30pm, closed Sun* ☎ *Tram 1, 2, 4, 5, 9, 13, 14, 16, 17, 24, 25 to Dam.*

Henri Prouvin's wine-tasting house is located in **Het Huys met de Gaper**, which takes its name from the head with a gaping mouth above the entrance (formerly a pharmacist's shop sign). The brown café interior is dimly lit by heavy lamps that look like upturned soup tureens and the walls are hung with an assortment of drawings. As well as wine, reasonably priced and substantial café food is offered.

Van Puffelen
Prinsengracht 377 ☎ *(020) 246270. Map 10D3. Open Mon–Fri 4pm–1am, Sat, Sun 4pm–2am. Open 6–10pm. Tram 13, 14, 17 to Westermarkt.*

The main reason for visiting this brown café, located on the western rim of the main canals, is to sample its exceptional cuisine. If you don't mind the somewhat cramped surroundings, you can eat excellent *nouvelle cuisine* here at a fraction of the price charged elsewhere. In addition, the portions are more substantial than in some of the more precious French establishments.

De Reiger
Nieuwe Leliestraat 34 ☎ *(020) 247426. Map 10C3. Open 9am–1am* ☎ *Tram 13, 14, 17 to Westermarkt.*

A brown café in the *Jordaan*, popular with the students and artists who now make up a large part of the population of this former working-class neighborhood. Its selection of 19thC watercolors with sentimental titles such as *Betwixt the Hills* and *A Peaceful Backwater* seems somehow not quite in keeping with the intense artistic milieu of the Jordaan. De Reiger opens earlier than most cafés of this genre, and is a pleasantly quiet place in which to pore over the newspapers.

Reijnders
Leidseplein 6 ☎ *(020) 234419.*
Map 6F3. Open 9am–1am. Tram
1, 2, 5, 6, 7, 10 to Leidseplein.
A cheerful, old-fashioned brown café on *Leidseplein* that attracts a fair cross section of Dutch society, from wisecracking billiards players who suddenly burst into sentimental song to glittering punks. The Dutch, despite their reputation for cleanliness, seem to prefer their cafés a little dingy, and Reijnders more than obliges with its smoke-stained walls and dusty old bottles above the bar.

Scheltema
Nieuwe Zijds Voorburgwal 242
☎ *(020) 232323. Map 11D4.*
Open 8am–11pm. Tram 1, 2, 5,
13, 14, 17 to Dam.
A comfortable, creaking, brown café that has the battered look of an old suitcase. To add to its shabby charm, Scheltema, like a slowly sinking barge, is at least 1m (3ft) below street level. Situated next door to the former offices of the newspaper *Algemeen Handelsblad* (now occupied by squatters), Scheltema was the haunt of journalists until the major newspapers fled to the suburbs. The walls are still plastered with caricatures of well-known journalists and other memorabilia, and a few nostalgic scribblers retire here at the end of the day. The learned mood is enhanced by the handsome newspaper reading table planted firmly in the middle of the café.

Schiller
Rembrandtsplein 26
☎ *(020) 249846. Map 7F5. Open*
4pm–1am. Tram 4, 9, 14 to
Rembrandtsplein.
Schiller's dilapidated covered terrace on Rembrandtsplein may be disconcerting, but it is worth venturing behind the heavy curtain to discover one of Amsterdam's most evocative Art Deco interiors,

which looks like a Roxy cinema about to be foreclosed. The ornate lamps that smear random patches of yellow light on the marble walls and the glittering mirrors create a sense of anticipation, though the only excitement these days happens when someone accidentally sits on the broken spring of a defeated sofa. The portraits of 1930s cabaret stars on the walls were painted by the café's former owner Frits Schiller.

't Smackzeyl
Brouwersgracht 101
☎ *(020) 226520. Map 11B4.*
Open 11am–1am. Tram 3 to
Haarlemmerplein.
This beautiful café is located in a cheerful red-faced canal house overlooking a picturesque cluster of stately bridges and creaking boats. It is a perfect café to stroll to on a Sun morning, to read the newspaper and watch the seagulls swoop around the ships' rigging as Vivaldi gently plays in the background.

't Smalle
Egelantiersgracht 12
☎ *(020) 239617. Map 10C3.*
Open 11am–1am. Tram 13, 14, 17
to Westermarkt.
An ivy-covered 18thC house in the s of the *Jordaan* overlooking Egelantiersgracht. The interior – originally the distillery and tasting house of Pieter Hoppe – has been tastefully restored, and the golden light that filters through the stained-glass windows gives the interior the mellow hue of a Rembrandt painting. 't Smalle is especially attractive on dark winter evenings with candles flickering at every table. The only drawback is that, as such a congenial place, it is almost always bursting at the seams.

Smits Koffiehuis
Stationsplein 10
☎ *(020) 233777. Map 12B6.*
Open Mon–Sat 8am–8.30pm,
Sun 9am–8.30pm. ≅ *Tram 1, 2,*
4, 5, 9, 13, 16, 17, 24, 25 to
Centraal Station.
Stepping out of Centraal Station into the cheerful confusion of trams, bicycles, street musicians and hurdy-gurdies, the first building to catch your eye is the ornate, wooden Smits Koffiehuis, formerly a tram station and now a tourist information office and café-restaurant. The attractive Old Dutch-style *koffiehuis* is an ideal

Cafés

place to catch your breath after a long journey or to meet friends off the train, and serves good coffee and reasonably priced food. In summer the café spills out onto a floating terrace overlooking the former harbor front.

De Smoeshaan
Leidsekade 90 ☎ (020) 250368. Map 6F2. Open 10am–1am ⧇ Tram 1, 2, 5, 6, 7, 10 to Leidseplein.
Actors and actresses gather in this very dark and simple brown café to launch new productions or mourn those that died. There is a good and inexpensive café menu, and a slightly more expensive restaurant upstairs (see *Restaurants*).

Tisfris
St Antoniesbreestraat 142 ☎ (020) 220472. Map 12D6. Open 11am–2am ⧇ Open 6–9.30pm. Tram 9, 14 to Waterlooplein.
Situated in Theo Bosch's Pentagon complex in the *Nieuwmarkt* district (where some of Amsterdam's best modern architecture can be found), this café is an intriguing modern design on three levels, with attractive views of canals through a multitude of windows. The food is above average.

De Wildeman
Kolksteeg 3 ☎ (020) 251310. Map 12C6. Open 3pm–1am, closed Sun. Tram 1, 2, 5, 13, 17 to N. Z. Kolk.
The Dutch association for the protection of historical monuments, which occupies a nearby 17thC corn exchange, should be proud of its local *proeflokaal*. Located in a medieval alley stubbornly resistant to change, De Wildeman is a handsomely restored shop with lofty windows, wood-paneled walls and magnificent brass lamps. The neat rows of jars on the shelves behind the counter and the gleaming tiled floor create something of the air of a pharmacy, but the merry regulars invariably take the chill off the place.

Wildschut
Roelof Hartplein 1 ☎ (020) 768220. Map 6I3. Open 9am–1am ⧇ Open 6–10pm. Tram 3, 5, 12, 24 to Roelof Hartplein.
The abandoned cinema fittings that decorate this café create a

nostalgic 1930s interior reminiscent of the moody paintings of Edward Hopper. Art Deco lamps throw dim pools of yellowish light on antique theater seats, as languid vocalists sing husky songs of the 1930s in the background. The location is appropriate: Wildshut's curving plate-glass windows overlook Roelof Hartplein, that dazzling architectural showpiece of the late 1920s intended as a prelude to the brave new world of *Amsterdam Zuid*.

After a fortifying *uitsmijter* and a strong espresso, you might enjoy a stroll through the streets of fanciful workers' housing south of here.

Wijnand Fockink
Pijlsteeg 31 ☎ (020) 243989. Map 11D5. Open 11am–8pm, closed Sun. Tram 4, 9, 16, 24, 25 to Dam.
The expansion of the **Hotel Krasnapolsky** (see *Hotels*) mercifully spared this charming little 17thC *proeflokaal*, with its half-shuttered windows and scrolled calligraphy. Shapely glasses are filled to the brim with the white, red, green or blue liqueur of your choice, and the bartender then explains, in any one of six languages, the proper etiquette of tasting. This requires you to bend over with your hands clasped behind your back to take the first sip – a wise precaution, since the stockbrokers and antique dealers who congregate here pack a mighty nudge. Once you have returned to the vertical, cast your eyes upward to admire the famous collection of rotund liqueur jars handpainted by impoverished students, and showing the portraits of Amsterdam burgomasters from the 16thC onward.

De IJsbreker
Weesperzijde 23 ☎ (020) 681805. Map 8H7. Open 10am–1am. Tram 6, 7, 10 or metro to Weesperplein.
An elegant *fin de siècle* café with mirrors, murals and slightly down-at-heel Art Nouveau lamps. The café is attached to a center for contemporary music and the ascetic minimalism of much of the work performed there seems a direct rebuke to the opulent 19thC eclectic architecture to be found on this once fashionable stretch of the *Amstel* river.

Nightlife and the arts

Dutch towns can be sadly staid and lifeless after hours, due to the combination of unreliable weather and Protestant morals, but Amsterdam is a conspicuous exception to this rule and remains buoyant 24 hours a day. Cultural activities are focused on Leidseplein, where many of Amsterdam's theaters, cinemas, discos, clubs and cafés are located. Rembrandtsplein forms a second, somewhat less vibrant, hub of activity, with its cinemas, bars and nightclubs.

The main attractions for visitors are classical music at the Concertgebouw, opera and dance at the Muziektheater, movies, pop concerts and jazz cafés. The **Amsterdams Uit Buro** (*Leidseplein 26* ☎ *(020) 211211, map 6F3.*) handles bookings for concerts, theater and dance, and publishes a monthly listing of events in the free *Uitkrant*.

Amsterdam has been famous since the 17thC for its red-light district, known colloquially as **De Walletjes** after the two canals Oude Zijds Voorburgwal and Oude Zijds Achterburgwal where most of the visible prostitution goes on. With a frankness that is perhaps unique to Amsterdam, sexily dressed women sit in the front windows of 17thC gable houses, with every pimple and dimple visible in the strong glow of red neon. This superlative exhibitionism has turned Amsterdam's red-light district into a major tourist attraction, and large bus parties are taken on what are reassuringly called "guided and guarded tours" through the maze of gaudy streets, like Dante being led through the Inferno. Some people may find the sexual explicitness offensive, but there is perhaps also a lighter side to it all, as in the ghastly bad taste of the brothel furnishings, and the sex shop signs announcing with the simple honesty of a corner grocery shop: "100% guaranteed porn." The women, too, have all the gifts of small entrepreneurs, and each "service" is performed at a fixed price.

Because of its popularity, the red-light district is fairly safe at night. If you do decide to visit it, however, keep to the crowded streets and, if you feel at all threatened, head into the nearest café.

Nightclubs featuring old-fashioned strip shows are mainly found on Thorbeckeplein; the statue of Thorbecke, who drafted the 19thC constitution of the Netherlands, discreetly faces away from the inviting neon signs.

Bars

Although bars may lack the Bohemian charm of brown cafés, they are quiet and comfortable for cocktails and conversation.

Amstel Hotel Bar
Prof. Tulpplein 1
☎ *(020) 226060. Map 8G7* AE
⊙ ⊙ VISA *Open 9am–1am. Tram 6, 7, 10 to Oosteinde.*
A quiet riverside bar. Live piano music lends romance to the setting.

Bass Pub
Doelen Crest Hotel, Nieuwe Doelenstraat 24 ☎ *(020) 220722. Map 11E5* AE CB ⊙ ⊙ *Open noon–1am. Tram 4, 9, 14, 16, 24, 25 to Muntplein.*
A confusing cross between a Dutch

brown café and a Victorian pub, where you can gently fall asleep after work on Fri drinking pints of British beer and listening to the slowest pianist in town.

Ciel Bleu
Okura Hotel (23rd floor), Ferdinand Bolstraat 333
☎ *(020) 787111* AE ⊙ ⊙ VISA *Open 6pm–1am. Tram 12, 25 to Cornelis Troostplein.*
The Okura Hotel's 23rd-floor bar is the ideal place to sip cocktails and listen to the house pianist as

the sun sinks behind the western suburbs.

Continental Bodega

Lijnbaansgracht 246
☎*(020) 239098. Map* **6***G3. Open Mon–Sat 3pm–9pm. Tram 1, 2, 5, 6, 7, 10 to Leidseplein.*
The Continental is an attractive sherry bodega.

Harry's American Bar

Spuistraat 285 ☎*(020) 244384. Map* **11***E4. Open Mon–Thurs 5pm–1am; Fri, Sat 5pm–2am; Sun 9pm–1am. Tram 1, 2, 5 to Spui.*
This bar is Amsterdam's answer to the famed watering-hole of Americans in Paris. Good cocktails are served.

Library Bar

Marriott Hotel, Stadhouderskade 19–21 ☎*(020) 835151. Map* **6***G2* AE ◑ ◐ VISA *Open noon–1am. Tram 1, 2, 5, 6, 7, 10 to Leidseplein.*
As its name suggests, the Library Bar of the Marriott Hotel is lined with old books, though the bias toward works by minor 19thC Dutch theologians may not be to everyone's taste.

Pulitzer Bar

Keizersgracht 234
☎*(020) 228333. Map* **10***D3* AE ◑ ◐ VISA *Open 11am–1am. Tram 13, 14, 17 to Westermarkt.*
Pleasant bar overlooking Keizersgracht, decorated with 17thC maps and prints.

Cinemas

Amsterdam has an excellent range of cinemas, often retaining original Art Deco furnishings. Films are almost always shown in their original language with Dutch subtitles, apart from children's matinees and films marked *Nederlands gesproken* (Dutch spoken). Programs change on Thurs and most cafés display the current listings. For insomniacs, there are *Nachtvoorstellingen* (night screenings), beginning around midnight.

Alfa

Hirschgebouw, Leidseplein
☎*(020) 278806. Map* **6***F3. Tram 1, 2, 5, 6, 7, 10 to Leidseplein.*
Four very comfortable theaters showing a good selection of international films, tucked into the back of a former department store modeled on Selfridges of London.

Alhambra

Weteringschans 134
☎*(020) 233192. Map* **7***H5. Tram 4, 6, 7, 10 to Frederiksplein.*
Slightly down-at-heel Art Deco cinema showing good foreign films.

Amsterdams Filmhuis

Ceintuurbaan 338
☎*(020) 623488. Map* **8***I6. Tram 3 to 2ᵉ v.d. Helststraat.*
Two-screen cinema showing avant-garde political films.

Bellevue Cinerama

Marnixstraat 400
☎*(020) 234876. Map* **6***F3. Tram 1, 2, 5, 6, 7, 10 to Leidseplein.*
Giant screens with Dolby stereo.

Cineac

Reguliersbreestraat 31
☎*(020) 243639. Map* **7***F5. Tram 4, 9, 14, 16, 24, 25 to Muntplein.*
Duiker's 1934 functionalist answer

to Tuschinski across the street. Notice the projectionist's room above the entrance.

Cinecenter

Lijnbaansgracht 236
☎*(020) 236615. Map* **6***F3. Tram 1, 2, 5, 6, 7, 10 to Leidseplein.*
A pleasant four-theater complex with an attractive café where you can wait for the film to begin.

City

Kleine Gartmanplantsoen 13–25
☎*(020) 234579. Map* **6***F3. Tram 1, 2, 5, 6, 7, 10 to Leidseplein.*
A six-theater complex showing mainstream films. The tower is all that remains of the original 1935 cinema designed by Jan Wils.

Desmet

Plantage Middenlaan 4a
☎*(020) 273434. Map* **8***E7. Tram 7, 9, 14 to Plantage Kerklaan or metro to Waterlooplein.*
Small Art Deco movie theater showing avant-garde films and old favorites.

Filmmuseum/Cinematheek

Vondelpark 3 ☎*(020) 831646. Map* **6***G1. Tram 1, 2, 5, 6 to 1ᵉ Constantijn Huygensstraat; tram 3, 12 to Overtoom.*
The avant-garde Filmmuseum is

incongruously located in a grand pavilion that was built as a fashionable café in the heady 1880s. Films shown here vary from vintage German Expressionism to W.C. Fields comedies.

Kriterion
Roetersstraat 170
☎*(020) 231708. Map **9**G8. Tram 6, 7, 10 to Roetersstraat.*
Two-theater complex showing avant-garde films hot from the Berlin or Venice film festivals. The Kriterion also has a very attractive café. The sort of cinema that can be counted on to show *Death in Venice* at least once a year.

The Movies
Haarlemmerdijk 161
☎*(020) 245790. Tram 3 to Haarlemmerplein.*
An attractive three-theater complex built in 1912 in Egyptian Art Deco style. The complex offers a good selection of international films with an emphasis on Latin countries.

Tuschinski
Reguliersbreestraat 26
☎*(020) 262633. Map **7**F5. Tram 4, 9, 14, 16, 24, 25 to Muntplein.*
Amsterdam's most opulent Art Deco cinema, with six screens showing international successes.

Classical and modern music
The obvious advantage of music is the absence of a language barrier, and Amsterdam offers a broad spectrum of styles from traditional opera to experimental modern music.

Concertgebouw
Van Baerlestraat 98
☎*(020) 718345. Map **6**H2* AE
⊙ ⊙ *Box office open 10am–3pm. Tram 3, 5, 12, 16 to Museumplein.*
The elegant Classical Concertgebouw (concert hall), home of Holland's foremost orchestra the Concertgebouworkest, was built in 1888 by A. L. van Gendt. The Concertgebouw boasts faultless acoustics (though its foundations are a little shaky). Watch out for special events such as the inexpensive *Zomeravondconcerten* (summer evening concerts, early Aug–early Sep) and the free lunchtime concerts (every Wed at 12.30pm). Formal dress is not obligatory to attend Concertgebouw concerts, and younger people tend to wear colorful, casual clothes.

Engelse Kerk
Begijnhof 48 (entrance on Spui)
☎*(020) 249665. Map **11**E4. Tram 1, 2, 4, 5, 9, 14, 16, 24, 25 to Spui.*
Sat afternoon concerts (*Zaterdagmiddagconcerten*) begin at 4pm in a neat little church in the center of Amsterdam where the Pilgrim Fathers once worshiped.

IJsbreker
Weesperzijde 23
☎*(020) 681805. Map **8**H7. Tram 6, 7, 10 or metro to Weesperplein.*
The photographs on the walls of the café IJsbreker give an idea of what to expect in this small concert hall specializing in international avant-garde music.

Mozes & Aäronkerk
Waterlooplein 57
☎*(020) 221305. Map **12**E6. Tram 9, 14 or metro to Waterlooplein.*
Occasional performances of traditional Indian dance and music are held in this former 19thC church on Waterlooplein.

Het Muziektheater
Amstel 3 ☎*(020) 255455. Map **7**F5. Tram 9, 14 or metro to Waterlooplein.*
With its view of the river Amstel, and its varied program of classical and modern opera and ballet, Amsterdam's new Muziektheater has brought renewed life to the former Jewish area of Amsterdam. Home to the national ballet (Het Nationale Ballet) and the Dutch opera company (De Nederlandse Opera), the Muziektheater also features performances by major foreign companies on tour.

De Nieuwe Kerk
Dam ☎*(020) 268168. Map **11**D4. Open Mon–Fri 9am–5pm. Tram 1, 2, 4, 5, 9, 13, 14, 16, 17, 24, 25 to Dam.*
Organ concerts on Sun 4–5pm.

Oude Kerk
Oude Kerksplein 1 ☎*(020) 249183. Map **11**D5. Tram 4, 9, 16, 24, 25 to Dam, then a 5min walk.*
Occasional organ concerts in Amsterdam's oldest (and coldest) church.

Nightlife and the arts

Sonesta Koepelzaal
*Kattengat 1. Map **11**C5. Tram 1, 2, 5, 13, 17 to Martelaarsgracht.*
Sun concerts by small ensembles at 11am in an unusual 17thC round Classical church.

Stedelijk Museum
Paulus Potterstraat 13
☎*(020) 5732911. Map **6**H2. Tram 2, 3, 5, 12 to Van Baerlestraat.*
Contemporary music concerts take place on Sat at 3pm, Sept–June.

Tropeninstituut
Mauritskade 63
☎*(020) 5688200. Map **9**G9. Tram 9, 10 to Mauritskade.*
Occasional performances of non-Western dance and music in the main hall of the *Tropeninstituut*.

Waalse Kerk
*Oude Zijds Achterburgwal 157. Map **11**D5. Tram 4, 9, 16, 24, 25 to Dam, then a 5min walk.*
Occasional chamber music concerts.

Cultural institutes
As in other major cities there are several cultural institutes in Amsterdam. **The British Council** (*Keizersgracht 343* ☎*(020) 223644, map **10**E3, tram 1, 2, 5 to Keizersgracht*) shows British films, and the **Maison Descartes** boasts a bistro offering French *cuisine bourgeoise* in a tiled kitchen (*Vijzelgracht 2* ☎*(020) 224936, map **7**G4, tram 16, 24, 25 to Prinsengracht*). German films are screened at the **Goethe Institut** (*Herengracht 470* ☎*(020) 230421, map **7**F4, tram 16, 24, 25 to Herengracht*). Occasional Italian cultural events are held at the **Instituto Italiano di Cultura** (*Keizersgracht 564* ☎*(020) 265314, map **7**F4, tram 1, 2, 5 to Keizersgracht*).

Discos
Discos around Leidseplein tend to be crowded with young people, while older Amsterdammers prefer places slightly off the beaten track. Some Amsterdam discos are, strictly speaking, private clubs and will only admit you, if at all, after you have purchased a temporary membership. Most discos do not really begin to swing until about 1am when cafés close.

Boston Club
Kattengat 1 ☎*(020) 245561. Map **11**B5. Open 10pm–5am. Tram 1, 2, 5, 13, 17 to Martelaarsgracht.*
Exclusive disco for older swingers, in Sonesta Hotel basement.

Club la Mer
Korte Leidsedwarsstraat 73
☎*(020) 242910. Map **6**F3. Open Mon–Fri 10pm–4am, Sat, Sun 10pm–5am. Tram 1, 2, 5, 6, 7, 10 to Leidseplein.*
Amsterdam's bronzed elite squeeze into this cramped disco to listen to Motown and soft disco.

Fizz
Nieuwe Zijds Voorburgwal 165 ☎*(020) 271997. Map **11**D4. Open Tues–Sun 11pm–4am, Fri, Sat 11pm–5am. Tram 1, 2, 5 to Dam.*
A cosmopolitan New Wave disco close to the Dam, with a large, empty room for dancing on the ground floor and a spacious café with video and billiards upstairs.

Homolulu
Kerkstraat 23 ☎*(020) 246387. Map **6**F3. Open Sun–Thurs 10pm–4.30am, Fri, Sat 10pm–5.30am. Tram 1, 2, 5, 6, 7, 10 to Leidseplein.*
Gay disco, with restaurant.

Juliana's
Apollolaan 138 ☎*(020) 737313. Open 10pm–4am. Tram 16 to Emmastraat.*
The Amsterdam Hilton's elite discotheque, named after the former queen of the Netherlands.

Mazzo
Rozengracht 114
☎*(020) 267500. Map **10**D2. Open Sun–Thurs 11pm–4am, Fri, Sat 11pm–5am. Tram 13, 14, 17 to Westermarkt.*
Mazzo's wall-to-wall audiovisual entertainment makes it popular with Amsterdam's avant-garde artists, musicians and fashion designers, who arrive on old black bicycles from nearby ateliers in the Jordaan.

't Nijlpaardenhuis
*Warmoesstraat 170. Map **11**D5.
Open Thurs–Sat 8pm–1am, Sun
1–5.30pm, 8pm–1am. Tram 4, 9,
16, 24, 25 to Dam.*
Amsterdam's only roller-skate
disco in the basement of a parking
garage behind the Bijenkorf.

Odeon
*Singel 460 ☎(020) 249711. Map
11E4. Open Sun–Thurs
10pm–5am, Fri, Sat 10pm–6am.
Tram 1, 2, 5 to Koningsplein.*
In 1782 John Adams negotiated
the first US-Dutch loan in this
17thC neck gable house designed
by Philips Vingboons. A beautiful
oval concert hall, added in 19thC,
has been sensitively converted into
a discotheque, while the stately
voorkamer (front room), with its
Baroque painted ceilings, now
functions as a late-night café.

't Okshoofd
*Herengracht 114 ☎(020)
227685. Map **11**D4. Open Sun–
Thurs 11pm–6am; Fri, Sat 2am–
7am. Tram 1, 2, 5 to Spui.*
Located in the cellar of a stately
Herengracht mansion, 't Okshoofd
is Amsterdam's oldest disco. It
attracts a lively crowd of night

owls, ranging from aging hippies
to youthful yuppies.

36 op de schaal van Richter
*Reguliersdwarsstraat 36
☎(020) 261573. Map **6**F4. Open
Sun–Thurs 11.30pm–4am, Fri,
Sat 11.30pm–5am. Tram 4, 9, 14,
16, 24, 25 to Muntplein.*
If you feel at ease in *Café
Oblomow*, you'll probably like
this chic disco nearby. A décor of
shattered mirrors and brick rubble
is intended to suggest the
aftermath of an earthquake
measuring a theoretically
impossible 36 on the Richter scale.
Entry at the discretion of the bouncer.

Zorba the Buddha
*Oude Zijds Voorburgwal 216
☎(020) 259642. Map **11**D5.
Open Sun–Thurs 9pm–2am, Fri,
Sat 9pm–3am. Tram 4, 9, 16, 24,
25 to Dam.*
Although this large disco is run by
Bhagwan disciples, most of the
people who come here are solely
interested in the dance floor. The
relaxed and friendly atmosphere
is appreciated by teenagers, who
flock here on weekends, on quieter
weekdays it attracts a loyal band of
slightly older Amsterdammers.

Jazz, blues and Latin American music
The **Jazzline** (☎*(020) 267764*) gives recorded information
(in Dutch only) of forthcoming jazz concerts.

Café Alto
*Korte Leidsedwarsstraat 115
☎(020) 263249. Map **6**F3. Open
8pm–2am (concerts begin
9.30pm). Tram 1, 2, 5, 6, 7, 10 to
Leidseplein.*
This intimate, cosmopolitan jazz
café offers a tranquil escape from
the crowds thronging Leidseplein.

Bamboo Bar
*Lange Leidsedwarsstraat 66
☎(020) 243993. Map **6**F3. Open
8pm–2am (concerts begin
10pm). Tram 1, 2, 5, 6, 7, 10 to
Leidseplein.*
Tropical décor, friendly
atmosphere and live groups.

BIMhuis
*Oude Schans 73–77
☎(020) 233373. Map **12**E6.
Concerts Thurs–Sat at 9pm. Café
open Mon–Thurs 8pm–2am, Fri,
Sat 8pm–3am (Thurs–Sat
8pm–midnight, café open to
ticket holders only). Tram 9, 14 or
metro to Waterlooplein.*
The BIMhuis is a bright, crisp jazz
center on the E side of town, not far

from the Rembrandthuis. It was
set up in the 1970s by the
Beroepsvereniging van
Improviserende Musici BIM
(Professional Jazz Musicians'
Union) in a former warehouse.
Concerts are given Thurs–Sat in
the spacious amphitheater, while
informal workshops featuring new
musicians take place Mon–Wed.
The **BIMcafé** offers a good range
of beers, cocktails and Indonesian
snacks such as *lemper* (rice mixed
with spiced meat) and *pisang
goreng* (fried banana).

Cab Kaye's Jazz Pianobar
*Beulingstraat 9 ☎(020) 233594.
Map **11**E4. Open Tues–Sat 9pm–
3am. Tram 1, 2, 5 to Koningsplein.*
Discreet piano bar.

De Engelbewaarder
*Kloveniersburgwal 59
☎(020) 253772. Map **11**E5.
Open 11am–1am. Tram 9, 14 to
Waterlooplein or metro to
Nieuwmarkt.*
Literary café featuring jazz
sessions every Sun afternoon.

Nightlife and the arts

De Kroeg
Lijnbaansgracht 163
☎ *(020) 250177. Map 10E2.
Open Sun–Thurs 10pm–4am, Fri,
Sat 10pm–5am. Tram 7, 10, 17 to
Elandsgracht.*
Jazz and salsa concerts begin most
evenings around 10.30pm in this
dark dive at the w limit of the
Jordaan. Though the back room
bears a distinct resemblance to
Edward Kienholz's horrific
Beanery in the *Stedelijk Museum*,
the atmosphere is friendly and
relaxed.

Joseph Lam Jazzclub
Van Diemenstraat 8
☎ *(020) 228086. Open Fri, Sat
9pm–3am, Sun 8pm–2am. Tram 3
to Zoutkeetsgracht (terminus).*
Atmospheric Dixieland jazz club
in a remote part of the old harbor,
best reached by taxi.

Maloe Melo
Lijnbaansgracht 160
☎ *(020) 253300. Map 10E2.
Open 10pm–3am. Tram 7, 10, 17
to Elandsgracht.*
The smallest of the
Lijnbaansgracht trio of music
cafés, specializing in blues.

Pianobar Le Maxim
Leidsekruisstraat 35
☎ *(020) 241920. Map 6G3. Open
9pm–3am. Tram 1, 2, 5, 6, 7, 10 to
Leidseplein.*
Crowded piano bar for those who
like to sing along to sentimental
oldies.

Rum Runners
Prinsengracht 277
☎ *(020) 274079. Map 10C3.
Open noon–3pm, 6–11pm
(restaurant); noon–1am (bar).
Tram 13, 14, 17 to Westermarkt.*
Caribbean restaurant with Latin
American music on Wed at 8pm
and Sun at 2.30pm and 8pm.

Stip
Lijnbaansgracht 161
☎ *(020) 279692. Map 10E2.
Open 10pm–4am (concerts begin
at 11pm). Tram 7, 10, 17 to
Elandsgracht.*
The most traditional and least
cramped of the Lijnbaansgracht
music cafés, with a varied program
of jazz, blues, reggae and pop,
often with a 1960s flavor. The
mezzanine floor, where food is
available, offers a good view of the
stage.

Multifunctional/Alternative centers
Peaceful backwaters of 1960s idealism, featuring programs of
pop, poetry and politics.

De Meervaart
Osdorpplein 205
☎ *(020) 107393. Tram 1 to
Osdorpplein.*
A modern cultural center in an
attractive garden city on the w edge
of Amsterdam. Specialties include
jazz, blues and pop music, as well
as poetry.

Melkweg
Lijnbaansgracht 234a
☎ *(020) 241777. Map 6F3. Open
Wed, Thurs 6pm–12.30am, Fri–
Sun 6pm–1.30am. Closed Mon,
Tues. Tram 1, 2, 5, 6, 7, 10 to
Leidseplein.*
Occupying a large converted dairy
off Leidseplein, the Melkweg
(Milky Way) is a somewhat
fossilized relic of the 1960s, where
you can watch films, listen to live
bands or buy soft drugs from a
quaint shop that resembles an old-
fashioned grocery store. Perhaps
the most evocative corner of the
complex is the tearoom on the top
floor, which has the languid
atmosphere of a party that has gone
on too long. The **Labyrinth**

bookshop (specializing in zany
postcards) and the **Melkweg** café
(decorated like a 1950s milk bar)
are open during the day (*Open
Wed–Sun 10am–6pm. Entrance at
Marnixstraat 405*). However, at
night the complex is only
accessible by means of an iron
drawbridge, which is to be found
behind the Stadsschouwburg.

Paradiso
Weteringschans 6–8
☎ *(020) 264521. Map 6G3. Tram
1, 2, 5, 6, 7, 10 to Leidseplein.*
Still famous from the Sixties, this
19thC church repainted black
serves as Amsterdam's main spot
for pop, rock, blues and reggae
bands.

Vondelpark
*Map 6F3. Tram 1, 2, 5, 6, 7, 10 to
Leidseplein.*
During the summer months,
concerts, poetry readings and plays
take place in the Vondelpark, in
the open-air theater close to the
round blue teahouse. Pleasant on
fine evenings.

Theater and dance

The famous "tomato protest" in 1969, when the cast in a production of Shakespeare's *The Tempest* at the **Stadsschouwburg** was bombarded with tomatoes, signaled the end of conventional theater in Amsterdam. However, if you are interested in experimental, fringe drama and dance, Amsterdam has a flourishing alternative circuit, which features Dutch and foreign companies. A glance at the Uit Buro's files of reviews might give you an idea of what is being offered. Bear in mind that plays can be produced in Dutch, English, French or German.

ART Theater
Kerkstraat 4 ☎ *(020) 259495. Map* **6***F3. Tram 1, 2, 5 to Keizersgracht.*
The main English-speaking theater group in the Netherlands, specializing in contemporary American drama.

De Brakke Grond
Nes 45 ☎ *(020) 240394. Map* **11***D5. Tram 4, 9, 14, 16, 24, 25 to Dam.*
Dutch and Flemish theater and other cultural activities. Restaurant.

Theater Carré
Amstel 115–125
☎ *(020) 225225. Map* **7***F5. Tram 6, 7, 10 or metro to Weesperplein.*
Opened in 1887 as a circus, this imposing Dutch Renaissance building on the Amstel still occasionally features international circus troupes, as well as ballet, modern dance, theater and cabaret.

Frascati
Nes 63 ☎ *(020) 235723. Map* **11***D5. Tram 4, 9, 14, 16, 24, 25 to Spui.*
Alternative theater, dance and music.

De Kleine Komedie
Amstel 56–58 ☎ *(020) 240534. Map* **7***F5. Tram 4, 9, 14 to Rembrandtsplein.*
Established in the 18thC as a French theater, De Kleine Komedie now features a mixed program of Dutch theater, cabaret and opera.

Mickery
Rozengracht 117
☎ *(020) 236777. Map* **10***D2. Tram 13, 14, 17 to Westermarkt.*
After the night of the angry tomatoes at the **Stadsschouwburg** in 1969, the Mickery was set up in a former cinema in the Jordaan to provide Amsterdam with a forum for international experimental art.

Nieuwe de la Mar
Marnixstraat 404
☎ *(020) 233462. Map* **6***F2. Tram 1, 2, 5, 6, 7, 10 to Leidseplein.*
Cabaret, musicals and mainstream Dutch theater.

Shaffy Theater
Keizersgracht 324
☎ *(020) 231311. Map* **10***E3. Tram 13, 14, 17 to Westermarkt.*
A center of experimental drama, film and dance named after the Dutch actor Ramses Shaffy. The theater occupies the splendid 18thC Neoclassical temple of the *Felix Meritis* society. Brahms, Schumann and Grieg were among the 19thC Romantics who performed in this building, where now a stern Minimalist philosophy prevails.

Soeterijn
Linnaeusstraat 2
☎ *(020) 5688500. Map* **9***G9. Tram 9, 10 to Mauritskade.*
A pleasant, small theater attached to the *Tropenmuseum* and featuring unusual and often exotic programs of non-Western dance, music, theater and films.

Stadsschouwburg
Leidseplein 26 ☎ *(020) 242311. Map* **6***F3. Tram 1, 2, 5, 6, 7, 10 to Leidseplein.*
This gloriously ornate neo-Renaissance theater on Leidseplein, which was shaken to the foundations by the famous "tomato protest" of 1969, now offers an indecisive mixture of traditional and contemporary theater and dance.

De Suikerhof
Prinsengracht 381
☎ *(020) 227571. Map* **10***D3. Tram 13, 14, 17 to Westermarkt.*
Minuscule café-theater featuring international cabaret and theater groups. De Suikerhof occasionally includes performances in English.

Shopping

Famous for diamonds, antiques and tulips, Amsterdam also boasts numerous excellent fashion boutiques, jewelers and bookshops, together with specialized shops devoted exclusively to such items as toothbrushes, Indian jewelry, bottled beers, beads and herbs.

The main shopping area runs from Centraal Station to Muntplein, with large department stores along Damrak and Rokin, while smaller chain stores are located along Nieuwendijk and Kalverstraat. Nieuwendijk has a young, rebellious image, while Kalverstraat is slightly more exclusive.

The true genius of Amsterdam, however, shines through in the small, specialized boutiques that tend to be somewhat off the beaten track. One of the best areas to explore is the series of parallel streets running w from Spuistraat to Prinsengracht. These streets lead into the Jordaan, which contains a mixture of fashionable boutiques and run-down shops selling bric-à-brac.

Tax-free shopping

People buying goods in the Netherlands may be entitled to a refund of the 20 percent sales tax (b.t.w. in Dutch) they have paid, provided that the goods cost more than Fl.890 and the buyer can show that the item was exported unused from the Netherlands almost immediately. Non-EEC residents should obtain a *certificaat van uitvoer OB90* (export certificate) from the shop, which they should hand to the customs officer. This will be returned to the shop, which will then refund the tax to the customer.

Residents of other EEC countries taking goods out of the Netherlands merely require proof of importing the goods into the country of destination. This should be sent to the shop to obtain refund of tax. Some shops, such as those at Schiphol Airport, will deduct tax on the spot.

Antiques

Rokin is the main center for antique dealers, but there is also a cluster of less forbidding shops on Nieuwe Spiegelstraat, which begins opposite the Rijksmuseum and looks like an extension of the Department of Sculpture and Applied Arts. It is worth shopping around before making a major purchase, and obtaining a signed certificate of authenticity from the dealer.

Amsterdam Antiques Gallery
Nieuwe Spiegelstraat 34
☎(020) 253371. Map 7F4. AE
CB VISA
Twelve antique dealers gathered under one roof, offering icons, dolls, 19thC paintings and pieces of 16thC Spanish armour.

Jan Best
Keizersgracht 357
☎(020) 232736. Map 10E3.
Art Nouveau and Art Deco lamps.

Couzijn Simons
Prinsengracht 578 ☎(020)
232654. Map 7G4 AE ◑ CB
Antique dolls and toys in a beautiful 18thC interior.

Degenaar en Bijleveld
Nieuwe Spiegelstraat 45–60
☎(020) 277774. Map 7F4 AE ◑
VISA
Antique clocks and scientific instruments.

Italiaander Galleries
Prinsengracht 526
☎(020) 250942. Map 6F3 AE ◑
CB VISA
Primitive and traditional Asiatic art, including Indonesian puppets.

E. Kramer
Nieuwe Spiegelstraat 64
☎(020) 230832. Map 7F4 ◑
CB VISA
Dutch tiles and old clocks.

Leidelmeijer
Nieuwe Spiegelstraat 58
☎ *(020) 254627. Map **7F4*** AE ⊕
⊙ VISA

Leidelmeijer, yet another antique
shop to be found among the many
others on Nieuwe Spiegelstraat,
specializes in Art Nouveau and Art
Deco objects. These include the
distinctive Amsterdam School
lamps that are a feature of so many
of Amsterdam's brown cafés.

Van Os & Yu
Nieuwe Spiegelstraat 68
☎ *(020) 220740. Map **7F4*** AE ⊕
⊙ VISA

Mechanical music boxes.

C. P. J. van der Peet
Nieuwe Spiegelstraat 33–35
☎ *(020) 235763. Map **7F4*** AE ⊙
VISA

Japanese woodcuts and specialized
books on Japan and China.

Auctions
Watch out for *kijkdagen* (viewing days) advertised at the
various auction houses. Both **Christie's** (*Cornelis Schuytstraat
57* ☎ *(020) 642011*) and **Sotheby's** (*Rokin 102*
☎ *(020) 275656, map 11E5*) have branches in Amsterdam.
Van Gendt (*Keizersgracht 96–98* ☎ *(020) 234107, map 11C4*)
specializes in books, prints and maps.

Books and newspapers
Amsterdammers are highly cosmopolitan in their reading
interests, and have no hesitation about picking up books in
English, French or German. Their tastes are also highly
eclectic, so that you can find almost any book, new or secondhand, in Amsterdam. Book-hunting is made particularly
pleasurable by the wealth of attractive bookshops, mainly on
the canal ring formed by Singel and Kloveniersburgwal.

Allert de Lange
Damrak 62 ☎ *(020) 246744.*
*Map **11C5**.*
A serious literary bookshop with a
wide range of Dutch, English,
French and German novels,
together with excellent travel and
art sections.

American Discount Book Center
Kalverstraat 185
☎ *(020) 255537. Map **11E4**.*
Discount imported US novels,
magazines and unusual subjects
such as Japanese classics, gay
fiction, body-building and sci-fi.

Architectura & Natura
Leliegracht 44 ☎ *(020) 236186.*
*Map **10C3**.*
Every day that goes by, the piles of
unsorted books seem to increase in
this bookshop devoted to the
owner's two consuming passions,
architecture and the natural world.
A must for all lovers of Frank
Lloyd Wright or England's
threatened hedgerows.

Athenaeum Boekhandel & Nieuwscentrum
Spui 14–16 ☎ *(020) 226248.*
*Map **11E4**.*
Beautiful 1904 Art Nouveau shop
with a labyrinthine interior

designed in the 1960s.
Amsterdammers flock here on Sat
to buy literature, be it in Dutch,
English, French, Spanish or Latin.
There is also a small section
devoted to Dutch literature in
translation. The adjoining
newspaper shop (☎ *(020) 242972*)
is stocked with newspapers and
magazines flown in from every
corner of the world.

Au Bout du Monde
Singel 313 ☎ *(020) 251397. Map*
11E4.
Occult books and music.

The Book Exchange
Kloveniersburgwal 58
☎ *(020) 266266. Map **11E5**.*
Well-organized secondhand
bookshop devoted to English
paperbacks and hardbacks.

Ciné Qua Non
Staalstraat 14 ☎ *(020) 255588.*
*Map **11E5**.*
Cinema posters and new and
secondhand books for film buffs.

De Slegte
Kalverstraat 48–52
☎ *(020) 225933. Map **11E4**.*
Remaindered books on the ground
floor, and a vast treasure trove of
rare antiquarian books upstairs.

Shopping

Erasmus
Spui 2 ☎ *(020) 230535. Map* **11E4**.
Art, architecture and antiquarian
books.

International Theater
Bookshop
Leidseplein 26 ☎ *(020) 226489.*
Map **6F3**.
Books and periodicals in seven
languages on theater, ballet, opera,
cabaret, circus and magic.

Intertaal
Van Baerlestraat 76
☎ *(020) 715353. Map* **6H2**.
The Dutch hunger for foreign
languages is evident in this
beautiful bookshop stocking
textbooks, dictionaries, cassettes,
videos and computer programs in
about 120 languages, with titles
ranging from *English for Bank
Cashiers* to *Basic Tagalog for
Foreigners and Non-Tagalogs*.

Kinderboekwinkel
I *Bloemdwarsstraat 23*
☎ *(020) 224761; Nieuwe Zijds
Voorburgwal 344* ☎ *(020)*
227741. Maps **10D3** *and* **11E4**.
Children's bookshop where young
readers are welcome to browse.

De Kloof
Kloveniersburgwal 44
☎ *(020) 223828. Map* **11E5**.
Chaotic secondhand bookshop full
of extraordinary books.

Kok
Oude Hoogstraat 14–18
☎ *(020) 231191. Map* **11D5**.
Large antiquarian and
secondhand bookshop.

De Kookboekhandel
Runstraat 26 ☎ *(020) 224768.*
Map **10E3**.
His devotion to the joys of eating
and drinking has earned
Kookboekhandel owner Johannes
van Dam the nickname "the
pudding professor," and chefs and
gourmets flock from all over the
world to his well-stocked
international cookbook shop.

Robert Premsela
Van Baerlestraat 78
☎ *(020) 624266. Map* **6H2**.
Avant-garde art bookshop
opposite the Stedelijk, specializing
in art, architecture, graphic design,
photography, ballet and fashion.

Scheltema, Holkema,
Vermeulen
Koningsplein 16–18
☎ *(020) 267212. Map* **7F4**.
Amsterdam's main university
bookshop, with a wide range of
novels, art books and textbooks in
Dutch, English, French and
German.

Straat Antiquaren
Rosmarijnsteeg 8
☎ *(020) 227904. Map* **10E4**.
A good selection of secondhand
English, French and German
novels, film magazines and French
fashion magazines dating back to
1803.

Xantippe
Prinsengracht 290
☎ *(020) 235854. Map* **10E3**.
An international women's
bookshop, named after Socrates'
wife.

Children's clothing
Fashions for children feature colorful, fun clothes that are
quite expensive: **Hobbit** (*Van Baerlestraat 42*
☎ *(020) 710502, map* **6H2** AE VISA) sells bright clothing for
teenagers; **Pauw** (*Van Baerlestraat 48* ☎ *(020) 731665, map*
6H2 AE ⊙ ⊙ VISA) stocks expensive clothes for trendy toddlers.

Delftware, glass and china
High-quality, hand-painted Delftware porcelain is still
produced by **De Porceleyne Fles** in Delft.

Focke & Meltzer
*P. C. Hooftstraat 65–67;
Kalverstraat 176*
☎ *(020) 642311 (for all
branches). Maps* **6H2**, **11E4** *and*
7H4 AE ⊙ ⊙ VISA
Good for classic Delftware, merry
Dutch tiles and serious
Scandinavian and German
glassware.

De Porceleyne Fles
Muntplein 12 ☎ *(020) 232771.*
Map **11F4**.
Situated in a dusky neo-
Renaissance building next to the
Munttoren, this shop stocks a
good selection of high quality
Delftware, Makkum porcelein,
tiles and dolls in traditional Dutch
costumes.

Rosenthal Studio-Haus
Heiligeweg 49–51
☎*(020) 245865. Map* **11E4**
AE ⊙ ⬛ VISA
The committee of German experts
that selects the items sold in
Rosenthal shops is clearly biased in
favor of clean-cut modern
Scandinavian design, judging by
the items that are on display,
although they also like the zany
New York ceramics of Dorothy
Hafner and the Danish fairy-tale
plates of Bjørn Wiinblad.

Crafts

Clog-making may be Holland's most curious craft, but you can
also find small potteries producing tasteful modern designs in
the Jordaan.

Jeroen Bechtold
Korte Leidsedwarsstraat 159
☎*(020) 249871. Map* **6G3**
AE ⊙ ⬛ VISA
Limited-edition of modern
ceramics.

Kleikollektief
Hartenstraat 19 ☎*(020) 225127.*
Map **10D2 – 11D3** AE
A small potters' collective
producing zany black and white
ceramics.

De Klompenboer
Spuistraat 3 ☎*(020) 230632.*
Map **11C5.**
The old craft of hewing clogs from
wood, in a downtown workshop.

De Voetboog
Voetboogsteeg 16
☎*(020) 260169. Map* **11E4**
AE ⊙
Small arts-and-crafts center
exhibiting tasteful ceramics,
postcards, watercolors etc.

Department stores

Amsterdam has only a few large department stores, which are
located mainly along Damrak and Rokin.

De Bijenkorf
Damrak 90a ☎*(020) 218080.*
Map **11D5** AE ⊙ ⬛
Amsterdam's most fashionable
department store, where next
season's colors are reflected in the
litter baskets, corkscrews, sofas
and table napkins, as well as in the
clothes and shoes. Good for
chocolates, international
newspapers and stationery. Its
restaurant, **La Ruche**, is
constantly dreaming up new and
enticing offers, such as the popular
"teatime buffet."

Hema
Nieuwendijk 174;
Reguliersbreestraat 10
☎*(020) 234176; (020) 246506.*
Maps **11C5** *and* **7F5.**
The Hema chain is a subsidiary of
De Bijenkorf (see above) and
stocks inexpensive clothes,
brightly colored kitchen utensils
and a limited range of good-value
wines.

Maison de Bonneterie
Kalverstraat 183 ☎*(020) 262162.*
Map **11E4** AE VISA
With its glittering chandeliers and
spacious interior, Maison de
Bonneterie struggles to retain an
old-fashioned elegance amid the

brash modernity of Kalverstraat.
Its fashions are rather conservative
for Holland, especially in the
men's department, although it has
recently begun introducing more
colorful and relaxed women's
clothes alongside the traditional
tweeds, tartans and cashmeres.
Upstairs, there is a small golf shop.

Metz & Co.
Keizersgracht 455
☎*(020) 248810. Map* **6F3**
AE ⊙ ⬛ VISA
Metz & Co., founded in 1740 by a
French draper from Metz,
occupies a striking corner building
laden with caryatides looking
down balefully on the flux of
Leidsestraat. In the early 20thC,
Metz encouraged furniture and
fabric designers such as Bart van
der Leck and Sonia Delaunay, and
in 1933 the architect Gerrit
Rietveld was commissioned to
design the rooftop exhibition
cupola (*koepel*), which he offered
as an example of "the space which
we need to preserve in our
structures." This De Stijl
addition offers a splendid
view of Amsterdam, as does the
striking post-modern café
on the sixth floor, designed by
Cees Dam. The other floors of

119

Metz – which is now owned by Liberty of London – are devoted to modern furniture, fabrics, kitchen utensils and gifts.

Vroom & Dreesmann
Kalverstraat 201
☎ *(020) 220171. Map 11E5* [VISA]
A branch of Holland's main department store chain.

Diamonds

The diamond trade was introduced to Amsterdam by refugee Jews in the 16thC, and in 1908 the world's largest diamond, the "Cullinan," was cut in Amsterdam by the Asscher Company. Today Amsterdam is one of the world's most important diamond centers. Demonstrations of diamond polishing can be seen in most factories and diamond shops, and visitors are under no obligation to buy. Outlets include the **Amsterdam Diamond Center** (*Rokin 1–5* ☎ *(020) 245787, map 11D5* [AE] [◆] [◯] [VISA]) *and Kalverstraat 56* ☎ *(020) 233979, map 11E4*), **Bonebakker** (*Rokin 86–90* ☎ *(020) 232294, map 11E4* [AE] [◆] [◯] [VISA]) and **Willem van Pampus** (*Kalverstraat 117* ☎ *(020) 236898, map 11E4* [AE] [◆] [◯] [VISA]). **Coster** (*Paulus Potterstraat 2–4* ☎ *(020) 762222, map 6H3* [AE] [◆] [◯] [VISA]) is where, in 1852, the Kohinoor (Mountain of Light) diamond was cut for the British Crown Jewels. Conveniently close to the *Rijksmuseum*, Coster allows visitors to view diamond polishers at work.

Fabrics

Bold, brightly colored traditional materials imported from Latin America, Africa and Asia are to be found in Amsterdam. **Capsicum** (*Oude Hoogstraat 1* ☎ *(020) 231016, map 11D5* [AE] [◯] [VISA]) is stocked with exotic fabrics from India, China, Japan, Africa, Thailand and Portugal, mostly handmade from natural fibers. The gentle Indian background music recalls the 1970s, as does Harold the Kangaroo's decorated column at the entrance.

Fashions

Amsterdam favors casual, loosely fitting clothes in bright colors. Sizes tend to be on the large side, however, apart from Italian and French lines. Successful Dutch designers often make their home on P. C. Hooftstraat, while younger designers may have a boutique in the Jordaan or in the increasingly fashionable area of Nieuwe Hoogstraat and Sint Antoniesbreestraat. See *Children's clothing, Men's fashions, Men's and women's clothing* and *Women's clothing*.

Food and drink

Holland produces interesting spirits, sturdy cheeses that travel well and delicious chocolates – so the figure conscious should beware. Good-quality tea, coffee, cigars, bottled beers and French wines are imported. There are some interesting specialty delicatessens in Amsterdam.

Berkhoff
Leidsestraat 46 ☎ *(020) 240233. Map 6F3.*
Homemade candies and cookies; elegant *salon de thé.*

Brink's Wijnhandel
Staalstraat 6
☎ *(020) 233957. Map 11E5.*
Good choice of Dutch and foreign beers; some wines and spirits.

Henri Bloem's
Gravenstraat 8 ☎ *(020) 230886. Map 11D5.*
A friendly and informed wine merchant.

Crabtree & Evelyn
Singel 439 ☎ *(020) 224774. Map 11E4* [AE] [◯] [VISA]
A restored 19thC pharmacist's shop provides a fitting backdrop to

Shopping

Crabtree & Evelyn's nostalgic range of British natural products, such as herbal soaps, jams and old-fashioned hard-boiled sweets.

Eichholz
Leidsestraat 48 ☎ *(020) 220305. Map 6F3.*
An eclectic range of gourmet foods, including unexpected delights such as *Hungry Jack Pancake Mix* from the USA.

Geels & Co.
Warmoesstraat 67
☎ *(020) 240683. Map 11C5.*
A friendly coffee and tea shop on the edge of the red-light district.

P. G. C. Hajenius
Rokin 92–6 ☎ *(020) 237494.*
Map 11E4. AE ◉ ◎ VISA
This famous tobacconist has the air of an English gentlemen's club, with its dark mahogany cabinets and gleaming marble walls. Although you can buy a simple pack of cigarettes here, the assistants are happiest when explaining the merits of pipes or the temperament of different cigars, including Hajenius' famous *Grande Finale*.

Hart's Wijnhandel
Vijzelgracht 27 ☎ *(020) 238350. Map 7G4.*
A ravishing Art Nouveau interior stocking a carefully chosen selection of French wines at all prices, some tempting beers and a good collection of Dutch liqueurs.

Holtkamp
Vijzelgracht 15 ☎ *(020) 248757. Map 7G4.*
Fine candies.

Jacob Hooy & Co.
Kloveniersburgwal 12
☎ *(020) 243041. Map 12D6.*
The heady aroma of spices and herbs wafts across Nieuwmarkt from Jacob Hooy, which has been curing Amsterdammers' aches and pains since 1743. This doggedly old-fashioned shop stocks some 500–600 spices and herbs in a magnificent array of 19thC wooden drawers and earthenware jars labeled in Latin. Jacob Hooy also sells 38 types of *drop* – a peculiar Dutch licorice delicacy.

Robert Kef
Marnixstraat 192
☎ *(020) 262210. Map 10D2.*
Store with a good selection of imported French cheeses.

Keijzer
Prinsengracht 180
☎ *(020) 240683. Map 10D3.*
Tea and coffee shop furnished in Old Dutch Granny style.

Banketbakkerij Lanskroon
Singel 385 ☎ *(020) 237743. Map 11E4.*
This superb German *Konditorei* (coffeehouse) is popular with local office workers, who steal out in the afternoon to tuck into giant slices of strawberry or bilberry tart. Lanskroon also bakes delicious early-morning croissants.

Leonidas
Damstraat 11 ☎ *(020) 253497. Map 11D5.*
Delicious Belgian candies.

Meidi-Ya
Beethovenstraat 18
☎ *(020) 737410.*
Specialty food shop importing *sake*, Kirin beer, exotic seaweeds and other essentials of Japanese cuisine.

De Notenbar
Singel 437 ☎ *(020) 241801. Map 11E4.*
It's difficult to resist the smell of freshly roasted cashew nuts wafting from this shop, which sells a range of nuts and dried fruit.

d'Oude Gekroonde
Huidenstraat 21
☎ *(020) 237711. Map 10E3.*
Specialized beer shop with some 500 types of bottled beer and a wide range of matching glasses.

Pâtisserie Pompadour
Huidenstraat 12
☎ *(020) 239554. Map 10E3.*
A portrait of Madame de Pompadour looks down with smiling approval on Arnold Reijers' 45 varieties of handmade candies, which can be sampled individually in the exquisite Louis XVI-style tea room.

Spiga d'Oro
Spuistraat 60 ☎ *(020) 273983. Map 11C4.*
Fresh Romagna pasta in bright colors, and other Italian delicacies.

Wout Arxhoek
Damstraat 23 ☎ *(020) 229118. Map 11D5.*
Small shop with good selection of Dutch cheeses for export, including the unusual *Friese nagelkaas* (Frisian clove cheese).

121

Household articles

Amsterdammers have a taste for bizarre clocks, lamps and espresso machines.

Studio Bazar
Reguliersdwarsstraat 60
☎ *(020) 220830. Map 6F4*
AE ◐ ◉ VISA

A wide selection of kitchen utensils, ranging from dazzling chrome espresso machines from Italy to frivolous pickle picks from England and cress scissors from Denmark.

Clockwitz
Herengracht 305
☎ *(020) 242706. Map 11E4*
◉ VISA

Eccentric clocks designed by

Yvonne Holzhaus and Frank Clewitz.

Het Magazijn
Keizersgracht 709
☎ *(020) 222858. Map 7F4*
AE ◐ ◉ VISA

Hi-tech kitchen accessories for yuppies.

De Witte Tandenwinkel
Runstraat 5 ☎ *(020) 233443.*
Map 10E3.

An esthetic display of dental accessories ranging from the utilitarian to the bizarre.

Jewelry

Traditional jewelers tend to be found along Kalverstraat, while avant-garde boutiques, specializing in brightly colored and highly imaginative designs, occupy tiny shops in narrow streets such as Grimburgwal.

Hans Appenzeller
Grimburgwal 1–5
☎ *(020) 268218. Map 11E5.*
AE ◐ ◉ VISA

Elegant, expensive modern jewelry by one of Holland's leading designers.

Baobab
Elandsgracht 128
☎ *(020) 268398. Map 10E2.*
Thea de Vegte has turned a nondescript shop in the Jordaan into an Aladdin's Cave packed with Oriental treasures. Her main interest is jewelry, but she has also brought back from her Far Eastern travels, furniture, carpets and utensils, which are arranged in such a way that you feel you are entering a Nepalese temple or a Javanese home.

Jorge Cohen
Singel 369 ☎ *(020) 238646.*
Map 11E4.
Exquisite jewelry made on the premises by Jorge Cohen, born in Argentina. Some pieces are inspired by the red and black décor of the Tuschinski cinema, while others incorporate fragments of old jewelry found in Paris flea markets.

André Coppenhagen
Bloemgracht 38
☎ *(020) 243681. Map 10C3.*
Huge selection of beads in different colors and sizes for home-made jewelry.

Grimm
Grimburgwal 9 ☎ *(020) 220501.*
Map 11E5 AE VISA
This small boutique specializes in low-cost avant-garde jewelry by young Dutch designers: light, colorful and delicately constructed objects showing traces of De Stijl and the 1950s.

Novanta Nove
Utrechtsestraat 99
☎ *(020) 270797. Map 7F5.*
This chic gallery retains an old-fashioned frieze of tile tableaux depicting wholesome country activities, a contrast to the boldly innovative, often bizarre, jewelry, pottery and art on sale.

Schaap en Citroen
Kalverstraat 1 ☎ *(020) 266691;*
Rokin 12 ☎ *(020) 255666. Maps*
11D4 and 11D5 AE ◐ ◉ VISA
Exclusive silver jewelry. The shop on Kalverstraat is a curious Expressionist work by Amsterdam School architect Th. Wijdeveld, while the Rokin branch shows a distinct De Stijl influence.

The Turquoise Tomahawk
Berenstraat 16 ☎ *(020) 257106.*
Map 6E3 AE ◐ ◉ VISA
Turquoise *Amsterdammertjes* (the local word for traffic posts) announce this unusual shop specializing in imported New Mexican and South American Indian jewelry and all kinds of other crafts.

Maps

The voyages of discovery of the 17thC seem to have given the Dutch a taste for travel, and specialized maps and guides can usually be found in Amsterdam.

A la Carte
*Spui 23 ☎ (020) 250679.
Map 11E4*
An international selection of travel books and guides, as well as a range of maps covering everything from New York's East Village to the planet Mars.

L. J. Harri
*Schreierstoren, Prins Hendrikkade 94–5 ☎ (020) 248035.
Map 12C6.*
Sailing books, sea charts and nautical instruments in a 16thC tower covered with bronze plaques commemorating historic sea voyages.

Pied à Terre
*Singel 393 ☎ (020) 274455.
Map 11E4*
Crammed with detailed maps and guidebooks. Excellent if you are planning a cycling trip or walking vacation.

Jacob van Wijngaarden
*Overtoom 136 ☎ (020) 121901.
Map 6G1.*
Amsterdammers seized with wanderlust instinctively make a beeline for this store, whose specialized map collection covering virtually the whole world is crammed into one of Amsterdam's smallest shops.

Markets

Amsterdam's specialized markets are particularly fascinating, but it is also interesting to visit one of the many food markets, if only to witness the size of Dutch vegetables.

Antiekmarkt De Looier
Elandsgracht 109 ☎ (020) 249038. Map 10E2.
A sprawling indoor market on the edge of the Jordaan, where you can find everything from rusty scythes to street organs. Its claim to be an antique market should not be taken too literally. Closed Fri.

Bloemenmarkt
Singel (between Koningsplein and Muntplein). Map 7I4.
Amsterdam's spectacular floating flower market.

Albert Cuypstraat
Albert Cuypstraat. Map 7I4.
Exotic, cosmopolitan open-air food market.

Boekenmarkt
Oudemanhuispoort. Map 11E5.
An unusual passage containing 18 tiny shops dating from the 18thC, mostly occupied by antiquarian booksellers.

Plantenmarkt
Amstelveld. Map 7G5.
Colorful plant and seed market held early on Mon mornings (May–Oct), while the rest of Amsterdam is still fast asleep.

Postzegelmarkt
Nieuwe Zijds Voorburgwal (opposite Amsterdams Historisch Museum). Map 11E4.
Makeshift stamp and coin market held on Wed and Sat, close to numerous philately shops.

Noordermarkt
Noordermarkt. Map 10B3.
Crowded flea market held on Mon mornings, which spills over into Westerstraat. On Sat, a bird market.

Waterlooplein
Waterlooplein. Map 12E6.
"Lying there were headless nails, toothless saws, bladeless chisels, locks without springs, keys without locks, hooks without eyes and eyes without hooks, buckles without prongs." This description of Amsterdam's flea market, penned by the writer Multatuli in the 19thC, still rings true today, although the atrocities of World War II robbed it of its distinctive Jewish identity. Amsterdammers will tell you that its heyday is long past, but Waterlooplein is still a good place to hunt for second-hand clothes, old books, prints and other curiosities.

Men's fashions

Suits are rare; Dutch men tend to wear casual, comfortable clothes.

Shopping

Barbas
P. C. Hooftstraat 140
☎ *(020) 713537. Map 6H2.*
AE ⊕ ⊙ VISA
Baggy trousers; chunky knitwear.

Hij
Kalverstraat 87 ☎ *(020) 263452.*
Map 11E4 AE
Chain store stocking casual styles.

Martijn van Kesteren
Reestraat 25 ☎ *(020) 256371.*
Map 10D3.
A small shop that stocks a good
selection of colorful shirts, ties and
trousers, together with some arty
Italian woolens.

Matinique
Kalverstraat 88–90
☎ *(020) 237283. Map 11E4*
AE ⊕ ⊙ VISA
Predominantly Italian and French

fashions that are particularly
appealing to young men.

Nero
Kalverstraat 134
☎ *(020) 230003. Map 11E4*
AE ⊕ ⊙ VISA
Attractive Italian fashions in
adventurous colors.

New Man Mode
P. C. Hooftstraat 116
☎ *(020) 799319. Map 6H2.*
Casual styles for men are a feature
of this store.

Pauw
Van Baerlestraat 88
☎ *(020) 646653. Map 6H2*
AE ⊕ ⊙ VISA
Situated on Van Baerlestraat near
the museum quarter, Pauw sells
chic fashions for young men; also
blazers and bankers' overcoats.

Men's and women's clothing

Several shops specialize in fashions for both sexes, such as
Hartman en Hartman (*Prinsengracht 176* ☎ *(020) 248718,
map 10D3* AE ⊕ ⊙ VISA *and P. C. Hooftstraat 38*
☎ *(020) 710688, map 6G2* AE ⊕ ⊙ VISA), which sells casual,
attractive men's and women's fashions and accessories.
Nieuwe England (*Koningsplein 6* ☎ *(020) 245721, map 11E4*
AE ⊕ ⊙ VISA) stocks classic fashions for men and women of all
ages. **Sissy Boy** (*Kalverstraat 210* ☎ *(020) 260088, map 11E4*
AE ⊙ VISA) sells loose-fitting clothes, suitable for both sexes.

Clothing sizes
When shops give clothing sizes in inches or centimétres, use
the following conversion scale to determine the correct size

12 in	16	20	24	28	32	36	40	44	48
30 cm	40	50	60	70	80	90	100	110	120

When standardized codes are used, although these may be found
to vary considerably, the following provides a useful guide.

Women's clothing sizes

UK/US sizes	8/6	10/8	12/10	14/12	16/14	18/16
Dutch sizes	34	36	38	40	42	44
Bust in/cm	31/80	32/81	34/86	36/91	38/97	40/102
Hips in/cm	33/85	34/86	36/91	38/97	40/102	42/107

Men's clothing sizes

European code (suits)	44	46	48	50	52	54	56
Chest in/cm	34/86	36/91	38/97	40/102	42/107	44/112	46/117
Collar in/cm	13½/34	14/36	14½/37	15/38	15½/39	16/41	16½/42
Waist in/cm	28/71	30/76	32/81	34/86	36/91	38/97	40/102
Inside leg in/cm	28/71	29/74	30/76	31/79	32/81	33/84	34/86

Men's and women's shoe sizes

UK/US sizes	3/4¼	4/5½	5/6½	6/7½	7/8½	8/9½	9/10½	10/11½	11/12½
European	36	37	38	39	40	41	42	43	44

Postcards

Specialized postcard shops stock a wide range of imaginative, witty and bizarre cards as an alternative to the ubiquitous tulips and windmills.

Art Unlimited
Keizersgracht 510
☎*(020) 248419. Map 6F3.*
Art Unlimited publishes postcards to suit every whim, including art reproductions, cats, Amsterdam bicycles, Dutch costumes, teddy bears, misty polder landscapes, eccentric Italian furniture, tulips, ballet dancers' toes and many other themes. The big sellers, such as the famous *Maja* nude, are also available in poster format.

Cards for Days
Huidenstraat 26
☎*(020) 248775. Map 10E3.*
Greetings cards for every eventuality are sold in this store,

which imports cards from New York, California, London and Paris.

Labyrinth
Marnixstraat 405
☎*(020) 268797. Map 6F2.*
Attached to the **Melkweg** (see *Nightlife and the arts*) Labyrinth's specialties are esoteric books and weird postcards. The entrance to the store is on Marnixstraat.

Putman
Rusland 29 ☎*(020) 239845. Map 7E5.*
This eccentric antiquarian bookshop sells an eclectic collection of old postcards.

Records

Amsterdam's specialized record shops cover classical, jazz and pop music, as well as more esoteric styles. **Boudisque** (*Haringpakkerssteeg 10–18* ☎*(020) 232603)*, has a good selection of new and secondhand pop, rock and reggae records. **Concerto** (*Utrechtsestraat 60* ☎*(020) 235228, map 7F5*) stocks a large collection of classical and pop records including reduced-price new records and secondhand rarities in good condition. An enthusiastic and well-stocked jazz record shop complete with Art Deco furnishings is **Jazz Inn** (*Vijzelgracht 9* ☎*(020) 235662, map 7G4*).

Shoes and leather goods

Shoe fashions are colorful and creative.

Fred de la Bretonière
Sint Luciensteeg 20
☎*(020) 234152. Map 10E4.*
AE VISA
Exclusive leather shoes, belts and bags traditional and modern.

Candy Corson Leeratelier
Sint Luciensteeg 19
☎*(020) 248061. Map 10E4*
⊙ ⊙⊙ VISA
Attractive leather bags and accessories in a range of colors.

Cinderella
Kalverstraat 177
☎*(020) 233617. Map 11E4.*
Bright, youthful shoe styles.

Dr Adam's
P. C. Hooftstraat 90
☎*(020) 623835. Map 6G2.*
AE ⊙ ⊙⊙ VISA
Tough, attractive shoes made to survive Amsterdam's notorious sidewalks.

Dungelmann
Heiligeweg 2–6
☎*(020) 221866. Map 11E4*
⊙⊙ VISA
Classic men's and women's shoes.

Jan Jansen
Rokin 42 ☎*(020) 251350. Map 11E4.*
Astonishing fashion shoes in a remarkable Post Modern interior.

't Klompenhuisje
Nieuwe Hoogstraat 9
☎*(020) 228100. Map 12E6.*
Sturdy wooden clogs, gaudy souvenir clogs and, for the sensible, some health sandals.

Pisa
Van Baerlestraat 19
☎*(020) 710741; Kalverstraat 14*
☎*(020) 245910. Maps 6H2 and 11D4.* AE ⊙ ⊙⊙ VISA
Exclusive shoes in just about every color imaginable.

Shopping

Stationery and art supplies
Excellent art supplies shops cater to all forms of art; stationery is flamboyant.

Van Beek
Stadhouderskade 63–5
☎*(020) 621670. Map* **7***H4* AE
Artists' supplies shop opened in 1895, with paintings from former customers, such as the Impressionist George Breitner.

't Japanse Winkeltje
Nieuwe Zijds Voorburgwal 177
☎*(020) 279523. Map* **11***D4.*
Imports the best of Japanese design, including calligraphic materials, origami paper, porcelain tea sets and kimonos.

Van der Linde
Rozengracht 38 ☎*(020) 242791. Map* **10***D3.*
Professional art supplier in the street where Rembrandt spent his last years.

Posthumus
Sint Luciensteeg 25
☎*(020) 255812. Map* **10***E4.*
Elegant writing paper, *ex libris* labels, unusual monogram and pictogram rubber stamps and other printing equipment. Closed Sat.

Women's clothing
Warm, comfortable, multilayered clothes for winter; loosely fitting and lighthearted styles for summer.

Agnès B
Rokin 126 ☎*(020) 271465. Map* **11***D4* AE ⊕ ⊙ VISA
Quietly sophisticated French designs that use colors sparingly.

Marga Albers
Sint Antoniesbreestraat 126
☎*(020) 223214. Map* **12***E6* ⊕ VISA
A small but attractive collection, including designs by Marga Albers.

Jacques d'Ariège
P. C. Hooftstraat 98
☎*(020) 710918. Map* **6***H2.* AE ⊕ VISA
Elegant, seductive clothing.

Azzurro
Van Baerlestraat 17
☎*(020) 716804. Map* **6***H2.* AE ⊕ VISA
Glittery Italian clothes and shoes.

Benetton
Heiligeweg 23 ☎*(020) 269150;
P.C. Hooftstraat 72* ☎*(020) 795706. Maps* **11***E4 and* **6***G2.*
Italian chain store specializing in fashion knitwear in many colors.

Carmina
Prinsengracht 496
☎*(020) 247523. Map* **6***F3.*
Theatrical costumes, drawings and curiosities.

Colombine Instant White
Nieuwe Hoogstraat 6
☎*(020) 231599. Map* **12***E6* AE ⊕ ⊙ VISA
Elegant, Parisian-style fashions by Colombine Sarraïlhé.

Edgar's Boutique
Beethovenstraat 57
☎*(020) 627460.* AE ⊕
Opened by Edgar Vos to offer Dutch designers' work to a wider public; mainly for older women.

Gin and Tonic
2ᵉ Tuindwarsstraat 6
☎*(020) 267830. Map* **10***C3.*
Bright fashions from Britain.

Frank Govers
Keizersgracht 500
☎*(020) 228670. Map* **6***F3.*
Dutch designer clothes.

't Haasje
Elandsstraat 121 ☎*(020) 238507. Map* **10***E2.* AE ⊕ VISA
Bright, tropical colors.

Kenzo
Van Baerlestraat 66
☎*(020) 626253. Map* **6***H2.*
AE ⊕ ⊙ VISA
Creative Parisian designs.

Het Kimonohuis
Singel 317 ☎*(020) 258882. Map* **11***E4* AE ⊙
Exquisite imported kimonos.

Fong Leng
P.C. Hooftstraat 77
☎*(020) 738427. Map* **6***H2.*
Elegant, imaginative prêt-à-porter collection for younger women.

Look-Out Kleding
Sint Luciensteeg 22
☎*(020) 277649; Utrechtsestraat 91* ☎*(020) 255032. Maps* **11***E4 and* **8***G6* AE ⊕ VISA

Attractive pullovers, Slippely T-shirts and the colorful fashions produced by Oilily of Alkmaar.

Pauw
Heiligeweg 10 ☎ *(020) 244780;*
Leidsestraat 16 ☎ *(020) 265698;*
Van Baerlestraat 72
☎ *(020) 717322;*
Beethovenstraat 82
☎ *(020) 713299. Maps 11E4,*
7F4, and 6H2 AE ① ⓒ VISA
Highly successful Amsterdam chain of fashion boutiques stocking elegant but casual clothes in rather large sizes. No two shops are the same, and there are also branches to be found for men and children.

Puck en Hans
Rokin 66 ☎ *(020) 255889.*
Map 11D4.
Sleek, simple, slightly futuristic Dutch designer clothes.

Liesbeth Rooyaards
Prinsenstraat 6 ☎ *(020) 265026.*
Map 11C4 ⓒ
Stylish, original designs.

Sheila
Rokin 50 ☎ *(020) 265364.*
Map 11D4 ① ⓒ VISA
Exclusive evening dresses by Sheila de Vries.

Claudia Sträter
Kalverstraat 179–181
☎ *(020) 220559;*
Beethovenstraat 9
☎ *(020) 736605. Map 11E4* AE
① ⓒ VISA
Elegant clothes in large sizes.

Edgar Vos
P. C. Hooftstraat 134
☎ *(020) 626336. Map 6G2* AE
①
Exclusive clothes at affordable prices for older women.

Toys, games and models
Amsterdam has several well-stocked toy shops that appeal to adults and children alike.

Authentic Shipmodels
Bloemstraat 191
☎ *(020) 246601. Map 10D2*
AE ① ⓒ VISA
Located on a run-down canal where most of the houseboats have sunk, Authentic Shipmodels stocks a wide range of finely detailed wooden ships, including IJsselmeer fishing boats.

Cladder
Utrechtsestraat 47
☎ *(020) 237949. Map 7F5.*
Makeup and carnival masks.

Matrioška
Nieuwe Leliestraat 43
☎ *(020) 221172. Map 10C3.*
Beautiful Russian dolls and other traditional handicrafts in a Chekhovian interior complete with nostalgic family snapshots.

E. Kramer Poppendokter
Reestraat 18–20
☎ *(020) 265274. Map 10D3.*
E. Kramer is an old-fashioned doll doctor, and his shop is crammed with dolls, puppets and soft toys, as well as a range of candles.

Speel-Goed
P. C. Hooftstraat 95
☎ *(020) 629304. Map 6H2.* AE
① ⓒ VISA
Wooden toys, games and dollhouse furniture.

Speelgoed Boon
Heiligeweg 26 ☎ *(020) 221122.*
Map 11E4.
Amsterdam's biggest toyshop, offering everything from dolls to Danish lollipops.

Teken aan de Wand
Huidenstraat 6 ☎ *(020) 256241.*
Map 10E3.
It is impossible not to smile as you squeeze gingerly among the dangling marionettes, swooping birds and exclusive kites in this enchanting toyshop. Teken aan de Wand (literally "the writing on the wall") is a paradise for model builders, bird kite fanciers, Snoopy fans and anyone who enjoys good old-fashioned nuttiness.

Het Treinenhuis
Bilderdijkstraat 94
☎ *(020) 181255. Map 10E2.*
A must for model railway enthusiasts. The store stocks almost 1,000 trains, over 2,000 pieces of rolling stock and a vast selection of accessories including Old Berlin streetlamps, inner-city slums, a flock of sheep and a burning customs post.

Vliegerwinkel
Gasthuismolensteeg 8
☎ *(020) 233450. Map 11D4.*
Kite and boomerang shop offering friendly advice to the novice.

Excursions

Amsterdam is surrounded by fascinating cities rich in history, art and architecture, each with a quite distinctive personality. Among the most interesting are the former Zuider Zee ports of Enkhuizen and Hoorn; the university towns of Utrecht, Leiden and Delft; the huge, modern port of Rotterdam; the stubbornly old-fashioned town of Haarlem; the aloof diplomatic city of Den Haag; and the cheese-making towns of Gouda and Alkmaar.

There are also numerous small, undisturbed villages within a few miles of Amsterdam, such as Broek in Waterland and Edam to the N, and Ouderkerk, Abcoude and Breukelen to the S. Although a few unfortunate ones such as Marken and Volendam have become overwhelmed by tourism, even these still retain a certain charm at quiet times of the year.

Despite such a concentration of cities, towns and villages, which makes this one of the most densely populated conurbations in the world, it is still possible to discover beautiful areas of typical Dutch landscape, such as Waterland to the N of Amsterdam and the area of lakes (*plassen*) to the S, while in spring the bulbfields to the W are a sight not to be missed.

Holland's main bulbfields are found in the area between Leiden and Haarlem, where fields are magically transformed into vivid blocks of color in Apr and May. A train journey from Haarlem to Leiden is the simplest way to view the bulbfields, after which you can take a bus (*NZH 50, 51*) to **Keukenhof ★** (*Stationsweg, Lisse* ☎ (02521) 19034 🖼 ⅍ 🍴 ⇨ *open end Mar/beg April to late May 8am–6.30pm*), a huge, landscaped flower garden packed with different varieties of tulips and daffodils. It is also possible to drive or cycle through the bulbfields; maps in English are available at VVV offices.

The Aalsmeer flower auction, **Verenigde Bloemenveilingen Aalsmeer ★** (*Legmeerdijk 313* ☎ (02977) 34567 🖼 ☀ ⇨ *open Mon–Fri 7.30–11.30am; bus CN 171, 172 from Amsterdam Centraal Station*) offers an intriguing glimpse of the commercial side of the bulb industry. Some 11 million flowers and one million plants are sold daily in this vast complex covering an area equal to 55 soccer fields. Visitors proceed along an elevated catwalk, which offers a panoramic view of the sorting, auction and distribution areas. Although efficiency is the main aim of the operation, the auction also possesses an undeniable romance: porters cycle by with huge bunches of flowers or toss stray red roses to the spectators above.

Amsterdam is also well placed for getting to the sea at **Zandvoort** (*30mins by train from Amsterdam Centraal Station; by car, on the N5*). The town is rather dull, even suburban, and there is little to do except sit on the fine, sandy beach, where even on crowded summer days the atmosphere is friendly and relaxed. The extensive dunes behind the beach are pleasant for walking or cycling.

The following cities and towns within easy reach of Amsterdam are described in the A–Z gazetteer below.

Art cities	Historic harbor towns	Cheese towns
Delft	Enkhuizen	Alkmaar
Den Haag	Hoorn	Broek in Waterland
Haarlem	Marken	Edam
Leiden	Monnickendam	Gouda
Rotterdam	Volendam	
Utrecht	Zaanstad	

Alkmaar

Noord-Holland, 40km (25miles) NW of Amsterdam.
Population: 83,900. Getting there: By train, 30mins from
Amsterdam Centraal Station; by car, on N5, then A9 **i**
Waagplein 3 ☎*(072) 114284.*

A compact market town located amid the prosperous polders N
of Amsterdam, Alkmaar is particularly cheerful on a Fri, when
an animated cheese market *(late Apr to mid-Sept 10am–noon)*
is enacted in the main square, **Waagplein**, beneath the
flamboyant Renaissance Waaggebouw, or weigh house. A
delightful mood of festivity infuses the town for the two hours
of the market, carillons, barrel organs and street musicians
filling the air with music, and the narrow streets around the
market are crammed with stalls selling cheeses and crafts. It is
worth arriving early in order to avoid the crowds, as the market
is a popular tourist attraction.

Sights and places of interest

The most seductive area of Alkmaar is the SE corner, which
from the station is reached by turning right along Stationsweg,
left down Geesterweg and, after crossing a canal, right down
Geest. This leads to a landscaped park, through which you can
walk to reach the **Molen van Piet**, an 18thC windmill built
atop a bastion. Cross Ritsevoort and then turn left down
Baanstraat and right along Parkstraat, a charming, though
quite unnecessary, detour, which eventually brings you back to
the outer canal. Continue along Kennemerpark – a leafy area of
19thC Art Nouveau houses – to reach the narrow canal
Baangracht, the perfect point at which to enter the city. Turn
left, then right along Oude Gracht until you come to the
impressive **Wildemanshofje** (no. 87), an 18thC almshouse.
Retrace your steps to cross the canal, then continue into the
heart of the town along Groot Nieuwland and Kapelstraat.

A wooden bridge then crosses Verdronkenoord, with the
small fish market to the left and the sprightly 17thC
Accijnstoren, where duty was paid on imported beer, to the
right. Continue straight ahead down Hekelstraat to another
bridge, which offers an exceptional view of the Renaissance
facade of the **Waag**, a 14thC Gothic hospice converted to a
weigh house in the 16thC. To reach Waagplein, continue down
the beguiling canal Kooltuin, then turn left along Dijk.

Across the next bridge, at Houttil 1, is the **Nationaal
Biermuseum "De Boom"** (☎*(072) 113801* 🖾 *open Mon–
Sat 10am–4pm, Sun 1–5pm),* attractively located in a former
18thC brewery. The exhibits are rather impenetrable to the
non-Dutch speaker, but you might enjoy the attractive
proeflokaal (tasting house) *(open Mon–Sat 10am–8pm, Sun 1–
8pm)* with its canalside terrace, which offers a choice of more
than 80 Dutch beers, including unusual Trappist brews
produced by the Schaapskooi brewery in Tilburg, and
Boombier, a traditional beer brewed specially for the museum
by a local brewery. A further attraction for epicures is the
Kaasmuseum *(Waagplein* 🖾 *open Apr–Oct Mon–Sat 10am–
4pm),* which demonstrates the art of cheese-making.

The **Stedelijk Museum** (*Doelenstraat 5* ☎*(072) 110737*🖾
open Tues–Fri 10am–noon, 2–5pm, Sun 2–5pm), reached
from Waagplein along the exceptionally narrow
Magdalenenstraat, contains some interesting paintings,
including an Altdorfer-like panorama of the siege of Alkmaar
in 1573, when the town successfully resisted a vastly superior

Spanish army, thereby turning the tide in the Dutch Revolt. The museum also contains collections of tiles, toys and facade stones.

$\rightleftharpoons$ If you are in the vicinity of the cheese market and want to eat something more than a *broodje kaas*, try the Indonesian restaurant **Deli** (*Mient 8* ☎ *(072) 154082* □ *last orders 10pm, closed Sun*).

Shopping

Clothing shops and department stores are tightly packed in the narrow streets s of the Waagplein, while the quieter streets to the N are favored by antique dealers and craft shops. Alkmaar is the home of the delightful, but expensive, Oilily children's clothes (*Houttil 3, off Waagplein*).

Broek in Waterland

Map **3**B4. *Noord-Holland, 12km (7 miles) N of Amsterdam. Population 2,670. Getting there: By NZH bus 110, 111, 114 or 115 from Amsterdam Centraal Station to Dorp; by car, through the IJ-tunnel, then N on E10.*

"Broek . . . is a little village so remarkable for the neatness of its appearance, as probably to be unique in the world," the writer Charles Tennant observed in 1824.

This very pretty village just N of Amsterdam has been a constant source of amusement to travelers because of its obsessive attention to cleanliness, which was essential for the local manufacture of cheese. Although you are unlikely nowadays to come across inhabitants scrubbing clean the trees – as one visitor observed – the town still has a decidedly prim and cared-for look, with its handsome 18thC wooden gable houses and its tidy streets where even the trees are carefully trained on wooden frames so as not to disturb the magisterial symmetry.

The most picturesque area is **Havenrak**, once a bustling harbor. The 16thC church lies to the w of here, and you can savor something of Broek's attentive domesticity by venturing farther w along streets such as Roomeinde and Leeteinde.

$\rightleftharpoons$ **De Witte Swaen** ✿ (*Dorpstraat 11–13* ☎ *(02903) 1525* □ *open 10am–9pm; closed Mon*), named after the white swan on Broek's coat of arms, is a favorite stop for cyclists, its typical N Holland interior decorated with attractive local watercolors. The delicious, sustaining pancakes are worth a detour, and of the 40 sweet and savory varieties on the menu, the *pannekoek Broekse heerlijkheid*, piled with apple, Calvados and cream, is particularly memorable. You can also sample the local specialty, *gerookte IJsselmeer paling* (smoked eel), but best avoid the Hertog Jan beer if you seriously intend to pedal back to Amsterdam.

Delft

Map **2**E2. *Zuid-Holland, 58km (36 miles) sw of Amsterdam. Population: 86,700. Getting there: By train, 55mins from Amsterdam Centraal Station; by tram, from Scheveningen and Den Haag CS; by car, on A4* **i** *Markt 85* ☎ *(015) 126100.*

"Delft is the most charming town in the world," sighed Hilaire Belloc in 1906, likening it to "a good woman in early middle age, careful of her dress, combed, orderly, not without a sober beauty." Today Delft inevitably conjures up images of mass-produced Delftware – of blue and white porcelain clogs and windmills – but it would be a pity to dismiss the town as just a tourist trap, for beyond the kitsch souvenirs, Delft has a rich history and a wealth of architectural interest.

In the early 16thC Delft was a major center of Catholic

humanism and the arts, counting among its painters the Master of Delft and the Master of the *Virgo inter Virgines*. The Reformation brought an end to Delft's monastic days, particularly after William of Orange took up residence in the Prinsenhof, turning Delft for a time into the capital city of the rebel Dutch provinces.

In the 17thC, however, Delft flourished again as a center of art and learning, producing painters such as Johannes Vermeer and Pieter de Hoogh, the pioneering microbiologist Anthonie van Leeuwenhoek and the legal philosopher Hugo Grotius.

Vermeer's exquisite paintings such as *The View of Delft* and *The Little Street in Delft* have done much to promote an idealized image of the town, and the reality may be somewhat disappointing, especially as most of the houses were shorn of their distinctive step gables in the 18thC. Giant industrial works on the N edge of Delft and a large modern university campus to the S threaten to destroy the town; yet you can still discover numerous quiet canals where the tranquil, almost monastic, mood of Vermeer's art survives.

Sights and places of interest
The town

Delft has not changed too much since Samuel Pepys described it in 1660 as "a most sweet town with bridges and a river in every street." The best way to see the town is to follow the canals (which Pepys took for rivers); those on the W side of town are urbane and prosperous, while those to the E have a more tranquil and forlorn air.

Begin at the railway station and walk through the narrow Barbarasteeg to reach **Oude Delft**, an old canal lined with handsome 17th–19thC houses. Turn left, past the former convent of St Barbara (no. 59), to reach, eventually, the **Gemeenlandshuis van Delfland** (no. 167), an exceptionally ornate late Gothic building dating from 1510 and attributed to Anthonis Keldermans. Just N of here is the **Prinsenhof**, whose gardens and bricked courtyards retain a medieval flavor. The **Volkenkundig Museum "Nusantara"** (*St Agathaplein 4* ☎ *(015) 120584* ◼ *open Tues–Sat 10am–5pm, Sun, hols 1–5pm*) contains a small, interesting collection of Indonesian artefacts. Opposite the Prinsenhof is the **Oude Kerk** (◼ ✠ *open Apr–Sept, Mon–Sat noon–4pm*), looking somewhat sullen with its 14thC leaning tower and unfinished late Gothic N transept, the work of Anthonis Keldermans and his son. Inside, the tomb of the naval hero Piet Heyn, designed in a solemn Classical style by Pieter de Keyser, is given pride of place in the main choir, while Admiral Maarten Tromp, who died fighting the English in 1653, is commemorated by a lavish Baroque monument designed by Jacob van Campen and Rombout Verhulst. The Oude Kerk also contains a tomb to the scientist Anthonie van Leeuwenhoek, and the simple grave of the painter Johannes Vermeer.

From the Oude Kerk, continue down Oude Delft to reach a weatherbeaten Gothic portal showing, apparently, St John the Evangelist on the island of Patmos. This leads to the former **Bagijnhof**, now somewhat disappointing except for the narrow alley to the right of no. 118, where the atmosphere of Vermeer's Delft has survived.

Return to Oude Delft and head N, past the attractive **Louis XIV house** (no. 118), to reach the small canal Kolk. If you are interested in enigmas, continue down Noordeinde to

Wateringse Vest and cross the road to the small park to discover, nestling in a dark glade, a tomb purported to be that of Louis XVII of France, who apparently lived in Delft under the alias Karl Wilhelm Naundorff until his death in 1845. Retrace your steps down Noordeinde and turn left along Kolk to Geerweg, where the modern buildings on one side contrast with the crumbling 17thC houses opposite. Don't miss the view down Verwersdijk to the spire of the Nieuwe Kerk.

Cross the footbridge opposite Kantoorgracht 70 to reach the **Pauwhofje** (*Paardenmarkt 54*), a pleasant almshouse established in 1707. Around the corner on Van den Mastenstraat is the 16thC **Hofje van Gratie**. Continue E to Verwersdijk and turn left. The first street you pass is Doelenstraat, where Rembrandt's gifted pupil Carel Fabritius was living when a gunpowder magazine in an expropriated convent nearby exploded, killing some 200 people including the young artist, and, according to an eyewitness, leaving "nothing but a pool of water."

To reach Markt, turn right off Verwersdijk down Voldersgracht, the famous *Little Street in Delft* painted by Vermeer, who lived in a house that backed on to this street until bankruptcy forced him to move in 1672. Turn left into the broad market square **Markt**, overlooked by the ornate Renaissance **Stadhuis** built in 1618 by Hendrick de Keyser.

Here is a convenient place to pause, after which you might continue down Oosteinde to reach Delft's only surviving city gate, the 14thC **Oostpoort**, embellished in the 16thC with elegant Burgundian towers. Return along the left-hand side of Oosteinde and turn left along Gasthuislaan and, later, left down Achterom to reach the Kapelsbrug, where you can still pick out many of the features that appear in Vermeer's *View of Delft*, which was painted from an upper window of a house, on the far side of the broad harbor, known as *De Kolk*. Dominating this corner of Delft is the **Armamentarium**, an arsenal established in the early days of the Dutch Republic and now housing the **Legermuseum** (National Army Museum) (🖾 *open Tues–Sat 10am–5pm, Sun 1–5pm*). Also of interest is the former seat of the Delft Chamber of the Dutch East India Company at **Oude Delft 39**, comprising three former houses grouped around a courtyard.

Nieuwe Kerk
🖾 & 🖾 *Open Apr–Sept, Mon–Sat 9am–5pm; Oct–Mar, Mon–Sat 10am–noon, 1.30–4pm. Closed Sun.*

The exterior of the Nieuwe Kerk is a baffling jumble of jarring styles and periods: the 15thC choir soars above the 14thC transepts, while the tower comprises a late 14thC base, a 15thC High Gothic tier, a 16thC late Gothic tier and a 19thC spire. However, the interior is surprisingly harmonious, with attention directed towards the choir, where a mysterious golden light is shed on the tomb of William of Orange.

Begun 40 years after the death of William, as a symbol to unify the country at a time of religious strife, the tomb is a cold, melancholy design by Hendrick de Keyser, laden with Renaissance obelisks and wailing cherubs. The four corner figures represent the virtues of Liberty (with a hat), Justice, Religion and Fortitude, while behind stands a trumpeting figure of Fame and, at William's feet, his loyal dog.

Numerous other monarchs, most of them called Willem (except for one queen, called Wilhelmina), are buried in the Nieuwe Kerk. The Delft-born jurist Hugo Grotius, who laid

the foundations of international law and is popularly
remembered for his escape from Loevestein Castle in a trunk,
is commemorated by a simple Classical monument.

Paul Tétar van Elven, Museum
*Koornmarkt 67 ☎ (015) 124206 ▧ K Open Tues–Sat
11am–5pm. Closed Sun, Mon.*
This curious 19thC house filled with nostalgic memorabilia
belonged to a minor painter who taught at the Delft
Polytechnische School and in his spare time assiduously
copied the Dutch Masters of the Golden Age. Van Elven's
favorite artist was Vermeer of Delft and he went to the length
of fitting leaded glass to his first-floor studio windows to
recreate the mellow light that suffuses Vermeer's works. The
museum contains an incongruous room in Louis XIV style on
the ground floor, which was rescued from a nearby house in
the 1970s.

Rijksmuseum Huis Lambert van Meerten
*Oude Delft 199 ☎ (015) 121858 ▧ Open Tues–Sat
10am–5pm, Sun, hols 1–5pm. Ring bell for entry.*
This small museum is famed for its huge collection of tiles,
which cover the walls of the house so completely that you

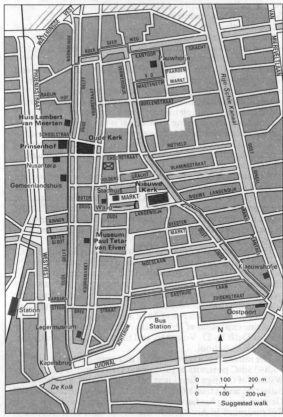

might think you have stumbled into a mosque.

The Delft industrialist Lambert van Meerten had this house built in 1891 in an unusual version of Old Dutch Renaissance style, and to make matters worse had genuine 16thC architectural fragments incorporated into the fabric, such as the pillars flanking the entrance and the magnificent Renaissance window on the staircase landing. Van Meerten intended his house to become a museum, but his plans were thwarted by his bankruptcy in 1902, and he committed suicide shortly afterwards.

Some friends tried nevertheless to open the house as a museum, although everything movable had already been sold. The architect Jan Schouten came to the rescue, however, presenting to the museum his unique collection of tiles. This includes early examples from Mediterranean countries, but its chief interest lies in the extensive range of blue and white Dutch tiles, naively decorated with children, ships, flowers and other cheerful subjects.

Despite these whimsical exhibits, the house is filled with a profound nostalgia for the Dutch Golden Age, especially in the bedroom, where Van Meerten had leaded glass windows and even a traditional cupboard bed installed.

Stedelijk Museum Het Prinsenhof ★

St Agathaplein 1 ☎ (015) 602357. Open Tues–Sat 10am–5pm, Sun, hols 1–5pm. From Oct 1–Nov 30, the annual art and antiques fair is held in the Prinsenhof, and the permanent collection is not on display.

This beautiful 15thC convent with its late Gothic tracery and sagging Burgundian roofs seems to come straight out of an early Netherlandish painting. In spring the museum is especially attractive to visit, with bunches of tulips in every niche and birds singing merrily in the courtyards. However, the main attraction of the Prinsenhof is the gloomy Moordzaal (rm 8), where William of Orange was assassinated in 1584 by Balthazar Gerards. The holes in the wall where the bullets struck can still be seen, together with several melodramatic 19thC prints depicting the event.

William took up residence in the Prinsenhof – previously a convent dedicated to St Agatha – in 1572 and conducted many of the crucial battles of the Dutch Revolt from here, including the dramatic relief of Leiden. It is popularly believed that the beautiful room at the front of the building which is known as the **Prinsenkamer** (rm 16), was where William used to sleep and work.

The Prinsenhof's moment of glory is recalled in the 16thC portraits hanging in the former chapel (rm 4), which show some of the leading protagonists of the Dutch Revolt. The museum boasts a fine collection of paintings by Delft artists – sadly no Vermeers are among them – which mainly depict the disasters that have befallen the city, such as the conflagration of 1536, the Stadhuis fire of 1618 and the gunpowder magazine explosion of 1654. Also of interest is the capricious view of Delft by D. Vosmaer, and the church interiors by the 17thC Delft School.

The museum also possesses an interesting collection of 16th–18thC portraits of prominent Delft families (rm 7, where William of Orange dined just before his death), a Delftware collection and a trunk (both rm 5); this last supposedly served Grotius during his famous escape from captivity (although the *Rijksmuseum* in Amsterdam makes the same claim about a chest in its historical collection).

When visiting the museum, go round: rms 3–7, 14–25 (first floor), then 8–13.

Located next to the Prinsenhof and occupying two 17thC houses, the **Museumhotel** (*Oude Delft 189* ☎ *(015) 140930* ☎ *38026* ▣ *30 rms* ▣▣▣ ▣ ▣ ▣) combines tasteful, modern décor with a few well-chosen antiques. If you want to splurge, book a room on the canal side for a splendid view of the Oude Kerk. Other hotels in Delft tend to be furnished in Old Dutch style, a classic example of which is **Leeuwenbrug** (*Koornmarkt 16* ☎ *(015) 123062* ☎ *33756* ▣ *34 rms* ▣▣▣▣▣), a friendly hotel with an interior bathed in mellow light.

≡ **Le Chevalier** (*Oude Delft 125* ☎ *(015) 124621* ▥▥ *to* ▥▥ ▣▣▣ ▣▥ *closed Sat lunch, Sun, July 20–Aug 10*), located in an 18thC town house on Delft's oldest canal, is consistently praised for its delicate, traditional French cuisine; **Redjeki** (*Choorstraat 50* ☎ *(015) 125022* ▣ ▣▣ *closed Mon*) offers Indonesian cuisine in pleasant surroundings; **Kleyweg's Stadskoffiehuis** (*Oude Delft 135* ☎ *(015) 124625* ▣ *closed Sun*) is a tasteful coffee house producing excellent pancakes and *broodjes* that draw gasps of admiration; and **Exprezzo** (*Oude Delft 140* ☎ *(015) 123108* ▣ *open 10am–7pm; closed Mon*) is a dazzling Post Modernist coffee bar popular with architectural students and homesick Italians.

Shopping
The only surviving producer of hand-painted Delftware porcelain is **De Porceleyne Fles** (*Rotterdamseweg 196* ☎ *(015) 560234, shop open Mon–Sat 9am–5pm, Sun 10am–4pm; bus 60 from railway station*).

Edam
*Map **3**A4. Noord-Holland, 22km (14 miles) N of Amsterdam. Population: 24,000. Getting there: By NZH bus 114 from Amsterdam Centraal Station; by car, through IJ-tunnel, then E10 **i** Speeltoren, Kleine Kerkstraat ☎ (02993) 71727.*

The neat, stately town of Edam was a major shipbuilding center in the 15th–16thC, and when the inland seas to the W such as the Beemster and Purmer were drained in the 17thC to create rich pastures, the town adroitly shifted its attention to the cheese trade. The round, red cheese that goes by the name of Edam is one of Holland's best-known exports, although the Dutch themselves much prefer Gouda.

Sights and places of interest
The **Edams Museum** (*Damplein 8* ▣ * open Easter–Oct Mon–Sat 10am–4pm, Sun 2–4pm*) occupies a remarkable late Gothic house built about 1550, its most mysterious feature being a floating cellar which rocks gently like a small boat. One local legend has it that this was installed by a retired captain to remind him of his days at sea, although a more plausible explanation is that it was to protect the fabric of the house from changes in the water table. Equally curious are three large portraits of local freaks: the exceptionally fat Jan Claeszoon Clees, the tall Trijntje Cornelisdochter Kever and finally Pieter Dirkszoon Langebaard, who traveled around Holland exhibiting his lengthy beard to raise money for the local orphanage. Another interesting painting shows the Edam shipbuilder Jacob Mathijsz Osterlingh proudly displaying the fleet of some 92 fishing boats and warships constructed in his shipyards. The labyrinth of dark rooms and steep stairs, cupboard beds and other unexpected details make this museum especially appealing to children.

135

Edam is a pleasant and interesting town to explore if you have some time. The most dignified canal is the **Schepenmakersdijk** (shipbuilders' dike), with its ornate tea houses and picturesque 18thC offices belonging to the Hoogheemraadschap van de Uitwaterende Sluizen (a body set up in the 16thC to reduce the danger of flooding in this part of Holland).

In contrast, the area N of the main square **Dam** is rather modest and in parts even rural, particularly along Nieuw Vaartje, where there is a farmhouse with chickens running loose in the yard, as well as a house with a puzzling decorated beam (no. 8). The quay opposite, known as Groenland, recalls Edam's former links with the Greenland whaling industry. Farther N is the huge **Grote Kerk**, which boasts a handsome late Gothic library on the S side. The **Kaasmarkt** (cheese market), with its 18thC weigh house (*open 10am–5pm*), is also worth a glance.

Enkhuizen
Noord-Holland, 62km (39 miles) NE of Amsterdam. Population: 15,750. Getting there: By train, 1hr from Amsterdam Centraal Station; by car, through IJ-tunnel, then A7 i Stationsplein 1 ☎ (02280) 13164.

Enkhuizen's flamboyant Renaissance houses and massive warehouses date mainly from the first quarter of the 17thC, when it boasted the largest herring fleet in Holland. The silting of the Zuider Zee in the late 17thC brought its prosperity to an end and by the 19thC Enkhuizen was one of the famous "dead towns of the Zuider Zee" to which travelers flocked in search of the old-fashioned and picturesque. Nowadays its harbors are crammed with a fascinating variety of sailboats, while the Zuiderzee Museum is a major crowd-puller. But you only have to walk a short distance away from the harbor to discover a lingering mood of melancholy decay. This is especially true in the quarter known as the **Boerenhoek**, where an almost rural disorder prevails.

During the summer months (*mid-May to mid-Sept*), passenger boats (taking bicycles) cross the IJsselmeer. One route goes from Enkhuizen to Urk, a former island now joined to the mainland by the Noord-Oost polder, and another to Staveren, which is linked by rail with attractive Frisian towns such as Hindeloopen (famous for its painted furniture), Workum (a former port) and Sneek (set among picturesque lakes). Another boat service connects Enkhuizen with the port of Medemblik to the N.

If the notion of setting sail on a traditional brown-sailed boat catches your fancy, contact **Zeilvaart Enkhuizen** (*Zuiderhavendijk 101 ☎ (02280) 12424*) for information on individual or group excursions lasting one or more days.

Sights and places of interest
The harbors
The best view of Enkhuizen's harbors is to be had from the gusty promontory at the end of **Wierdijk**, the old sea wall. From here, cross the bridge and turn left along the picturesque street **Bocht** which bends round to reach a second bridge. Across this bridge is the 16thC tower known as **De Dromedaris**, built to protect the harbor mouth and in the 17thC adorned with a merry Hemony carillon (*concerts Sat 4–5pm*). A second harbor is reached through the gate of the

tower. Here, turn right past the fish auction and along the harbor, then right again to reach a third harbor. Cross the bridge and turn right down Dijk, which brings you to the splendid **Snouck van Loosenhuis** (no. 34–6), built in the 1740s and adorned with an ornate cartouche. Just beyond the bridge, turn left down the quiet canal **Zuiderhavendijk** to reach the center of town.

The town

The distinctive late Gothic spire of the **Zuiderkerk**, with its curious onion-shaped top, indicates the center of the town. The **Stadhuis**, an imposing example of 17thC Classicism, is found just E of here in Bredestraat, while a short distance N is the **Stedelijk Waagmuseum** (*Kaasmarkt 8* 🖭 *open Tues–Sat 10am–noon, 2–5pm, Sun 2–5pm*), a jaunty 16thC Renaissance weigh house which contains the magnificent 17thC wood-paneled chamber of the Enkhuizen guild of surgeons, and an early 20thC hospital ward.

Enkhuizen's main shopping street, **Westerstraat**, runs W from here, passing the exceptionally ornate Renaissance **Weeshuis** (orphanage) dating from 1616 (*Westerstraat 109*), whose facade stone shows a schoolroom. Nearby is another late Gothic church, the **Westerkerk**, built in 1472–1519, with a curious wooden belfry incorporating ships' timbers.

Proudly proclaiming Enkhuizen's prosperity in the 17thC are the former Mint of Westfriesland at **Westerstraat 125**, and the house at **Westerstraat 158**, with the Maid of Enkhuizen adorning the gable top.

Just N of here lies the **Boerenhoek** (farmers' quarter), an intriguing area of Enkhuizen, where the canals have a distinctly unkempt appearance and huge pyramid-roofed farmhouses appear in the streets. To discover this pleasantly bucolic corner, turn right down the canal **Oudegracht**. This leads eventually to the site of the city walls, where a small 17thC watchtower stands guard over a gate through which small boats entered the city. Here, you can take a brisk walk along the ramparts, which offer glimpses of crowded market gardens and (in spring and early summer) bright bulbfields. Turn left and walk to the 17thC city gate known as the **Koepoort**. Just beyond here is an experimental flower garden, the **Summer Garden** (*open mid-July to Aug Mon–Sat 9am–5pm, Sun 1–5pm; closed if raining*). Westerstraat then leads back to the center of the city.

Zuiderzee Museum

Wierdijk 18 ☎ *(02280) 10122* 🖭 &. *only in Buitenmuseum* ✕ 🖭 ▬ *Binnenmuseum open mid-Feb to Dec Mon–Sat 10am–5pm, Sun, hols noon–5pm. Buitenmuseum open mid-Apr to mid-Oct 10am–5pm (last entry 4pm). Buitenmuseum can only be reached by a special ferry service from Enkhuizen railway station and from the parking lot just E of Enkhuizen on the road to Lelystad.*

The completion in 1932 of the Afsluitdijk (enclosing dike) across the N end of the Zuider Zee was the beginning of the end for the numerous fishing towns on this inland sea. Large-scale land reclamation caused former islands such as Urk and Schokland to vanish in the polder, while other ports such as Elburg and Harderwijk were suddenly transformed into inland towns. A mixture of guilt and nostalgia led to the establishment of the Zuiderzee Museum to provide a record of a vanished way of life.

This exceptionally interesting museum consists of two

parts: the **Binnenmuseum** (indoor museum), housed in a
series of magnificent old warehouses built by the Dutch East
India Company, and the **Buitenmuseum** (open-air museum)
whose 130 assorted buildings from Zuider Zee towns have
been grafted onto Enkhuizen to form a compact unit. It is best
to begin by visiting the Buitenmuseum (except in winter, when
it is closed). A ferry operates across the picturesque harbor of
Enkhuizen to the museum, which is to the NE of the town.
Allow three hours to visit the Buitenmuseum and a further
hour for the Binnenmuseum, which is located just to the left of
the exit from the Buitenmuseum.

Buitenmuseum
One of the main charms of the open-air museum is its lifelike
disorder, which is achieved by clustering houses into
picturesque *buurtjes*, or neighborhoods. Around the perimeter,
the *buurtjes* reflect the local styles of small fishing towns such
as Monnickendam (a port SW of Enkhuizen), Urk (a former
island with glossy wooden-fronted houses), Harderwijk (now
landlocked by the Flevoland polder) and Marken (with
picturesque black wooden houses). The inner area is occupied
by more opulent buildings representing market towns such as
Edam and industrial areas such as the Zaanstreek. The town
canal interestingly reflects the modest style of a Frisian town
on one side and a prosperous North Holland town on the other.
Among the attractive buildings overlooking the canal are a
16thC Gothic house from Edam (now a souvenir shop) and an
imposing green-fronted merchant's house from the Zaan
region, with a curious formal garden which includes parterres
of glass beads originally manufactured in Amsterdam as
trading tokens, and a spherical mirror to enlarge the apparent
size of the garden.

Many of the modest fishermen's houses have been furnished
in 1930s style and their cramped but genteel interiors
incorporate delightful period details such as goldfish bowls,
trays formally set for afternoon tea and neat rows of clogs by
the door. The museum even includes a church in which the
population of Den Oever (at the SW end of the Afsluitdijk) once
worshiped, together with gravestones uprooted from various
spots. The museum also has Den Oever's post office, which
suggests there cannot be very much to Den Oever nowadays.

There are also several shops including a baker's
(*banketbakkerij*) from Hoorn where you can buy home-made
chocolates, a grocer's (*kruidenier*) from Harderwijk where
delicious local sausage is sold and a novelty gift shop from
Monnickendam. A cheese warehouse from Landsmeer (one of
the buildings transported here by boat) serves as one of three
museum restaurants, while another boasts a remarkable
decorative tiled interior from a restaurant in Zandvoort.
Perhaps the most attractive place to pause, however, is in the
café perched on the dike above the harbor.

Demonstrations are given of traditional activities such as
tanning, boat building and house painting, while there are
working models of a 19thC windmill (which maintains the
water-level in the museum) and a steam laundry from near
Kampen. Occasional trips are also organized on the
reconstructed Texel fishing boat, which is moored in the
Marken harbor.

There is hardly a corner of the museum that is not
beguilingly picturesque, but one of the loveliest areas to
explore is hidden behind the souvenir shop, and includes an

unusual *leugenbank*, literally a liars' bench, where fishermen traditionally gathered to exchange yarns.

Binnenmuseum

It is worth visiting the Binnenmuseum simply to enjoy the complex of vast 17thC warehouses set around a courtyard. The main building is the **Peperhuis**, a double step-gabled warehouse built in 1625 and later used by the Dutch East India Company. Mementos of Enkhuizen's maritime past include the gable stone, on the Peperhuis, illustrating a herring boat and another at Wierdijk 22 showing sailing ships struggling through a stormy sea.

The large **ships' hall** (rm 1) contains a number of **boats** that once sailed on the Zuider Zee and the inland waters of North Holland, ranging from stocky fishing boats to elegant pleasure yachts. The museum also has a collection of **figureheads** and other decorations (rm 2), **ship models** (rm 9) and an interesting **display of methods of fishing and duck hunting** (rm 8).

The low-beamed **attic** (rm 4) contains a collection of **hand-painted furniture and sleighs** from isolated fishing communities such as Marken and Workum. These marvelous examples of folk art are illustrated with mythological or biblical episodes copied from artists' prints. The examples of Classical furniture (rm 7) are very sober by comparison. Another attic (rm 6) is devoted to traditional trades such as boat-building, weaving cloth for sails and cheese-making. There are also several sleighs of the type that feature in the skating scenes of Avercamp.

Finally, the museum contains a series of detailed furnished rooms (rms 13–15) illustrating the extraordinary variety of costumes and interiors found around the Zuider Zee. The interiors come from the islands of Terschelling, Urk and Marken, the manufacturing area NW of Amsterdam known as the Zaanstreek, a West-Friesland farmhouse and the former ports of Spakenburg and Volendam.

≈ Probably the most attractive restaurant in Enkhuizen is **Die Drie Haringhe** (*Dijk 28* ☎ *(02280) 18610* 🖃 ⦿ ⦿ 🖃 *last orders 10pm; closed Tues*), its name recalling the three herrings on the town's coat of arms. Located in a former Dutch East India Company warehouse overlooking the Oude Haven, it specializes in delicate French cuisine. The restaurant's waterside terrace is a pleasant spot for a drink on sunny days, while its basement bar offers a retreat on days of blustery winds. **De Boei** (*Havenweg 5* ☎ *(02280) 14280* ☐ 🖃 ⦿ *last orders 10pm*) is a simple, affordable fish restaurant overlooking Buiten Haven, where the house specialty is all the plaice you can eat. Or head for one of the many fish shops found on the harbors, where you can pick up a *lekkerbekje* (piece of fried fish), *maatjes haring* (cured young herring) or perhaps a huge Dutch gherkin.

Gouda

Map 2E3. Zuid-Holland, 53km (33 miles) s of Amsterdam. Population: 60,000. Getting there: By train, 50mins from Amsterdam Centraal Station or Amstel; by car, on A2, then A12 i Waag, Markt 27 ☎ (01820) 13666.

The compact market town of Gouda is principally famed for its flat round yellow cheeses, which the Dutch consume in large quantities. Those whose palates are accustomed to vigorous French cheeses might complain that Gouda is a touch bland, but the Dutch come stoutly to the defense of their beloved national food, and point out that there are five different types of cheese according to age, not to mention exotic varieties with cumin (*komijn*) or cloves (*nagel*). The youngest Gouda, *jong*, is a creamy soft cheese about four weeks old; *jongbelegen* (eight weeks), *belegen* (four months) and *oud* (ten months) are increasingly hard, while one-year-old *overjarig* is particularly crumbly. A traditional cheese market is enacted in the large market square on Thurs (*mid-June to Aug 9am–noon*), with much of the action taking place in the **Waag**, designed in 1668 by Pieter Post and decorated with an impressive facade stone by Balthazar Eggers depicting the weighing of Gouda cheeses.

Sights and places of interest
The town
Gouda's most striking building is its **Stadhuis** in the middle of Markt, built in 1450 in a soaring Gothic style and adorned with sculptures of prominent Burgundian counts and countesses. An ornate Renaissance staircase with unusual caryatids was added in 1603.

From Markt, head down Kerksteg to reach the **Sint Janskerk**, then walk along the outside of the church to reach a small park. Just beyond here, a short distance to the right down Molenwerf, is a small bridge that offers an almost Venetian view down a canal. Retrace your steps to reach Jeruzalemstraat, where the remains of a 12-sided chapel dating from about 1500 are visible. Turn right down Spieringstraat, passing on the left the 17thC orphanage with its attractive courtyard and on the right the colorful 17thC portal of a former almshouse. Walk through the park at the end of the street and turn right past a windmill to reach a picturesque canal, **Oosthaven**, which you should follow N.

The **"De Moriaan" Museum** (*Westhaven 29* ☒ *open Mon–Sat 10am–5pm, Sun noon–5pm*) is located in a 17thC tobacconist and coffee shop, which advertises itself to passers-by with a row of tobacco bales and a figure of a North American Indian holding a clay pipe. The labyrinthine interior contains some curious clay pipes, tiles and Art Nouveau ceramics.

Also worth a visit is the **Stedelijk Museum Het Catharina Gasthuis** (*Achter de Kerk 14* ☒ *open Mon–Sat 10am–5pm, Sun noon–5pm*), located in a hospice dating from the 14thC. You can enter from Oosthaven through the *gasthuis* (hospice) chapel (no. 10), or through the Lazaruspoortje, a picturesque 17thC gateway on Achter de Kerk decorated with sculpture alluding to the building's function as a hospital.

The museum contains several 17th–19thC period rooms, including the delightful *gasthuis* kitchen (complete with a turtledove in a cage), a reconstructed apothecary's shop, the Gouda surgeons' guild room, a schoolroom and a toy collection.

The museum's collection of paintings includes medieval altarpieces from Gouda churches, 17thC civic guard group portraits, 19thC landscapes by the Barbizon and Hague Schools and some interesting modern works.

Sint Janskerk ★
Achter de Kerk 16. Open Mon–Sat 9am–5pm.
Many Dutch churches can be given a miss, but not the Sint Janskerk, with its astonishing Renaissance stained-glass windows. Most of these were designed in the 16thC by the brothers Dirk and Wouter Crabeth while Gouda was still a Catholic city, and the scenes are mainly religious and

mythological. Works by these brothers include: *King Solomon receiving the Queen of Sheba* (window 5); *Judith and Holofernes* (window 6); *The Last Supper*, donated by Philip II of Spain who is shown with his wife Queen Mary Tudor of England (window 7); *Jonah and the Whale* , given by the Guild of Fishmongers (window 30); *The Nativity* (window 12); *John the Baptist* (window 14); *The Baptism of Jesus* (window 15) and *Christ Preaching* (window 16).

The stained-glass windows craze continued after Gouda turned Protestant in the late 16thC, the themes then shifting to heroic episodes in Dutch history, such as the dramatic relief of Leiden, given by the city of Delft and designed by the burgomaster of Leiden (window 25). A more tenuous Dutch connection is alluded to in the illustration of the Capture of Damietta by Dutch crusaders in 1219 (window 2), and the cornerstone of the Dutch constitution is illustrated in the symbolic group of figures representing Freedom of Conscience (window 1).

Many of the windows were restored in the late 19thC by Jan Schouten of Delft, who created a number of curious, almost surreal, windows using leftover fragments of glass (windows 1A–C, 20 and 21). Finally, a window depicting Occupation and Liberation was added after World War II (window 28A).

Den Haag *(The Hague)*

*Map **2**D2. Zuid-Holland, 60km (37 miles) sw of Amsterdam. Population: 445,200. Getting there: By train, 55mins from Amsterdam Centraal Station (change at Leiden for Den Haag Centraal Station) or from Amsterdam RAI and Zuid WTC; by car, on A4 **i** Kon. Julianaplein (in Babylon complex, next to Centraal Station) ☎(070) 546200.*

Much admired in previous centuries for its elegant avenues and extensive parks, Den Haag (its full name is 's-Gravenhage, which the English simplified to The Hague) is today a rather staid city which has been knocked about mercilessly by urban planners. Yet it still retains a stately air thanks to its numerous royal palaces, government offices, embassies and multinational organizations, and it boasts excellent museums and art galleries, parks and shops. There is also much to keep children amused, particularly as the beach at Scheveningen is only a short tram ride away.

> The Hague is Hampton-Court turned into a large town.
> William Hazlitt, *Notes of a Journey through France and Italy* ,
> 1826

Event: The main event every year is the JVC North Sea Jazz Festival, a friendly and sprawling festival held in mid-July which brings together some of the biggest names in jazz. It is held in the **Congresgebouw**, a building designed in the 1960s by J. J. P. Oud in his distinctive nautical style *(for further info ☎(070) 502034 🖝33430).*

Sights and places of interest
The town
The most rewarding area of Den Haag to explore lies between the Binnenhof and Javastraat. From the Mauritshuis, head N along Korte Vijverberg to Lange Vijverberg, a pleasant chestnut-lined avenue bordering the Vijver. A number of imposing buildings overlook this pond, including the

Sebastiaansdoelen (*Korte Vijverberg 7*), a pedimented Classical building designed by Arend van 's-Gravesande in 1636, and now housing the historical museum of Den Haag (☎ *(070) 646940* ☎ *open Tues–Fri noon–4pm*).

Continue w along the Vijver and turn right down Kneuterdijk past the Classical home at Kneuterdijk 6 of the Raadspensionaris Johan de Witt, who in 1672 was murdered by a mob following the French invasion of the Netherlands. The rather overbearing **Paleis Kneuterdijk** (*NW corner of Kneuterdijk*) was built in 1717 by Daniel Marot and in 1816 was acquired by King William I, who lived there with his Russian wife Anna Paulovna.

A short detour down Heulstraat, then right along Noordeinde brings you to the small mock-Gothic **art gallery** built at the back of the Paleis Kneuterdijk by the Anglophile William I. Opposite is the restored 17thC **Paleis Noordeinde**, built in Dutch Classical style by Jacob van Campen and Pieter Post.

Retrace your steps to Kneuterdijk and continue straight ahead to reach the Lange Voorhout, a beautiful tree-lined avenue which in early spring is carpeted with crocuses. The last surviving step gable in Den Haag, at Lange Voorhout 6, was built in 1618 for the state ordnance officer. Cannons were stored in the choir of the nearby Kloosterkerk.

The most imposing building on Lange Voorhout is the former **Koninklijke Bibliotheek** (Royal Library) at no. 34, which was built by Daniel Marot as a five-bay-wide town house in 1734–38 and was extended on both sides by Pieter de Swart in 1761.

A short detour left down Vos in Tuinstraat, then right along Maliestraat leads to an unexpectedly picturesque spot where two canals meet. Unfortunately, this charm does not extend very far in any direction, so having taken in the wisteria-drenched houses, retrace your steps straight back to the Lange Voorhout.

The reserved Classicism of Pieter de Swart is evident in the house (now belonging to the royal family) he built in 1760–64 for the banker John William Hope at the E end of Lange Voorhout, and also in the unfinished palace he built for Princess Caroline van Nassau in 1760, now the **Koninklijke Schouwburg** (*Korte Voorhout 3*).

Clingendael

Wassenaarseweg 🖾 🚍 *Open dawn-dusk. Japanese Garden open early May to mid-June 9am–8pm. Bus 18 from Centraal Station to Laan van Clingendael.*

Located in the grounds of the Van Brienens' 18thC country house, Clingendael is one of the most attractive parks in Den Haag, with its masses of rhododendrons in the star-shaped **Sterrebos**, its Rosarium and its 18thC Old Dutch Garden (Oud-Hollandse Tuin). But its greatest glory is the Japanese Garden (Japanse Tuin), which is open to the public for a mere six weeks every year while the azaleas and cherry trees are at their best.

This enchanting miniature garden, begun in the early 20thC, is correct in every detail, from the stone lanterns placed in symbolic settings beside the winding paths, to the striking red lacquered bridge across the pond. Every corner of the garden cries out to be photographed, but the view through the Moon Window of the replica Tea House is perhaps the most picturesque.

Haags Gemeentemuseum ★

Stadhouderslaan 41 ☎ (070) 514181 📷 💻 Open Tues–Fri 10am–5pm, Sat, Sun, hols 1–5pm. Tram 10 to Stadhouderslaan.

The fascinating and diverse collection of the municipal museum of Den Haag is housed in an attractive building designed by H. P. Berlage in 1935. The ivy-clad brick walls and ornamental lily ponds are particularly picturesque, while the interior possesses a certain ceremonial grandeur, especially in the **Erezaal** (Hall of Honor) above the main entrance, where Eric Orr's remarkable *Light Space* highlights the awesome dimensions of Berlage's design. The Gemeentemuseum's display cases, lamps and litter bins were also designed by Berlage, who died shortly before the building was completed.

The ground floor is mainly devoted to applied art and includes some intriguing Spanish and Italian apothecaries' jars, examples of Chinese porcelain and a magnificent 18thC dollhouse. The five rooms furnished in 18thC styles (*stijlkamers*) are also worth a glance, particularly the exquisite Japanese room, rescued from a house that was demolished to make way for the Vredespaleis. For many, the most interesting feature of the Gemeentemuseum is its extensive **collection of musical instruments**, ranging from a 14thC wooden flute dredged up from a moat to a remarkable 19thC Viennese pyramid piano, lavishly adorned with Egyptian motifs. It is also worth seeking out the **Nederlands Kostuummuseum**, which has an engaging gallery of fashions covering everything from 18thC corsets to 20thC punk clothing.

The layout of the upper floor, devoted to the museum's collection of 19th and 20thC painting, is rather baffling and it is easy to miss large sections of the collection. The best rooms to begin with are those devoted to 19thC Romantics such as Wijnand Nuijen and early Impressionists such as Jan B. Jongkind. Be sure not to miss Monet's vibrant *Quai du Louvre* or his much later, almost abstract, *Glycine*, painted in the 1920s in his garden at Giverny.

The collection of paintings by the **Hague School** contains attractive seascapes such as Jacob Maris' *Bomschuit* and J. H. Weissenbruch's *Strandgezicht*, which capture the breezy atmosphere and silver-gray light of the Dutch coast. There is also an excellent collection of Impressionist works by Breitner, including a view of the Zandhoek in Amsterdam, a startling cavalry charge and the exquisite *Red Kimono* (1893).

A room is devoted to Jan Toorop, a Dutch artist who tried various modern styles before settling into a rather tormented Symbolism.

The museum's **collection of Mondrian paintings** spans his diverse styles, and includes some early landscape paintings of the river Gein and the dunes at Domburg, as well as a series of tree studies which show his development from the style of late Van Gogh (*Red Tree, 1908*) to complete abstraction (*Composition: Trees II*). The museum also has works by Theo van Doesburg, including a painting whose diagonal lines threw Mondrian into a rage.

Finally, don't miss the atmospheric **Dijsselhofkamer**, an Art Nouveau room dating from 1895.

Huygens Museum Hofwijk

Westeinde 2, Voorburg ☎ (070) 872311 📷 🚃 Open Wed, Thurs, Sat, Sun 2–5pm. Tram 10, or train to Voorburg Station.

Hofwijk was a country retreat on the river Vliet belonging to

the statesman, poet and scientist Constantijn Huygens
(1596–1687), who helped Rembrandt gain major commissions.
The house, an elegant Classical box, was designed by Huygens
with help from Jacob van Campen.

Suburban sprawl has now swallowed up most of the estate,
while the constant throb of traffic destroys the idyllic
atmosphere. Yet the interior retains the charm of the Golden
Age with its tiled kitchen and intimate library.

The museum contains memorabilia such as portraits, letters,
scientific instruments and books, including Huygens' 2,824-
line poem in praise of Hofwijk, and his plan for a broad,
straight boulevard between Den Haag and Scheveningen (now
the Scheveningse Weg).

On leaving Hofwijk, turn right to reach Voorburg's
attractive main street Herenstraat, which is assumed to be the
old Roman road that led to the settlement of Forum Hadriani.
The main sights in Voorburg are the 15thC church, the
handsome Renaissance double step gable of Swaensteyn, a
former inn, and the pleasant park **Vreugd en Rust**, designed
by the 19thC landscape gardener J. D. Zocher.

Madurodam ★
Haringkade 175 ☎*(070) 553900* 🖾 ♿ 🖳 ⚕ 🚻 🚐 *Open
Apr–June 9.30am–10.30pm; July–Aug 9.30am–11pm; Sept
9.30am–9.30pm; first three weeks Oct 9.30am–6pm. Tram 1,
9 to Madurodam. No dogs.*
Founded in memory of a Dutch soldier who died in Dachau
concentration camp, the miniature town of Madurodam has
been assembled with painstaking attention to detail. Because
Madurodam is intended to reflect every aspect of Dutch
society, the models include not only historic buildings, trains,
airplanes and ships, but also a sewage works, a car accident and
a nudist beach. The miniature vegetation is equally precise and
at night the town is illuminated by 50,000 miniature lamps.

Mauritshuis, Koninklijk Kabinet van Schilderijen ★
Plein 29 ☎*(070) 469244* 🖾 *Open Tues–Sat 10am–5pm,
Sun, hols 11am–5pm. Tram 3, 7, 8 to Centrum.*
A visit to the Royal Picture Gallery in the Mauritshuis is
doubly delightful since its superb collection of 17thC Dutch
Masters is housed in an architectural gem dating from the
Golden Age.

The Mauritshuis was commissioned by Johan Maurits, a
popular governor of the ill-fated Dutch settlement in Brazil. It
was built on the edge of the Vijver by Jacob van Campen in
1633–44 in a mixture of mellow brown brick and yellow-gray
sandstone and epitomizes the quiet contentment associated
with the Golden Age.

The Mauritshuis is particularly renowned for its
Rembrandts, including two self-portraits: the rather haughty
Self-portrait as a Young Man, painted around 1629 when
Rembrandt was still living in Leiden, and the quietly resigned
Late Self-portrait, painted shortly before his death. The
Mauritshuis also possesses Rembrandt's first major
commission, *The Anatomy Lesson of Dr Tulp*, painted in 1632 –
one year before the Mauritshuis was begun – to hang in the
surgeons' hall of the Waag in Amsterdam.

Equally remarkable are the two paintings by Vermeer: the
astonishingly tender *View of Delft* painted in an uncertain
moment between sunshine and rain, and the snapshot-like
Head of a Girl.

The Mauritshuis also boasts 13 paintings by Jan Steen,

illustrating his delight in providing compact moral tales
enhanced with touches of bawdy humor. The most boisterous
scene illustrates the old Dutch adage "The way you hear it is
the way you sing it" – a warning against children imitating
their parents – in which Steen includes himself offering a clay
pipe to a child.

Other popular works are Jacob van Ruisdael's *View of
Haarlem* and Paulus Potter's remarkably realistic *Young Bull*;
but possibly the most endearing painting in the collection is
the *Goldfinch* painted by Rembrandt's unfortunate pupil Carel
Fabritius, who was killed in a gunpowder explosion in Delft in
1654. Many of his works perished in the disaster, while others,
which had been bought by the Czar of Russia, were lost in a
shipwreck, leaving only eight surviving works.

Although the accent is on 17thC Dutch paintings, the
Mauritshuis also contains several works by Flemish Masters,
such as Rogier van der Weyden's *Lamentation*, and works by
Holbein and Rubens.

Museon

Stadhouderslaan 41 ☎*(070) 514181* 🖼 💻 ⚥ 🚗 *Open
Tues–Fri 10am–5pm, Sat, Sun, hols noon–5pm. Tram 10 to
Stadhouderslaan.*

The Museon is the catchy new name for the former Museum of
Education, which was founded in 1904 as a progressive science
museum for children. The attractive new building was
designed by Gerardus Quist to harmonize with Berlage's
Gemeentemuseum, and the interior design creates just the
right sense of adventure. The main subjects covered are
geology, biology, physics, history, ethnology and human
rights, and each section is packed with exhibits such as a
Bedouin tent, a prehistoric shelter and a model of the Rhine.

Omniversum

President Kennedylaan 5 ☎*(070) 545454* 🖼 ♿ 💻 ⚥ 🚗 *Open
daily* ☎ *for times of screenings. Tram 10 to
Stadhouderslaan. Commentary only in Dutch.*

View the Panorama Mesdag first, then visit Omniversum to
see an attempt some 100 years later to achieve a similar illusion
of three-dimensionality on a two-dimensional surface.
Omniversum uses a giant domed cinema screen similar to a
Planetarium, plus a computer and a vast array of loudspeakers
to create a highly convincing sensation of movement (scenes
involving flight are particularly stomach-churning).

Programs last one hour and consist mainly of documentaries
on themes such as space travel (*The Dream is Alive*), computer
technology (*The Magic Egg*) and Dutch landscapes and cities
(*Picture Holland*). Don't be deceived by the titles into
expecting English commentary: everything is in Dutch,
although the visual effects can be enjoyed in any case.

Panorama Mesdag ★

Zeestraat 65b ☎*(070) 642563* 🖼 🎦 ⚥ *Open Mon–Sat
10am–5pm, Sun, hols noon–5pm. Tram 7, 8 to Mauritskade.*

The Panorama Mesdag, one of the few surviving 19thC
panorama paintings in the world, is a 120m (400ft) long and
14m (45ft) high circular view of the village of Scheveningen
and the North Sea coast, seen from the Seinpostduin (a dune).
Its main fascination is due to its uncanny realism, which is
achieved by creating a three-dimensional *faux terrain* between
the viewing platform and the canvas, so that there appears to
be no dividing line between the painting and the viewer. The
fame of the Panorama Mesdag lies not merely in its technical

virtuosity, but also its artistic merit. It was painted in 1881 by
the famous Dutch marine painter H. W. Mesdag, assisted by
his wife, who painted the village of Scheveningen, Th. de
Bock, who was responsible for the sky and dunes and the
Amsterdam Impressionist G. H. Breitner, who painted the
cavalry and artillery on the beach.

The viewing platform incorporates Mesdag's sketching
cylinder, and a set of peepholes at the exit provides a glimpse
behind the scenes. The museum also contains a small
collection of paintings by Mesdag, together with a permanent
exhibition on the panorama phenomenon in the 19thC.

Postmuseum
_Zeestraat 82 ☎(070) 624531 ▨ & ▣ Mon–Sat 10am–5pm,
Sun, hols 1–5pm. Tram 7, 8 to Vredespaleis._

The recently-modernized Postmuseum is concealed behind a
white Neoclassical facade near the Panorama Mesdag. The
museum charts the development of post and
telecommunications in the Netherlands, from the slow horse-
drawn boats known as _trekschuiten_ to modern fiber optics. The
exhibits include a beautiful reconstructed post office, a
collection of mailboxes, delivery vans, a sorting machine,
radios, telephones and a huge international stamp collection.

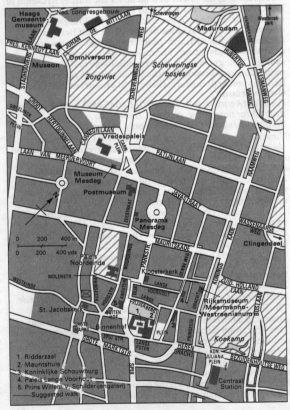

1. Ridderzaal
2. Mauritshuis
3. Koninklijke Schouwburg
4. Paleis Lange Voorhout
5. Prins Willem V, Schilderijengalerij
—— Suggested walk

Prins Willem V, Schilderijengalerij
Buitenhof 35 ☎ (070) 638963 ⌷ Open 11am–2pm. Tram 7, 8 to Kneuterdijk.

This old-fashioned art gallery was founded in 1774 by Prins Willem V as the first public gallery in the Netherlands. It is perhaps most interesting as a curiosity, as it retains its 18thC appearance, with the walls of the long gallery and small antechamber covered from floor to ceiling with paintings.

The 130 or so paintings in the collection are mainly 17thC Dutch and Flemish works, showing familiar subjects such as church interiors, still lifes, prim towns and romantic landscapes. The smaller paintings are difficult to appreciate and it takes a huge work like Bloemaert's *Marriage of Peleus and Thetis* (1638) to catch one's attention. W. van Haecht's strange treatment of *Alexander the Great Visiting the Studio of Apelles* shows a gallery similar to that of Prins Willem V.

Ridderzaal
Binnenhof 8a ☎ (070) 646144 ⌷ ✗ compulsory. Open Mon–Sat 10am–4pm. Tram 3, 7, 8 to Centrum.

Begun in the 13thC by Count William II and completed by his son Floris V, the Ridderzaal is the oldest and most imposing building of the Binnenhof complex. During the Middle Ages, the Binnenhof served as an administrative center for the provinces of Holland and Zeeland, and after the Revolt of the Netherlands it became the seat of government of the new Republic.

Restored in the 19thC, the Ridderzaal remains the symbol of Dutch government, although it is only used on ceremonial occasions such as the state opening of parliament. Everyday government business is conducted in the surrounding buildings of the Binnenhof, which date mainly from the 18th and 19thC. The elected Tweede Kamer (Second Chamber) meets in a grand Neoclassical ballroom, built by Stadholder William V shortly before he was forced to flee from the invading Napoleonic army, and the provincial representatives of the Eerste Kamer (First Chamber) meet in the 17thC assembly room of the States General.

Rijksmuseum Meermanno-Westreenianum
Prinsessegracht 30 ☎ (070) 462700 ⌷ Open Mon–Sat 1–5pm. Ring bell for entry. Tram 1, 9 to Zuid–Hollandlaan.

This striking Neoclassical town house contains an extensive collection of antiquities and rare books, begun in the 18thC by Gerard Meerman and extended by Baron van Westreenen in the 19thC. Interesting temporary exhibitions on contemporary book design are organized by the **Museum van het Boek**, which was established in 1960. The interior of the building is worth a glance, both for the delightful 18thC rooms on the ground floor, and the 19thC museum and library above.

Rijksmuseum H. W. Mesdag
Laan van Meerdervoort 7f ☎ (070) 635450 ⌷ Open Tues–Sat 10am–5pm, Sun, hols 1–5pm. Ring bell for entry. Tram 7, 8 to Vredespaleis.

While the crowds push to see the spectacular Panorama Mesdag, the home and private collection of the marine painter H. W. Mesdag gets so few visitors that it is threatened with closure. Yet for anyone interested in the quiet, meditative landscapes of late 19thC French and Dutch artists, this museum is a must.

The top floor of the museum is devoted to Mesdag's collection of paintings by the Romantic Barbizon School, the largest collection of works by this group outside France. It includes landscapes by Millet, Daubigny, Corot and Courbet.

The rest of Mesdag's collection concentrates on the artists of the Dutch Hague School, including Israels, Roelofs, Willem and Jacob Maris, Bosboom and Mesdag. These artists depicted the dunes, polders and sea near Den Haag in the same melancholy dark browns and greens favored by the Barbizon artists.

Scheveningen

✤ *Tram 1, 7, 8, 9 to Gevers Deijnootplein.*

Originally a fishing village dating back to the 15thC, Scheveningen became one of Europe's most fashionable resorts in the late 19thC, due largely to its proximity to Den Haag.

The recently-restored Kurhaus is one of the last relics of this *fin de siècle* elegance, although it is now surrounded by a brash explosion of modern buildings which is Scheveningen's way of competing with Mediterranean resorts.

Apart from the Kurhaus, with its frescoed Kurzaal café, bars, restaurants and casino, the main attraction of Scheveningen is the modern pier, which offers a fine view of the usually gray sea from its observation tower. The replica **Nautilus** from Jules Verne's *Twenty Thousand Leagues Under the Sea* is curiously fascinating with its antiquated iron fittings, ghostly organ music and mechanized exotic fish.

Scheveningen's other attractions are its broad sandy beach and *golfslagbad* – a swimming pool with artificial waves, a gym, sauna and solarium.

Vredespaleis

Carnegieplein 1 ☎(070) 469680 ▨ X compulsory. Open Mon–Fri; guided tours at 10am, 11am, noon, 2pm, 3pm; also 4pm June–Aug. Tram 7,8 to Vredespaleis.

Den Haag was the scene of the first international peace conference in 1899, which was held in the splendid if somewhat unsuitable **Oranjezaal** of the Huis ten Bosch, whose vast Baroque murals depicted the heroic exploits of Frederik Hendrik. It was later decided to set up a permanent court of arbitration in Den Haag and the Scottish-born steel magnate Andrew Carnegie donated 1.5 million dollars for the construction of a peace palace.

The French architect Louis Cordonnier won the competition for the design of the palace with a grandiose eclectic design which originally included four corner towers. But even Carnegie could not afford to sponsor such splendor and the palace was eventually built with only one tower, giving it a decidedly lopsided appearance.

The interior is an intimidating display of opulence, and contains various unusual items donated by member states of the United Nations such as wood paneling, chandeliers and tile tableaux. Perhaps the most delightful items are the fountain in the courtyard, which was donated by Denmark, and the Japanese wall hangings. The most impressive gift, however, is the main staircase of the Vredespaleis, which was given by the city of Den Haag.

Begun in 1907, the Vredespaleis was completed just before the outbreak of World War I put an end to its noble aspirations.

The guided tour takes in the Permanent Court of Arbitration and the International Court of Justice, which was added in 1922.

Westbroekpark

Kapelweg, Scheveningen ☎ *Open 9am–8pm. Tram 1, 9 to
Nieuwe Duinweg.*
A landscaped park in the Scheveningse Bosjes just N of
Madurodam and famed for its Rosarium of some 20,000 roses,
which are at their best from about July–Sept.

🛏 The **Hotel des Indes** (*Lange Voorhout 54–6* ☎ *(070) 469553*
📠*31196* ▥ ⒶⒺ ⒸⒷ ① ⓪ ⓥⓘⓢⓐ) is one of the last souvenirs of Den
Haag's glittering past, its name at once an evocation of French elegance
and colonial grandeur. Built in 1859, it was converted to a hotel in 1881.
The spy Mata Hari frequented Des Indes in the years before World
War I and the ballerina Anna Pavlova died here of pleurisy in 1931 after
a performance at the nearby theater. Despite its fame, Des Indes
remains a discreet hotel, popular with diplomats.
    The **Steigenberger Kurhaus** (*Gevers Deijnootplein 30*
☎ *(070) 520052* 📠*33295* ▥▥ ⒶⒺ ① ⓪ ⓥⓘⓢⓐ) is Den Haag's other great
hotel, a relic from the days when Scheveningen was a chic spa resort.
Saved from demolition a few years ago, the Kurhaus has been given a
new lease of life by the careful addition of modern facilities such as a
financial center and fully-equipped conference rooms, but the center of
attraction is still the magnificent Kurzaal, with its frescoes of sea
nymphs. Because the Kurhaus now caters mainly to business visitors,
rates drop markedly on weekends.
    Located in the center of Den Haag, the **Parkhotel De Zalm**
(*Molenstraat 53* ☎ *(070) 624371* 📠 *33005* ▯ ⒶⒺ ① ⓪) is an
inexpensive hotel retaining an old-fashioned charm. But generally, if
looking for something cheaper, it is advisable to stay clear of the city
center. For example, the **Sweelinck** (*Sweelinckplein 78* ☎ *(070) 608058*
▯) is a quiet hotel overlooking the stately Sweelinckplein – a must for
those who enjoy the whimsicalities of 19thC eclectic architecture. Or, if
Art Nouveau is preferred, try the comfortable **Bel Park**
(*Antwerpsestraat 18* ☎ *(070) 556831* ▯), or the inexpensive **Van
Zanen** (*Leuvensestraat 39* ☎ *(070) 554636*▯), both friendly hotels in
quiet, leafy streets, close to Scheveningen beach.

☎ Because of its links with the former Dutch colonies in the Far East,
Den Haag boasts numerous excellent Indonesian restaurants offering
exotic *rijsttafels*. A favorite with former colonial administrators is
Garoeda (*Kneuterdijk 18a* ☎ *(070) 465319* ▯ ⒶⒺ ① ⓥⓘⓢⓐ *closed Sun
lunch*), offering delicate and fragrant cuisine in an airy upstairs
restaurant overlooking the elegant Lange Voorhout. Close to the
Binnenhof and popular with politicians, **Raden Ajoe** (*Lange Poten 31*
☎ *(070) 644592* ▯ ⒶⒺ ① ⓪ *last orders 10pm*) is a luxurious
restaurant with a huge menu, strong in seafood and vegetable dishes and
offering a range of overflowing *rijsttafels*. Food and presentation are
equally impressive in its sister restaurant **Raden Mas** (*Gevers
Deynootplein 125* ☎ *(070) 545480* ▯ ⒶⒺ ① ⓪ ⓥⓘⓢⓐ *last orders
10.30pm*) in Scheveningen.
    Den Haag's other specialty is fish, which is landed at Scheveningen.
Restaurants come in all types, from the simple **Havenrestaurant BV
Wed. J. v. d. Toorn Mzn.** (*Treilerdwarsweg 2* ☎ *(070) 545783* ▯ ⒶⒺ
① ⓪ *last orders 7.30pm; closed Sun*) to the culinary heights of the
aristocratic **Saur** (*Lange Voorhout 51* ☎ *(070) 463344* ▥▥ ⒶⒺ ① ⓪
ⓥⓘⓢⓐ *closed Sat lunch, Sun*). In addition to its wood-paneled restaurant,
Saur boasts an oyster bar open from noon to midnight and a delicatessen
offering gourmet takeouts.
    Standing on the dune where Mesdag painted his Panorama, **Seinpost**
(*Zeekant 60* ☎ *(070) 555250* ▥▥ ⒶⒺ ① ⓪ ⓥⓘⓢⓐ *closed Sat lunch, Sun,
Mon*) offers the double attraction of a splendid sea view and exquisite
cuisine.
    An unexpected cluster of restaurants is located in the former fish
auction shed overlooking Scheveningen's harbor, including the
excellent **Golden Duck** (*Dr Lelykade 29* ☎ *(070) 541095* ▯ ⒶⒺ ①
⓪ *closed Tues*), where you can watch the sun set while
experimenting with the cuisine of Canton, Peking or Szechwan.
Inexpensive meals can be enjoyed at the tasteful **Brasserie Luden**

(*Frederikstraat 34* ☎ *(070) 601733* □ AE ⊕ ⊚ VISA *closed Sat lunch and Sun lunch*), the informal **Charcoal** (*Denneweg 130* ☎ *(070) 659788* □ *last orders 11pm*) or the vegetarian **Hortus** (*Prins Hendrikstraat 53* ☎ *(070) 456736* □ *last orders 8.45pm; closed lunch and Mon*), which offers an imaginative variety of international dishes in an elegant interior reminiscent of a winter garden.

▣ Old-fashioned courtesy is still found at the comfortable café **De Posthoorn** (*Lange Voorhout 39a, open 8am–1am*), where graying ex-cabinet ministers, artists and locals engage in animated disputes. On summer days, the chestnut-shaded terrace is particularly attractive. A similar mood pervades the café **Corona** (*Buitenhof 40–42*), which offers a bright street terrace and a darker wood-paneled interior. Another survival from grander days is the **Kurhaus** café in Scheveningen, which occupies a corner of the magnificent frescoed Kurzaal, where stars such as Edith Piaf, Duke Ellington and Marlene Dietrich have performed.

Describing itself as a *café-tabac animé*, **Schlemmer** (*Lange Houtstraat 17, open Mon–Wed 9.30am–8pm, Thurs–Sun 9.30am–1am*) was launched a few years ago to provide Den Haag with a literary café. The atmosphere is relaxed, meals (including Sun brunch) are served, and there is a pleasant garden at the back. Close to Centraal Station, **Lloyd's Loom** (*Herengracht 48, open 11am–1am*) is a modern white café popular with both office workers and students from the nearby art school.

Nightlife and the arts

At night a deadly hush descends on Den Haag as if a curfew has been imposed, and what nightlife there is tends to maintain a rather low profile, except in Scheveningen. Two lively, late cafés are found on the Dunne Bierkade, a nostalgic stretch of canal that has survived intact: **De Paas**, located in a 16thC building once owned by the landscape artist Jan van Goyen, attracts connoisseurs with its 90 types of beer and 40 brands of whisky; and **De Pakschuit**, a civilized café with an open fire, occupies a warehouse where goods were stored prior to shipment by *trekschuit* to Amsterdam.

Those searching for the atmosphere of the North Sea Jazz Festival should head for the jazz café **No Problem** (*Sumatrastraat 14, open 8am–2am*), run by Miss Kaboeia who is herself a singer.

Discos include **Confetti's** (*Lange Houtstraat 15*) and nearby **Toys** (*Casuariestraat 1*), both catering to youngish swingers.

Classic films are screened in the **Haags Filmhuis** (*Denneweg 56* ☎ *(070) 459900*), which is worth a visit simply for its magnificent Art Nouveau architecture.

Shopping

Major department stores, including a large branch of De Bijenkorf designed in 1926 by the Amsterdam School architect P. L. Kramer, are located on Grote Markt. Smaller boutiques are found along Lange Poten and its continuations Spuistraat and Vlamingstraat. Noordeinde, a pleasant street rich in Art Nouveau details, boasts some exclusive boutiques, antique shops and art galleries, while the Denneweg, which runs N from the former palace on Lange Voorhout, contains a lively mixture of antique shops, art galleries, boutiques, cafés and restaurants. The exclusive department store **Bonneterie en Pander** (*corner of Gravenstraat and Groenmarkt*) and the Neo-Renaissance Passage opposite are the last vestiges of Parisian elegance.

Shops near the Kurhaus in Scheveningen are usually open in the evenings and on Sun.

Haarlem

Map 2B3. Noord-Holland, 23km (14 miles) w of Amsterdam. Population: 152,500. Getting there: By train, 15mins from Amsterdam Centraal Station; by car, on A5 **i** *Stationsplein 1* ☎ *(023) 319059.*

Despite being almost a suburb of Amsterdam, Haarlem is a rather quiet and provincial city which has hardly changed since the 17thC. Its main claims to fame are the beautiful **Frans**

Hals Museum, the overwhelming **Grote Kerk** and the curious **Teylers Museum**. It is also a rewarding town to explore, especially s and w of Grote Markt, where narrow brick-paved streets are lined with rosy Renaissance gables, curious old-fashioned shops and secluded *hofjes*.

Sights and places of interest
Tour of the main sights
Perhaps the best approach is from the station (a grand Art Nouveau building built in 1908) down Jansweg, which passes the impressive **Hofje van Staats** (*Jansweg 39*) built in Louis XIV style in 1730, and then crosses the former moat to enter the old city. On the right is the 14thC **Janskerk** (*Jansstraat 38*), where the 15thC painter Geertgen tot Sint Jans lived. A tangle of crooked lanes to the E surrounds the 14thC **Waalsekerk** (formerly the Begijnhof chapel), which retains its charm despite a number of brothels in the vicinity. Towards the end of Jansstraat, notice the beautiful **portal of the St Barbara Gasthuis** (*Jansstraat 54*), with a colorful relief showing the interior of this 17thC hospital.

Turn left at the Grote Kerk and head down Damstraat to the river Spaarne, where you find the rugged 1598 **Waag** (weigh house), attributed to Lieven de Key, the **Teylers Museum** and the picturesque **Gravestenenbrug**. Cross the bridge and turn left along Spaarnwouderstraat to reach the unexpected **Amsterdamse Poort**, a 15thC city gate. Bakenessergracht is also worth a glance, particularly the exquisite late Gothic spire of the **Bakenesserkerk**. But the best of Haarlem lies s of Grote Markt: head down the homey Warmoesstraat (notice the patterned sidewalks) to Schagchelstraat, then across Gedempte Oude Gracht (formerly the town moat) and down the gently curving Groot Heiligland. The **Omvalspoort**, squeezed between Groot Heiligland 22 and 24, is a particularly attractive medieval lane. Facing the **Frans Hals Museum** are the **Gasthuishuisjes**, a harmonious row of 12 identical step gables, built about 1610 for the St Elisabeth's Gasthuis. (Notice the 1612 facade stone at Groot Heiligland 47 showing a woman being carried into the hospital on a stretcher, and the inscription: "Bodily sickness is a medicine for the soul.")

Continue w along Ravelingsteeg and Cornelissteeg to reach the spacious **Proveniershuis**, formerly belonging to the civic guard of St George (painted several times by Frans Hals), and converted to a home for old people in 1707. Continue w along Kerkstraat, at the end of which looms the grim Classical facade of the **Nieuwe Kerk**, erected by Jacob van Campen in 1645–49 alongside a jaunty Renaissance tower designed by Lieven de Key in 1613. Head N along Lange Annastraat, past the compact **Hofje van Guurtje de Waal** with its 1661 portal, and the 1586 **Brouwershofje** with its bright red and white shutters (*both open to the public*). Farther N, the former **Kloveniersdoelen**, rebuilt by Lieven de Key in 1612, is indicated by the crossed muskets above the entrance on Gasthuisstraat (*courtyard open to the public*). The civic guard of St Adrian, which was the subject of Frans Hals' finest group portrait, met here to exercise and banquet.

Turn right along Zuiderstraat and then continue along Jacobijnestraat, past a former monastic garden, which in the 18thC was planted with medicinal herbs. The monastery was once used by William of Orange as his residence (Prinsenhof), and its cloister (entered from Grote Markt) now forms part of the Stadhuis (town hall). An ideal place to pause is in one of the many cafés on the N side of Grote Markt, after which continue w down Zijlstraat to reach Witte Herenstraat, where you find the **Frans Loenenhofje** with its 1625 portal in Dutch Renaissance style, and the **Luthershofje** (*open to the public*), which contains an open-air pulpit that is attached to the Lutheran Church.

Frans Hals Museum ★

Groot Heiligland 62 ☎ (023) 319180 🔲 🔲 🚶 *in De Witstraat. Open Mon–Sat 11am–5pm, Sun, hols 1–5pm.*

The Frans Hals Museum is located in the beautiful Oudemannenhuis, a home for old men, built in 1608 by Lieven de Key. It retains several rooms in 17thC style overlooking exactly the sort of dull formal garden that caused David Hume to grumble in 1748 that: "Nothing can be more disagreeable than the heap of Dirt & Mud & Ditches & Reeds, which they here call a country, except the silly collection of shells and clipt evergreens which they call a garden."

The museum possesses a distinguished collection of Dutch paintings, including eight large group portraits by the Haarlem artist Frans Hals (1580–1666) which illustrate the development of his style. The earliest group portrait is the rather stiff *Banquet of the Officers of the Civic Guard of St George* (no. 123), painted in 1616 when Frans Hals was 36. By 1627, when he painted the *Banquet of the Officers of the Civic Guard of St Adrian* (no. 125) and again the *Officers of St George* (no. 124), his style had become more animated. His finest work is undoubtedly the 1633 *Assembly of Officers and Subalterns of the Civic Guard of St George* (no. 126), which shows the Kloveniersdoelen, where they met, in the background. The last group portrait, showing again the officers of the civic guard of St George, was painted in 1639 in a rather stiff style (no. 127). It includes a somewhat apprehensive self-portrait behind the two rotund officers at the bottom left. When in 1641 Frans Hals painted the *Governors of the St Elisabeth Hospital* (no. 128), he adopted a particularly somber style to depict the black-clothed officials who administered the hospital directly opposite the museum. His last group portraits, showing the governors (no. 129) and governesses (no. 130) of the Oudemannenhuis, were painted in 1664 when Frans Hals was himself an old man under their care. The bitterness of these works – notice the caustic depiction of a drunkard, with his hat set at a rakish angle – is sadly out of keeping with his cheerful early works.

Another painter to look out for is Jan van Scorel, who during a brief period of exile in Haarlem in the late 1520s painted the *Knightly Brotherhood of the Holy Land* (which includes a self-portrait, third from the right).

Haarlem artists of the 16thC included Cornelis Cornelisz. van Haarlem and the remarkable Maerten van Heemskerck, whose eccentric Mannerism is illustrated by the study of St Luke (patron saint of artists) painting the Virgin and Child. Hendrick Cornelisz. Vroom, also from Haarlem, captured the bustling prosperity of the 17thC in his maritime painting of the arrival of the Elector Palatine's fleet at Vlissingen in 1616, and in his view of Haarlem from the Noorder Spaarne. Jan van Goyen suggests a more sleepy mood in his 1649 *River Scene*, with a gently crumbling town (probably Leiden) in the background. The views of Haarlem by Gerrit Berckheyde, on the other hand, convey an almost surreal perfection.

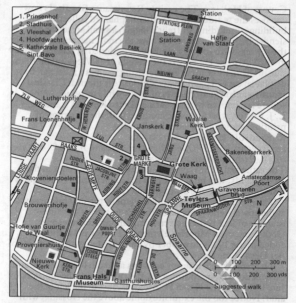

Key to map:
1. Prinsenhof
2. Stadhuis
3. Vleeshal
4. Hoofdwacht
5. Kathedrale Basiliek Sint Bavo

Grote Kerk ★
23 Oude Groenmarkt. Open Mon–Sat 10am–4pm, closed Sun.

Rising magnificently above the city is the Grote Kerk, one of the most popular subjects of Dutch painting. The oldest part is the late **14thC choir**, built of rough-hewn stone on the site of a 12thC church. Its **nave** dates from the 15thC, while the curious **Renaissance Baptistry** on the S side was added by Lieven de Key in 1600. The **spire** is a delicate late Gothic ornament built in 1520.

Perhaps the most remarkable feature of the church is the cheerful muddle of small shops clustered around the walls. At one time there were 37 separate shops that the church rented out to greengrocers, clog-makers, spectacle-sellers and the like. The church also received an income from the fish market (*Vishal*) which was built in 1603 against the N wall of the church.

Another curious feature of the Grote Kerk is its tiny entrance on the picturesque S side, from which a narrow corridor leads into the vast and rather bleak church, with its pavement of gray tombstones and its stark whitewashed walls. Most of the Gothic sculpture was destroyed during the Reformation, to be replaced by notice boards inscribed with the names of church officials in fine calligraphy.

The glory of the Grote Kerk is its **organ**, built by Christian Müller in 1738 and lavishly decorated with Baroque sculpture by Jan van Logteren. The organ, with its 4,295 pipes, has been played by Handel, Mozart (aged ten), Liszt and Saint-Saëns (*concerts Tues 8.15–9.15pm, Thurs 3–4pm.*).

Grote Markt
Haarlem's breezy main square stands on the site of a medieval tilting yard formerly overlooked by a hunting lodge of the

Counts of Holland. The mainly Renaissance **Stadhuis** now encloses the W side with its rather haphazard collection of buildings, including an Italian loggia, a small arcade and a slender late Gothic spire. Perhaps the most harmonious part is the N wing, with its lofty chimneys, designed by Lieven de Key in 1620. Also by De Key is the riotous 1603 **Vleeshal** on the S side of the market square, advertising itself as a meat hall by a display of carved oxen heads. Opposite is the neat Classical **Hoofdwacht** (guardhouse) of 1650, while the E side of the square is enclosed by the soaring **Grote Kerk**. A statue of L. J. Coster, who was once credited with the invention of printing, stands alongside the church.

Kathedrale Basiliek Sint Bavo
Leidsevaart 146 🎦 *Open Apr–Oct 9.30am–noon, 2–4.30pm. Bus 4, 8 from station to Emmastraat.*

The cathedral of St Bavo, one of the largest churches in the Netherlands, was built by Jos. Th. Cuypers in 1895 in a quiet residential area to the SW of the old city.

The picturesque confusion of chapels, turrets and gargoyles at the apsed E end (best seen from Emmastraat) is a fine example of late 19thC eclecticism, mixing Romanesque, Gothic and even Moorish elements. The towers at the W end, added in the 1920s, are sober by comparison, with just a hint of Art Deco at the top.

The remarkable interior contains a wealth of late 19thC and early 20thC art, including a set of Art Nouveau tile tableaux by Jan Toorop in the Kapel H. Aloysius, just to the left of the altar. Notice too the exquisite dome above the crossing, with its almost Moorish delicacy.

Teylers Museum ★
Spaarne 16 ☎ *(023) 316851* 🏛 🖾 *Open Tues–Sat 10am–5pm, Sun, hols 1–5pm. Closes 4pm Oct–Feb.*

The Teylers Museum is located E of the Grote Kerk on Haarlem's river, the winding Binnen Spaarne. Founded in 1778 by the wealthy draper Pieter Teyler van der Hulst, this ancient, gloomy relic with its splendid round entrance hall and Neoclassical Oval Room, is the oldest museum in the Netherlands. Its huge collection of scientific instruments, fossils and minerals was a model of enlightened 18thC thinking, but it all seems rather dull and melancholy now, particularly as the museum has stubbornly refused to make any concessions to modernity. Where else but in Haarlem would you still find museum rooms lit only by natural light filtering through grimy skylight windows, forcing the museum to close one hour earlier in winter months? But for those who enjoy such anachronisms and can stomach the creaking sepulchral gloom, Teylers Museum is worth a cautious detour.

The museum also has an extensive collection of drawings, including works by Raphael, Michelangelo and Lorrain, though only a few of these are ever displayed. The collection was augmented by paintings by the Dutch Romantics and Impressionists, including Breitner, Josef Israels and Weissenbruch. There are also some attractive views of cities by the museum's former curator, Wybrand Hendriks. Since the paintings are seen only by natural light, it is worth choosing a bright day to view the collection.

On leaving the museum, the spirit is lifted by a picturesque white wooden bridge across the Buiten Spaarne, overlooked by a pair of merry step gables that belonged to a 17thC brewery, De Oliphant (The Elephant).

➤ Worth noting among Haarlem's restaurants is **De Coninckshoek** (*Koningstraat 1–5* ☎ *(023) 314001* ∎∎ ∆∃ ⊙ ∨∃∆ *last orders 11pm; closed Sun*). This building was for some 300 years a wine merchant's shop. John and Marianne van Meurs converted the premises to a restaurant in 1972, with wood-paneled walls and leaded glass windows, and a splendid Mannerist fireplace that looks big enough to roast an ox. **De Coninckshoek** offers French *nouvelle cuisine* using local produce and takes advantage of its proximity to the port of IJmuiden to offer various fish specialties. The portions are generous and there is a wide range of interesting wines.

A beautiful late Gothic arch leads into the former Bank van Lening (lending bank), which has been expertly converted into a restaurant: **Peter Cuyper** (*Kleine Houtstraat 70* ☎ *(023) 320885* ∎∎ ∆∃ ⊙ *last orders 11pm; closed Sun, Mon*) has a pleasant brick-paved inner courtyard where you can enjoy an apéritif if the weather permits. Since you can almost smell the North Sea in Haarlem it is worth sampling a fish dish such as the *filets de sole cuits en croûte*.

◼ Haarlem's most popular cafés are mainly ranked along the N side of Grote Markt. Probably the most famous is the café-restaurant **De Kroon** (*Grote Markt 13, open Mon–Sat 9am–1pm*), occupying a 19thC neo-Renaissance building which fastidiously copies the bustling Mannerism of the Vleeshal on the opposite side of the square. The interior has been tastefully modernized and offers 13 types of coffee, a spicy local apple cake and almost anything else you might need. The nearby café-restaurant **Carillon** (*Grote Markt 27, open 7.30am–2am*) also offers a varied menu in an Old Dutch interior with wood paneling, comfortable armchairs and dim Art Deco cinema lamps.

Farther E is the **Proeflokaal De Uiver** (*Riviervischmarkt 13, open Mon–Sat 10am–2am, Sun 4pm–2am*), a tasting house located in a former fishmonger's shop, which boasts a magnificent tile tableau of fishing boats as well as some curious relics of Douglas DC-2 aircraft. **'t Stadscafé** (*Zijlstraat 56, open Mon–Sat 8am–midnight, Sun 2pm–midnight*) looks reassuringly old with its 1900 Art Nouveau facade, plump sofas and antique clocks, but in fact it only became a café in 1985. Equally deceptive is the **Café 1900** (*Barteljorisstraat 10, open 9am–1pm*), a former cinema that has been skillfully transformed into a Parisian-style café complete with round marble-topped tables, gleaming brass fittings and a fascinating mechanism for operating the ceiling fans that looks as if it belongs in the Teylers Museum.

Finally, do not leave Haarlem without glancing at the 1908 Art Nouveau station restaurant, which is the pride and joy of the Dutch railway system. Haarlem Station originally boasted no fewer than five waiting rooms, namely first, second, third class, women and lunatics.

Shopping

Haarlem's stubborn resistance to progress has left it with a number of traditional 18th and 19thC shop interiors which are a pleasure to enter even if only to buy a tube of toothpaste. Among many old-fashioned tobacconists are **W. H. Voet en Zonen** (*Kruisstraat 39*), located in an ornate Neoclassical interior, and **Prinsenhof** (*Jacobijnestraat 8*), named after the nearby building where William of Orange stayed in 1580. Haarlem-made Droste products, including cocoa sold in tins decorated with a nun, are available at **Haarlemmer Halletjes** (*Kruisstraat 37*), while traditional Dutch *drop* (liquorice) is, for some obscure health reason, sold at pharmacists (*drogisterijen*) such as **A. J. van der Pigge** (*Gierstraat 3*).

Antique shops, which Haarlem has in abundance, congregate in Zijlstraat, Kruisstraat and the area S of Grote Markt. Book-lovers should make a point of visiting **H. de Vries** (*Gedempte Oude Gracht 27*), which is furnished in the style of a 17thC Dutch painting, with brass chandeliers, solid oak furniture and old stone fireplaces. Though this shop is particularly famous for its books on sport, it also offers a good range of art books and English novels.

For chain stores, the main shopping street is Grote Houtstraat, which runs S from Grote Markt and passes close to the main department store, **Vroom & Dreesmann** (*Gedempte Oude Gracht*). Barteljorisstraat has a few slightly more unusual fashion shops.

Hoorn

Noord-Holland, 43km (27 miles) N of Amsterdam.
Population: 50,470. Getting there: By train, 30mins from
Amsterdam Centraal Station; by car, through IJ-tunnel, then
A7 i Nieuwstraat 23 ☎ (02290) 18342.

Hoorn was one of the foremost Dutch ports in the 17thC and
produced a host of mariners and explorers, including Willem
Schouten, who named Cape Horn after his home town; Abel
Tasman, who discovered Tasmania and New Zealand; and Jan
Pieterszoon Coen, who founded the Dutch colony of Batavia,
now the Indonesian capital Jakarta. After the silting of the
Zuider Zee in the late 17thC, Hoorn's fortunes rapidly
declined and it became in the 19thC one of the famous dead
towns of the Zuider Zee. In recent years, however, Hoorn has
risen from the grave and it is now a bustling center for
excursions on the IJsselmeer.

During the summer months (mid-June to mid-Sept)
gleaming steam trains depart from Hoorn railway station amid
clouds of black smoke and head N to the port of Medemblik.
Passenger boats connect Medemblik with Enkhuizen railway
station, so that it is possible to make a round trip in either
direction. Contact NS (Dutch Railways) for details of special
excursion rates.

Not to be outdone, an enterprising skipper has restored the
jaunty steam tug *Gabriëlle*, built in Brandenburg in 1903.
Excursions (*late June – Aug Wed and Sun afternoon only*) depart
from the pier in front of the Hoofdtoren.

For information about excursions on traditional wooden
sailing boats, contact **Lagemaat Schepenverhuur**
(*☎ (02290) 17695*).

Sights and places of interest
The harbors

From the railway station, follow signs to "Havens" to reach
the Westerdijk, which follows the broad sweeping bay known
as the Hoornsche Hop. The dike leads eventually to the plump,
round **Hoofdtoren**, built in 1532 to protect the harbor and
adorned with a bell tower in 1651. The sculptural group on the
harbor wall shows three boys from a seafaring romance set in
the 17thC.

Veermanskade has a splendid row of step-gabled merchants'
houses dating from the early 17thC when Hoorn's prosperity
was at its peak. A pleasant detour can be made along
Korenmarkt; then cross the bridge to reach Bierkade, where
the warehouse **Dantzig** at no. 8 dates from the time when
Hanseatic ships unloaded beer shipments on this quay.

Returning to the harbor, turn left, then pass two jaunty
Renaissance houses at Oudedoelenkade 17–19 and 21, with
ships carved on the gable stones and names indicating that the
merchant on the left traded with the Baltic while his neighbor
dealt with the Mediterranean. Cross the wooden bridge on the
right at the end of the harbor and continue straight ahead to
reach the former Chamber of the Dutch West India Company,
sited in a rather isolated spot. From here walk back along the
promontory known as Baatland to obtain a superb panorama of
the harbor front.

After recrossing the bridge, continue straight ahead down
Slapershaven to discover the curious three houses known as
the **Bossuhuizen**, which are decorated with magnificent
friezes depicting the Battle of the Zuider Zee in 1573 at which a

fleet of Dutch rebels defeated Admiral Bossu's Spanish fleet.
The town
After completing the harbor route, explore the rest of the town
by turning left along Grote Oost, a dignified street of mainly
18thC houses running from the splendid 1578 Oosterpoort to
the **Rode Steen**. Side streets such as Schoolstraat provide
picturesque distractions, but do not miss the theatrical 17thC
Staten-College (now the Westfries Museum) or the dignified
Waag on Rode Steen, the main square of Hoorn.

Kerkstraat runs N from here past the Renaissance facade of
the **St Jans Gasthuis**, built as a hospital in 1563. Behind the
19thC **Grote Kerk**, which now contains shops and
apartments, are two 17thC gates, one of which gave access to
the Admiralty offices, while the other was the entrance to a
home for elderly women. Both buildings were established in
former convents, which were abolished under the
Reformation.

A picturesque lane leads through a former cloister to
Nieuwstraat. The **Statenpoort** at Nieuwstraat 23 was built in
Dutch Renaissance style in 1613 as the meeting place for
representatives from the seven cities of West Friesland.
Nearby, in Muntstraat, is the late 17thC office of the Hoorn
Chamber of the Dutch East India Company. Continue N along
Korte Achterstraat, passing the Protestant Orphanage, where
Admiral Bossu was imprisoned after the Battle of the Zuider
Zee. Farther N is the 17thC hall of the Guild of St Sebastian.
Turn left at the end of this street and you will come across the
attractive Munnickenveld, with a small *hofje* which was
founded in 1682.
Westfries Museum ★
*Rode Steen 1 ☎(02290) 15597 ☒ Open Mon–Fri
11am–5pm, Sat, Sun 2–5pm.*

The museum of West Friesland is devoted to the history of the
area N of the IJ, bounded to the w by the North Sea and to the
E by the IJsselmeer (formerly the Zuider Zee). The museum
occupies the splendid 1632 College of the States of West
Friesland, a dazzling masterpiece of Dutch Mannerism. The
growling lions that hold aloft the coats of arms of the seven
cities of West Friesland (Alkmaar, Hoorn, Enkhuizen,
Medemblik, Edam, Monnickendam and Purmerend) are a
reminder of the former importance of these now slumbering
satellites of Amsterdam. Though the exhibits are labeled only
in Dutch, the Westfries Museum is well worth visiting to catch
the flavor of the Golden Age.

The chilly 14thC cellars (rms 1–5) are all that survive of the
house on this site occupied by the representative of the Bishop
of Utrecht. Among the facade stones salvaged from
demolished buildings are two ornate 17thC stones, one
showing Mary Queen of Scots and her unfortunate husband
Darnley, the other, which may once have decorated the house
of a Scottish merchant resident in Hoorn, depicting James I
and Anne of Denmark.

The three floors directly above preserve fine 17thC
Mannerist paneled rooms, connected by steep staircases that
creak like old galleons. The delegates of the seven cities used to
assemble in the magnificent room at the front of the building
(rm 7), which is now overwhelmed by huge 17thC Civic Guard
group portraits. The attic (rm 12) is also appealing, and offers
intriguing glimpses of the open water on one side and the Waag
and Grote Kerk on the other.

The final rooms occupy the 18thC Rococo annex and are furnished in various French styles, with pastel colors and delicate moldings that contrast vividly with the bold detailing and robust construction of the 17thC rooms.

🍽 In an area of Holland in which eating well is sometimes regarded as a deadly sin, **De Oude Rosmolen** (*Duinsteeg 1 (off Nieuwe Noord)* ☎*(02290) 14752* 𝄆𝄇 ▮ ▮ ▮ *last orders 9.30pm; closed lunch and Thurs*), a small restaurant located in a characteristic 17thC house, is unique. The friendly owner, Constant Fonk, claims a lifelong dedication to all aspects of the culinary arts, displaying a photograph of himself as a young boy proudly bearing a birthday cake he had baked. The inventive cuisine, carefully selected wines (including some rare white wines from Dutch Limburg) and a groaning cart of home-made gateaux amply demonstrate his commitment. Nor does the experience end with dessert: coffee is served with an irresistible selection of *petits fours*.

Located directly opposite Hoorn railway station, **Azië** (*Veemarkt 49* ☎*(02290) 18555* ▯ ▮ ▮ ▮ *last orders 11pm*) offers exquisite Chinese cuisine, ranging from delicate Cantonese to fiery Szechuan dishes, together with a range of *rijsttafels*. The specialty menu, offering a range of unusual dishes, is particularly good value.

Shopping

Most shops are located on the pedestrianized Grote Noord. Schoolstraat contains an interesting cluster of antique shops, including one that specializes in dolls and another that sells Wurlitzers, street organs and circus paraphernalia. Hoorn's most attractive shop is **P. Kaag Antz.** (*Breed 38*), selling tea, coffee and tobacco in a beautiful 19thC building with a gable stone showing a horse-drawn barge.

Leiden

Map 2D2. Zuid-Holland, 41km (26 miles) sw of Amsterdam. Population: 104,260. Getting there: By train, 30mins from Amsterdam Centraal Station, RAI or Zuid WTC; by car, on A4 **i** *Stationsplein 210* ☎*(071) 146846.*

Located on a branch of the Rhine, Leiden was a very prosperous city in the Middle Ages due to its cloth and beer industries. In 1573–74 the city, besieged by the Spanish, was eventually relieved in Oct 1574 when William of Orange broke the dikes to flood the surrounding countryside, allowing Admiral Boisot's fleet to sail up to the city walls.

In recognition of Leiden's stoic stand against the Spanish, William granted the town its own university, the first to be established in Holland. As a result Leiden became a major center of Protestant learning in the 17th–18thC, and its intellectual and religious tolerance attracted refugees such as the printer Louis Elsevier from the southern Netherlands. It was here, too, that the Pilgrim Fathers, led by John Robinson, settled in 1609 before they departed for the New World in 1620.

The names of numerous artists are linked with Leiden, including Jan van Goyen, Gabriel Metsu, Jan Steen (who ran a tavern on Lange Brug) and Rembrandt, born here in 1606.

Like the untidy study of a forgetful professor, the old city of Leiden now possesses a somewhat disheveled charm, which is best preserved in the narrow streets around the two enormous churches. Despite several heroic attempts at restoration, Leiden seems to be in permanent decline, and even in the 17thC paintings of Jan van Goyen has an air of neglect. Perhaps this is only superficial, however, for in the secluded world of Leiden's *hofjes* a brisk orderliness reigns, while its museums catalog everything from stuffed birds to clay pipes with an academic precision.

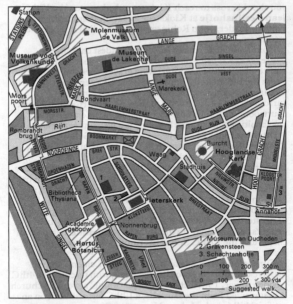

1. Museum van Oudheden
2. Gravensteen
3. Schachtenhofje

0   100   200   300 m
0   100   200   300 yds
Suggested walk

Sights and places of interest
The town
Boat tours of Leiden (*mid-June to early Sept*) depart from
Beestenmarkt, skirting the edge of the old city on the outward
journey and returning through the city along the Rhine.
However, you have to walk through the town to discover the
hidden *hofjes* and picturesque corners and lanes that are the
particular charm of Leiden.

From Beestenmarkt, head down Morsstraat to the 17thC
Morspoort and turn left to reach the **Rembrandtbrug**, whose
name recalls that Rembrandt was born just s of here in 1606.
However, the only building hereabouts that Rembrandt might
have seen is the **Renaissance house** built in 1612 on the
Stadstimmerwerf, where the municipal carpenters worked.
Head s down Weddesteeg and Rembrandtstraat to
Groenhazengracht, a picturesque canal of crumbling brick
houses. The figure of St George adorns a flamboyant gateway
that once led to the Civic Guard exercise ground.

Continue to Rapenburg and turn right past the dignified
Bibliotheca Thysiana, a pleasing 17thC Classical building
designed by Arend van 's-Gravesande, to reach the
Academiegebouw, a former convent chapel which was given to
the university in 1581.

One of Leiden's secret delights is its **Hortus Botanicus**
(*Rapenburg 73; open daily; closed Sat Oct–Mar*), one of the
world's oldest botanical gardens, dating from 1575. A
reconstruction of the original garden, the Clusiustuin (named
after the 17thC Leiden botanist Carolus Clusius), is reached
from the main garden by a bridge. From here, follow
Zegersteeg and Kaiserstraat to reach the picturesque spot
where the river Vliet enters the city. Follow the river N to
Rapenburg, then turn left to reach the Nonnenbrug, which

159

you should cross to reach Kloksteeg. A plaque on the 17thC
Jean Pesijnshofje at Kloksteeg 21 recalls that the Pilgrim
Fathers' leader, John Robinson, lived and died in a house that
stood here.

Dominating the square is Leiden's oldest church, the
Pieterskerk (*open 1.30–4pm*), a gracefully soaring 15thC
edifice which has a few interesting gravestones and guild relics.
From the Pieterskerk, head w past the **Gravensteen**, a
picturesque jumble of buildings of various vintages
surrounding a 14thC prison of the Counts of Holland. Former
courtrooms and cells now accommodate Leiden university's
law faculty. Opposite the building is a pleasant *koffiehuis*.

On the corner of Schoolsteeg is the **Latin School** which
Rembrandt attended from 1614–20. It was built in 1599 by
Lieven de Key, as was the splendid 1595 **Stadhuis** on
Breestraat, which can be reached along Pieterskerkchoorsteeg.
Beyond the Stadhuis, turn left and cross the Nieuwe Rijn by
the Koornbrug, then continue right to Middelstegracht, a
filled-in canal that formed part of an ambitious 17thC
extension plan modeled on that of Amsterdam. The grandeur
of Amsterdam was never attained, however, and the main
delights on this canal are the 16thC **St Annahof** with its own
chapel and the 17thC **Schachtenhofje** (*both open to the
public*).

Turn left down Kloosterpoort to reach Leiden's second
massive church, the **Hooglandsekerk**, with its curious 14thC
wooden tower, 15thC choir and squat 16thC nave. The church
is best viewed from the **Burcht**, a 12thC fortress built on an
artificial hill (reached along Nieuwstraat).

Boerhaave, Museum
Reopens 1990 in the restored Caeciliacomplex.
Named after Leiden's distinguished professor of medicine
Herman Boerhaave (1666–1738), the museum reflects the
intense scientific atmosphere at Leiden University with its
marvelous collection of globes, planetaria, apothecaries' jars,
clocks, microscopes and surgical instruments.

Rijksmuseum van Oudheden ★
*Rapenburg 28 ☎ (071) 146246 ▨ ሌ Open Tues–Sat
10 am–5pm, Sun, hols 1–5pm.*
Founded in 1818, the national museum of antiquities contains
objects from the ancient civilizations of the Mediterranean,
together with archeological finds from the Netherlands.

The Egyptian Temple of Taffeh forms a dramatic and
somewhat menacing centerpiece to the collection. Built in the
district of Nubia in the 1stC AD, the temple shows evidence of
alterations made in the 4thC when winged sun-discs and
friezes of crowned cobras were added by worshipers of the
goddess Ibis. It was later used as a Christian temple and finally
as a house before being dismantled in 1960 during the
construction of the Aswan dams. It was then presented to the
Netherlands in recognition of Dutch assistance in the rescue of
the Nile temples.

The museum's **Ancient Egyptian collection** has always
been its chief glory and includes numerous mummies,
sarcophagi, tombs and chapels, as well as less gloomy relics
such as writing equipment and toys. The three statues from the
tomb of Tutankhamun's minister, Maya, are particularly
impressive.

The Ancient Roman rooms contain several interesting finds
from the Netherlands, such as the remarkable **Simpelveld**

sarcophagus, decorated inside with reliefs of a reclining figure surrounded by various pieces of furniture. Other remarkable finds are the altars dedicated to the goddess of merchants and seamen, Nehallennia. These were lifted from the sea off the coast of Zeeland in 1970.

An unusual feature is the **Panorama of Archeology,** which presents parallel displays of artifacts from different civilizations from 5000BC to AD500.

Rijksmuseum voor Volkenkunde

Steenstraat 1 ☎ *(071) 211824* 🖼 📷 *Open Tues–Sat 10am–5pm, Sun, hols 1–5pm.*

The rather old-fashioned Dutch national museum of ethnography is in the throes of modernization. Nevertheless it is worth a visit for its excellent **Japanese lacquer boxes** (the museum was founded by the first European allowed to travel freely in Japan), its **furnished rooms** from Japan, Korea and Nepal, the **South American exhibits** and **Javanese sculpture** – a curious blend of Hindu and Buddhist art.

Stedelijk Molenmuseum De Valk

2de Binnenvestgracht 1 ☎ *(071) 254639* 🖼 ✳ ◁€ *Open Tues–Sat 10am–5pm, Sun, hols 1–5pm.*

This imposing 8-story-high working corn windmill was erected in 1743 on a bastion on the N edge of the city. It now houses an interesting museum of milling, with furnished living quarters on the ground floor, and storage and machinery rooms on the upper floors. The ascent by steep wooden steps is rewarded by a panoramic view of Leiden.

Stedelijk Museum De Lakenhal ★

Oude Singel 28–32 ☎ *(071) 254620* 🖼 *Open Tues–Sat 10am–5pm, Sun, hols 1–5pm.*

Leiden's municipal museum is housed in the former cloth hall, an attractive building in sober Dutch Classical style designed by Arend van 's-Gravesande in 1640.

The Lakenhal is best known for the **triptych** by Lucas van Leyden of the *Last Judgment* (rm S17). Painted for the Pieterskerk in 1526, this work shows a hesitant transition from Gothic to Renaissance style. Among the interesting 17thC works (rm S18) is a view of Leiden by Jan van Goyen and several "Vanity" pieces, whose morbid symbolism seems to have appealed to Leiden's collectors.

The **tile collection** (rms L3–4) illustrates the development of designs from the complex Islamic styles favored in the southern Netherlands in the 16thC to the whimsical blue Holland tiles of the 17thC.

The Lakenhal also contains several attractive period rooms, including an **18thC kitchen** (rm L7), the Louis XIV style **Groene Papezaal** (rm P23) and the mainly Louis XVI style **Gele Papezaal** (rm P24). Of the 17thC rooms on the first floor, the **Grote Pers** (L8) is the grandest, but the intimate **Staalmeesterskamer** (L10), where the syndics of the cloth guild met, is somehow more attractive. On the opposite side of the main hall is the charming **Bierbrouwerskamer** (L13), which was rescued from the demolished brewers' guild hall, with delightful 18thC paintings showing harvesting of the hops, the malting house, the brewery, transporting the beer, and the malting mill, De Juffer.

The historical collection (L15) contains some interesting maps of Leiden and a series of paintings by Isaac Swanenburg illustrating the cloth trade. The courtyard in front of the building, where the quality of cloth was examined in daylight, contains an intriguing collection of old gable stones, including one curiosity illustrating the five senses.

For overnight stays the **Nieuw Minerva** (*Boommarkt 23* ☎ *(071) 126358* ⬛ AE ⊡ ⬛ VISA) is a friendly hotel located in a row of 17thC houses overlooking the Rhine. A comfortable modern alternative, but only accessible by car, is the **Ibis** (*Elisabethhof 4, Leiderdorp* ☎ *(071) 414141* ☎ *30251* ⬛ ⬛ ⭢ ⬛ AE ⊡ ⬛ VISA), 2km (1 mile) SE of Leiden.

Leiden's most respected restaurant, **Oudt Leyden** (*Steenstraat 51* ☎ *(071) 133144* ⬜ *to* ⬛ AE ⊡ ⬛ *last orders 10pm; closed Sat lunch* (*Rôtisserie*) *and Sun*), is divided into a sophisticated *nouvelle cuisine Rôtisserie* and a modestly priced crêperie-restaurant, *'t-Pannekoekenhuisje*. The latter offers an excellent value Tourist Menu, as well as pancakes served on large blue Delft plates.

For Indonesian food try **Surakarta** (*Noordeinde 51* ☎ *(071) 123524* ⬜ AE ⊡ ⬛ VISA *last orders 10pm; closed Mon*), which offers delicate Javanese dishes in a brown café ambience. Students tired of traditional *hutspot* (Dutch stew) head for **Camino Real** (*Doelensteeg 8* ☎ *(071) 149069* ⬜ AE ⊡ ⬛ *last orders 10pm*), a spacious café-restaurant furnished in an eccentric Italian-inspired Post Modern style. Although specializing in Latin American dishes, it also offers traditional *broodjes* (sandwiches), and has the added attraction of a garden.

Interesting cafés include **Harmonie** (*Breestraat 16*), with its 19thC stained-glass windows showing roisterous drinking scenes, and **De Bonte Koe** (*Hooglandsekerkchoorsteeg 31*), a convivial local café decorated with giant tile tableaux of grazing cows. **Barrera** (*Rapenburg 56*) is a pleasant student café, while **Huis de Bijlen** (*Morsstraat 60*) has the double attraction of a spacious terrace and rowboats for rent.

Shopping

Department stores and a few interesting shops are found on Breestraat, while boutiques and chain shops are found along the meandering Haarlemmerstraat, originally a dike along the N bank of the Rhine. Unusual antique shops and specialized antiquarian bookshops abound in the narrow streets around the Pieterskerk.

Marken

*Map **3**B5. 18km (11 miles) NE of Amsterdam. Population: 2,000. Getting there: By NZH bus 111, hourly from Amsterdam Centraal Station; by car, through the IJ-tunnel, then N on E10; by boat, Marken Express, every 45mins from Volendam and Monnickendam Mar–Oct.*

The curious fishing community on the island of Marken in the Zuider Zee was discovered by French travelers in the 19thC, who were amazed at the eccentric locals dressed in bright costumes and living in remarkable black tarred houses on stilts. Soon steamboats were bringing flocks of visitors to the island and Marken became one of the earliest casualties of the tourist industry. Marken suffered a further blow to its identity when the enclosure of the Zuider Zee in 1932 destroyed its fishing industry, and since the construction of a causeway to the mainland in 1957, the community has increasingly become a self-conscious parody of itself.

But Marken is at least not vulgarized, and its tightly packed clusters of houses perched on hillocks (*werven*) are architecturally fascinating. Marken is particularly jolly on Mon, when large quantities of old-fashioned laundry (not a T-shirt or pair of fluorescent socks in sight) are strung along the clotheslines in a manner a touch too regimented to ring true.

The busiest areas of Marken are the **Havenbuurt** (harbor quarter) and **Kerkbuurt** (church quarter), and to the E are quieter *werven* such as **Rozenwerf**. A brisk walk along the dike leads to a lonely lighthouse.

Regular boat services are operated by Marken Express (☎*(02995) 1707*) from Marken to Monnickendam or Volendam. An interesting option for those without a car is the NZH C-toer, a combined boat-bus pass that allows one to take a bus from Amsterdam to Monnickendam, boat from Monnickendam to Marken and from Marken to Volendam, then bus back to Amsterdam (*tickets obtainable from kiosk at Centraal Station, opposite Victoria Hotel*).

Marker Museum
Kerkbuurt 44–47 🖾 & *Open Easter–Oct Mon–Sat 10am–4.30pm, Sun noon–4pm.*
This tiny house packed with bright furniture gives an idea of the remarkably cramped interiors of fishermen's dwellings on Marken. Slide shows (with commentary in English or German) portray life on the island and explain the significance of the local costumes, which range in color from bright red to black depending on the occasion.

🍽 **De Taanderij** (*Havenbuurt 1; open Tues–Sun 10am–9pm; Sept–Easter reduced hrs; closed Mon*) is a pleasant café-restaurant overlooking the harbor, with a pottery in the basement.

Monnickendam
Map 3B4. Noord-Holland, 16km (10 miles) N of Amsterdam. Population 9,500. Getting there: By NZH bus 111 from Amsterdam Centraal Station; by car, through IJ-tunnel, then E10 **i** *De Zarken 2 (in the Grote Kerk tower)* ☎*(02995) 1998 (closed Sun).*
Monnickendam is a small and rather sleepy fishing town with pleasant canals and attractive buildings. The main activity is centered around the harbor, where a few eel smokehouses survive and a ferry departs (*Mar–Oct*) to the former island of Marken (☎*(02995) 1707 for departure times*).

🍴 On Monnickendam's harbor front, where the smell of smoked eel wafts around enticingly, the café-restaurant **Nieuw Stuttenburgh** (*Haringburgwal 4* ☎ *(02995) 1398* ☐ *to* ▮▮ AE ☻ VISA) offers an interesting menu of fish and meat dishes, including the inexpensive *Monnickendammer twaalf uurtje* (a lunch platter of three types of smoked fish). The interior is engagingly eccentric, with its mechanical musical instruments, pond, stuffed alligator and canary.

Rotterdam
Map 2F2. Zuid-Holland, 76km (47 miles) SW of Amsterdam. Population: 555,350. Getting there: By train, 1hr from Amsterdam Centraal Station; by car, on A4, then A13 **i** *Stadhuisplein 19* ☎*(010) 4141400; kiosk at Centraal Station.*
Rotterdam is almost as old as Amsterdam, but virtually all traces of the old city have been erased, first by 19th and 20thC progress and more brutally by the Nazi bombing of 1940. The St Laurenskerk, which miraculously survived the attack, stands as the only Gothic relic, with a statue in front of the humanist scholar Erasmus, claimed by Rotterdam as its most famous son.

Strategically located where the rivers Rhine and Maas enter

the North Sea, Rotterdam has devoted itself so
single-mindedly to its port that the city and its activities seem
something of an afterthought. Moreover, it is impossible to
escape anywhere the influence of the port: even the postwar
architecture in Rotterdam, with its promenade decks,
portholes and bridges, looks as if it was designed by a naval
architect. The most astonishing example of this is at
Kruisplein, where the view N is completed by the
superstructure of an oil tanker. The Lijnbaan shopping center
typifies the neat, shipshape style of Rotterdam, which has
influenced much postwar architecture.

Recently, however, Rotterdam has begun to break out of its
straitjacket and to improve its cultural image. The architecture
at Blaak, the major exhibitions at the Boymans Museum and
the new historical, ethnographic and maritime museums
demonstrate Rotterdam's determination to become more
highbrow. All of which causes considerable annoyance to
Amsterdam, which has already seen its port ruined by
Rotterdam's dynamism and is in no mood to surrender its
cultural supremacy as well.

Sights and places of interest
Boymans-van Beuningen Museum ★
Mathenesserlaan 18–20 ☎_(010) 4360500_ 🖾 ᚛ 🖵 _Open
Tues–Sat 10am–5pm, Sun, hols 11am–5pm. Metro to
Eendrachtsplein; tram 5 to Witte de Withstraat._

The Boymans-van Beuningen Museum is named after F. J. O.
Boymans, who bequeathed his art collection to the city of
Rotterdam in 1847, and D. G. van Beuningen, who added his
in 1958. Over the years, the museum has developed into one of
the most important in Europe, and is particularly renowned for
its ancient and modern art, ceramics and industrial design.
The building is rather confusing, consisting of an old wing
opened in 1935, with a distinctive tower beckoning like a
lighthouse, and a new wing added in 1972.

Probably the best place to begin is the department of old
paintings, which is reached from the circular lobby in the old
building (take the staircase from rm 39). The collection of
Early Netherlandish Painting is exceptional, and includes
Pieter Bruegel the Elder's fearsome _Tower of Babel_, which
contains a wealth of fine detail. Boymans also boasts several
works by Hieronimus Bosch (rms 3–4), ranging from two
exquisite miniature portraits to the _Prodigal Son_ and the
Wedding at Cana, the latter filled with delightful details such
as the concealed onlookers. Jan van Scorel's _Young Scholar in a
Red Cap_ is an impressive example of humanist portraiture,
while Pieter Aertsen's _Christ in the House of Martha and Mary_
is a striking example of Dutch Mannerism.

The museum's director in 1935 had the inspired idea of
displaying the collection of **Dutch Masters** in a series of
intimate rooms modeled on 17thC painting cabinets
(rms 6–10). These contain works by Pieter Saenredam
including his view of the now-vanished Mariakerk in Utrecht,
and a number of genre paintings such as Gerrit Dou's _The
Quack_ and Jan Steen's heavily symbolic _Fortunes can change
(Soo gewonne, soo verteert)_.

An extensive collection of small-scale works by **Rubens**
(rm 11) includes an unusual series of seven scenes from the life
of Achilles.

The **Van der Vorm collection** should on no account be

missed (rms 19–24). As well as offering further fine examples of Dutch 17thC painting, it boasts works by Courbet, Corot, Sisley and Monet, and a small collection of 19thC Dutch painting, including Breitner's exquisite *The Earring*.

The Boymans' collection of **20thC painting** (rms 25–30) is somewhat neglected, although it contains a superb collection of Surrealist works by Dali, Magritte and Ernst, and works by Picasso, Klee and Kandinsky.

Be sure not to miss the two rooms (36–37) devoted to **Rembrandt and his pupils**, containing Rembrandt's affectionate portrait of his son Titus at his desk and a self-portrait by Rembrandt's most gifted pupil, Carel Fabritius.

The collection of decorative art and industrial design on the ground floor is also worth a glance. It includes a fascinating collection of glazed tiles from Persia, Spain and the Low Countries (rm 45) and a delightful 15thC tiled floor from Naples (rm 51). The ceramics collection is also extensive, ranging from vibrant Italian majolica (rm 41) to contemporary works (rms 47–48). Another highlight is the unusual collection of household utensils from the Middle Ages to the 18thC, many of which feature in paintings on display in the museum. The industrial design collection (rm 46) includes some eccentric examples of Post Modern Italian design.

When the weather is fine, the coffee shop terrace overlooking the museum garden is perhaps the most idyllic spot in Rotterdam. The ornamental pool is also a pleasant place to linger, with Claes Oldenburg's giant *Screwarch* lending a surreal touch to the setting.

Café De Unie
Mauritsweg 35 ☎ (010) 4117394 ▣ Open Mon–Thurs 8am–midnight, Fri, Sat 8am–1am, Sun 10am–midnight. Tram 3, 4, 5 to Mauritsweg.
Built in 1924 by J. J. P. Oud and destroyed during the bombardment of 1940, De Unie was rebuilt in 1986 on a nearby site as a café-restaurant and cultural center. The red, blue and yellow facade was inspired by Mondriaan's abstract paintings.

Delfshaven
Metro to Delfshaven; tram 4, 6 to Spanjaardstraat.
The tiny port of Delfshaven was founded by the city of Delft in 1389 and remained within its jurisdiction until 1825, when it was granted independent status, only to lose it again 61 years later to Rotterdam. Two decorated gable stones on the wall of the 17thC **Zakkendragershuisje** (House of the Guild of Grain Porters) recall that in its heyday Delfshaven was an important whaling and herring fishing port. Yet its main claim to fame is that it was from here that the Pilgrim Fathers departed for America in 1620. Their ship, the *Speedwell*, proved unseaworthy, however, and they put into Plymouth some days later, before setting sail again on the *Mayflower*.

The attractive historical museum **De Dubbelde Palmboom** (*Voorhaven 12 ☎ (010) 4761533 ▨ & ▣ open Tues–Sat 10am–5pm, Sun 11am–5pm*) contains interesting relics relating to local trades such as peat-cutting, shipbuilding and *jenever* distilling. Excellent information sheets are available in English.

Like all dead ports, Delfshaven possesses a somewhat desolate atmosphere, although the recent extension of the metro line may inject new life into this picturesque corner of Rotterdam.

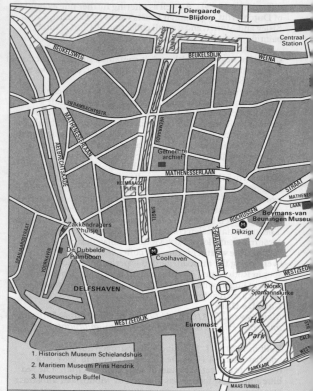

1. Historisch Museum Schielandshuis
2. Maritiem Museum Prins Hendrik
3. Museumschip Buffel

The port
The sheer size of Rotterdam's port reduces everything else in
Holland to Lilliputian proportions. Though it can no longer
claim to be the world's largest port, it is still by far the
world's busiest, handling some 250 million tonnes of goods
annually.

The best way to see the port is undoubtedly by **Spido
Havenrondvaart** (*Willemsplein ☎(010) 4135400 ⌧ ▣ ⚹
⪪ tours every day; tram 5 to Willemsplein*) which takes you
on a guided boat tour lasting 1hr 15mins, down the Nieuwe
Maas past tugs, dredgers, tankers, yachts, submarines, liners
and barges. The boats on these tours also enter some of the
docks, revealing ships in dry dock and mountains of
containers.

Harbor walk
Another way to see the harbor is to walk along the old harbor
front from the Euromast to Blaak. First follow the edge of
Het Park and continue along Westerkade to Veerhaven. For
those interested in 19thC architecture, **Calandstraat**, with
its sober warehouses, and **Parkstraat**, with its Art Nouveau
mansions, are worthwhile detours. **Westplein 5**, with its
tiled paintings of steamers, is one of a number of imposing

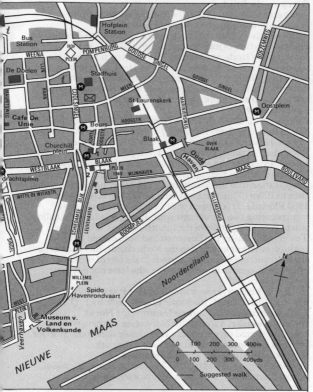

shipping offices in the vicinity. Continue down the E side of
Veerhaven passing a remarkably elegant Greek Revival
terrace, which is terminated by the delicate pastel-colored
Museum voor Land en Volkenkunde (museum of
geography and ethnography).

Beyond **Spido Rondvaarten**, head N along Leuvehaven,
which is crammed with Rhine barges. The **Maritiem
Museum Prins Hendrik** rides like a ship above the harbor
and forms a transition between the city and the port. Nearby
is the 19thC **Museumschip Buffel** and the **Historisch
Museum Schielandshuis**. The deserted Plein 1940 is
dominated by Ossip Zadkine's impressive monument *De
verwoeste stad* (The Destroyed City), erected in 1953 as a
memorial to those who died in the 1940 bombardment. From
here, continue along Wijnhaven (marked by the brightly
painted totem pole presented by the port of Seattle) and pass
under the railway bridge to reach **Oude Haven**, which is
overlooked by the Art Nouveau landmark **Het Witte Huis**
(The White House). This was Europe's tallest building at the
time of its completion in 1898. A cluster of attractive cafés
overlooking the harbor provides a pleasant conclusion to this
walk.

Diergaarde Blijdorp
Van Aerssenlaan 49 ☎*(010) 4654333* 🖼 💻 ✳ *Open 9am–5pm. Tram 3 to Diergaarde Blijdorp.*
This sensitively planned zoo designed in the 1930s contains an unusual mixture of modern and exotic buildings in a romantically landscaped setting. Major attractions include tigers, seals and birds of paradise. The Henri Martinhuis is interesting for its nocturnal animals and for the nonchalant acrobatics of the gibbons. There is an attractive café terrace and a superb adventure playground for children.

Euromast ★
Parkhaven 20 ☎*(010) 4364811* 🖼 ♿ 🍴 💻 ✳ ◁ *Open mid-Mar to mid-Oct 9am–10pm; mid-Oct to mid-Mar 9am–6pm (Space Tower 11am–4pm). Tram 6, 9 to Maastunnel.*
Rotterdam's tallest building, the 176m (560ft) Euromast offers splendid views of the port, with large ships heading down the Maas, helicopters flitting across the city and streams of cars disappearing into the Maastunnel. The lower part of the tower rises to 100m (320ft) and was built by H. A. Maaskant for the 1960 Floriade. It is capped with a distinctive crows' nest incorporating two restaurants with sloping windows that allow you to gaze straight down the funnels of ships. The Space Tower, added after the Euromast had been ousted from its position as tallest building in the Netherlands, incorporates a slowly revolving drum that ascends to the top of the mast, offering a magnificent view to those who have not got their eyes firmly closed.

The park below, known simply as **Het Park**, was landscaped in a 19thC Romantic English style by J. D. and L. P. Zocher. Its most curious feature is the **Norsk Sjømannskirke**, a church for Norwegian seamen, with brightly painted carvings and a remarkable slate roof. Stop for coffee in **Zocher**, a tranquil mansion in the park.

Historisch Museum Schielandshuis
Korte Hoogstraat 31 ☎*(010) 4334188* 🍴 *Open Tues–Sat 10am–5pm, Sun 11am–5pm. Metro or tram 6 to Churchillplein.*
Rotterdam's historical museum occupies the only Golden Age building to survive the 1940 bombardment: the Schielandshuis, built in 1662–65 for the powerful water board of the district of Schieland. The collection includes dollhouses, period rooms, paintings and films of the bombardment. Prints from the famous Atlas van Stolk are also exhibited.

Land en Volkenkunde, Museum voor
Willemskade 25 ☎*(010) 4111055* 🖼 🍴 *Open Tues–Sat 10am–5pm, Sun 11am–5pm. Tram 5 to Westplein.*
Rotterdam's museum of geography and ethnography occupies a distinguished Neoclassical building which was originally the clubhouse of the Royal Netherlands Yacht Club. The museum devotes considerable space to its temporary exhibitions, in which themes such as travel, festivals and ceremonies are treated with a combination of curiosity and concern. The restuarant's exotic menu is worth investigating.

Maritiem Museum Prins Hendrik
Leuvehaven 1 ☎*(010) 4132680* 🖼 💻 ✳ *Open Tues–Sat 10am–5pm, Sun 11am–5pm. Metro or tram 6 to Churchillplein.*
Holland's oldest maritime museum, founded by the seafaring Prins Hendrik in 1852, recently moved to a striking modern building overlooking the animated Leuvehaven. As well as

displaying a fascinating assortment of maps, globes, paintings and ship models, the museum has a small fleet of 19th–20thC barges and steam tugs moored in the harbor.

The most interesting of the ships is the turret-ram *Buffel* (Buffalo), a trim iron vessel built for the Dutch navy in 1868 and converted in 1896 to a barracks ship (▨ ▣ *on ship* ✽).

The officers' quarters are furnished in a plush Neoclassical Victorian style, and include a spacious captain's suite and an officers' Long Room which has something of the air of an exclusive London dining club. There are also working steam engines, models, charts and exhibitions on armaments and decoration.

Oude Haven
Metro or tram 3 to Station Blaak.

Devastated by a Nazi air raid in 1940, Rotterdam's old harbor area, the Oude Haven, now contains some of the most remarkable modern architecture in the Netherlands, including the pyramidal **Gemeentebibliotheek** (public library), which offers superb views of the city from the upper floors. Designed by the Van den Broek and Bakema Bureau, it shows obvious similarities to the Pompidou Center in Paris, particularly in the tangle of bright yellow ventilation ducts at the rear.

Farther s is a remarkable cluster of tilted cubic houses on poles designed by the Amsterdam-born architect Piet Blom. The complex incorporates a pedestrianized bridge lined with shops, which Blom modeled on the Ponte Vecchio in Florence. A number of avant-garde fashion boutiques have opened up in this futuristic environment, and various cafés line the attractive wharfside. The **Kijk Kubus** (*Overblaak 70* ▨ ✽ *open Apr–Oct Mon–Fri 10am–5pm, Sat, Sun 11am–5pm*) is well worth a visit.

▨ The **Parkhotel** (*Westersingel 70* ☎ *(010) 4363611* ☏ *22020* ▢ *to* ▥ ▣ ⊙ ▣) is probably the most interesting of Rotterdam's large business-class hotels, and includes a sauna, fitness center and art gallery. It is located close to the city center and the Boymans Museum; shops, restaurants and cafés are all within walking distance.

For those who enjoy watching ships and hearing foghorns boom in the night, the modern Scandinavian-style **Scandia** (*Willemsplein 1* ☎ *(010) 4134790* ☏ *21662* ▢ ▣ ⊙ ▣ ▣) is the only hotel overlooking the port and is conveniently positioned for Spido harbor tours. A slightly cheaper option is the **Savoy** (*Hoogstraat 81* ☎ *(010) 4139280* ☏ *21525* ▢ ▣ ⊙ ▣), a pleasantly furnished modern hotel not far from the architectural razzmatazz of Blaak.

Good, inexpensive hotels can be found in the streets behind the station. One of the best is **Bienvenue** (*Spoorsingel 24* ☎ *(010) 4669394* ▢ ▣ ⊙ ▣), which is attractively furnished in a crisp, modern style. The stairs are somewhat steep, but you are rewarded with a rare glimpse of a canal from the breakfast room. Another inexpensive and pleasant hotel withing walking distance of the station is **Holland** (*Provenierssingel 7* ☎ *(010) 4653100* ▢ ▣ ⊙ ▣), which overlooks another quiet stretch of canal.

▤ **La Vilette** (*Westblaak 160* ☎ *(010) 4148692* ▥ *to* ▥ ▣ ⊙ ▣ ▣ *last orders 10pm, closed Sat lunch, Sun*) is a stylish, modern restaurant offering businessmen a 60 min *Menu d'Affaires*, while those with more time are pampered with lengthy port and cigar menus; **Le Coq d'Or** (*Van Vollenhovenstraat 25* ☎ *(010) 4366405* ▥ *to* ▥ ▣ ⊙ ▣ ▣ *last orders 10pm, closed Sat, Sun, hols, Dec 24–Jan 1*) is a discreet and intimate restaurant offering superb cuisine; **Dewi Sri** (*Westerkade 20* ☎ *(010) 4360263* ▢ ▣ ⊙ ▣ *last orders 10.30pm; closed Sat lunch, Sun lunch*) is an Indonesian restaurant on the waterfront offering two *rijsttafels* (order the Sumatran at your peril); the modern **Café Lux** ❦ (*'s-Gravendijkwal 133* ☎ *(010) 4762206* ▢) offers excellent,

inexpensive Italian cuisine, with a summer terrace to complete the
Mediterranean atmosphere.

▦ Nostalgic brown cafés, their walls covered with faded photographs of
old liners, are concentrated along the Oude Binnenweg. However, the
progressive spirit of Rotterdam is better expressed by its modern white
cafés, such as **Radio Rijnmond** (_Delftsestraat 23_), attached to a local
radio station close to Hofplein, and **Dizzy** (_'s-Gravendijkwal 127_),
a spacious jazz café with a secluded garden for sultry summer evenings.
Recently, a cluster of cafés has sprung up on Oude Haven, and these
spread out on to the waterfront terrace on summer days. The café **De
Spaanse Poort** (_Haringvliet 637_) offers an interesting list of some 46
types of beer, as well as simple, inexpensive meals.

Nightlife and the arts

Probably the friendliest night-spots in Rotterdam are the jazz cafés such
as **Dizzy** (☎ (010) 4773014, concerts Tues 10pm, Sun 4pm) and
Harbour Jazz Club (_Weena 221_ ☎ (010) 4114958, concerts Fri, Sat
9.30pm). Jazz and blues also feature at **Theatercafé Plan-C**
(_Slepervest 1_ ☎ (010) 4124352).
  Bluetiek-In (_Karel Doormanstraat 12; open Thurs-Sun from 8.30pm_)
is Rotterdam's hottest discotheque, offering endless video and laser
distractions.
  For classical music see the program of **De Doelen** (_Schouwburgplein
50_ ☎ (010) 4132490). The cinema **Venster** (_Gouvernestraat 129_
☎ (010) 4364998) shows classic and avant-garde films.

Shopping

Major department stores are clustered around Beursplein, while other
shops are found in the pedestrianized Lijnbaan shopping center to the w
of here. The Binnenweg becomes increasingly interesting as it heads w,
and there is a small cache of fashionable boutiques in the remarkable
Promenade Overblaak.

Utrecht

_Map **3**D4. 35km (22 miles) s of Amsterdam. Population:
230,400. Getting there: By train, from Amsterdam Centraal
Station or Amstel; by car, on A2 **i** Vredenburg 90
☎(030) 314132; also information desk at Stationstraverse 5,
Hoog Catharijne._
Originating in the 1stC AD as a Roman outpost on the Rhine
frontier, Utrecht grew to become a major religious center in
the Middle Ages, and much of its interest lies in its numerous
churches and convents, and in the sculpture and painting that
developed during this period. During Holland's Golden Age,
Utrecht declined into a quiet backwater, and the hurricane of
1674 which toppled most of its church towers did nothing to
boost morale. The mood of melancholy continued into the
18thC, when the Scottish writer James Boswell, sent to
Utrecht by his father to study law, complained: "I groaned
with the idea of living all winter in so shocking a place."
  The development of the Hoog Catharijne shopping and
office complex in the 1970s has brought a new, restless energy
to the city, although there are still areas such as Nieuwegracht
where the mood of genteel decline has not totally vanished.

Sights and places of interest
The town
Like it or not, a visit to Utrecht is bound to begin in the brash
Hoog Catharijne complex, which contains the railway station
and parking lots, as well as shops and offices. Its only
redeeming feature is the Vredenburg concert hall, a
sympathetic modern design by Herman Hertzberger. As you

leave this building, you may be puzzled by some fragments of masonry below the bridge. These are all that remain of an Italianate fortress built in the 16thC by Charles V to keep the rebellious citizens in check. The strangest relic of all is the gun emplacement in the cellar below the VVV office. Several fragments from a demolished Art Nouveau office building, **De Utrecht**, also decorate the tourist office.

On leaving Vredenburg, cross the square of the same name and head down the lane Drie Haringstraat to reach Oude Gracht, a sunken canal with deserted quays, winding gracefully through the old city. Several medieval tower houses survive on Oude Gracht, notably **Oudaen** (no. 99), dating from 1320, and **Drakenborch** (no. 114), built in 1280. By descending to the lower quay, you can discover numerous lamppost consoles with modern sculpture illustrating scenes from Utrecht's history.

Head s down Oude Gracht, pausing on the bridges to enjoy the lively scene, completed by the exquisite cathedral tower. After passing the **Stadhuis**, continue down Vismarkt and turn left along Servetstraat, which leads to the cathedral tower. Just before you come to the tower, a gate on the right leads into a quiet garden **Flora's Hof** (*open Mon–Sat 10am–5pm*), which formerly belonged to the bishop's palace. A narrow lane leads from here to **Domplein**, the site of the nave of the cathedral, which was brought down by a hurricane. Cross the road and walk through the cathedral cloister, the **Dom Kloostergang** (*Domplein* ◙ *open mid-Oct to Mar Mon–Fri 10am–5pm, Sat, Sun 11am–5pm, and to 6pm Apr to mid-Oct; also June–Aug Thurs 6–9pm*), to reach Achter de Dom. Turn left, past the **Museum van Hedendaagse Kunst** (*Achter de Dom 12–14* ☎ *(030) 314185* ◙ ▣ *open Tues–Sat 10am–5pm, Sun, hols 1–5pm*), which exhibits Dutch and international art of the 1970s and 1980s, and right down Voetiusstraat to reach the tranquil precinct of the **Pieterskerk.**

On leaving the square, turn right and follow Achter St Pieter to Keistraat. The unusual corner house (no. 8) was built by a 17thC eccentric, Everard Meyster, who won a bet by persuading the people of Amersfoort to drag an enormous boulder into the center of the town, where it is still to be seen. The pretzel-shaped doorhandle is a reminder of the feast of beer and pretzels that Meyster threw, and the famous episode is also remembered in the street name **Keistraat** (Boulder Street).

Keistraat leads into the Janskerkhof, which boasts several dignified buildings, especially the neat 17thC Classical house at **Janskerkhof** 13. Yet this former precinct of the Janskerk is now a rather frantic area of town, and to get back to more tranquil parts, head back down the canal Drift, then turn left along Kromme Nieuwegracht, a quiet canal of 18thC town houses that follows a former loop in the Rhine. This leads to **Pausdam**, a picturesque convergence of quiet streets and canals, which is overlooked by the beautiful late Gothic **Paushuisje**, built in the early 16thC by Adriaen Florisz., who in 1522 became the first (and only) Dutch pope.

Nieuwegracht is a deep 14thC canal with deserted, overgrown quays along the waterside and quiet streets of 18thC houses above. A rusticated 17thC portal at Nieuwegracht 7 leads into a courtyard containing a fragment of an 11thC Benedictine abbey, which formed one church in a cross of churches built by the ambitious Bishop Bernold. The

Baroque gables at Nieuwegracht 15–17 are unusually flamboyant for Utrecht, while the house at Nieuwegracht 37 is a fetching example of miniaturized Classical architecture.

A short detour can be made to the left down Herenstraat, turning right down Oude Kamp and left down Brigittenstraat, to reach a quiet landscaped park overlooked by elegant 19thC villas. Turn right here to reach the **Bruntenhof**, a row of 17thC almshouses built by the city wall. The **Governors' Chamber** (no. 5) was reached through an ornate Renaissance portal adorned with melancholy symbols of mortality.

Walk along Bruntenhof to the **Gasthuis Leeuwenberg** – a 14thC hospital for plague victims – and turn right along Schalkwijkstraat to reach Nieuwegracht. Turn left and follow Nieuwegracht to the SE corner of the old city, where a Classical portal (no. 205) marks a *hofje* founded in 1651 by Maria van Pallaes. The simple almshouses are located around the corner in Agnietenstraat, while a second *hofje* – the late 16thC **Beyerskameren** – is discovered by turning right into Lange Nieuwstraat. From here enjoy also the full effect of the 18thC Rococo facade of the **Fundatie van Renswoude**, an enlightened orphanage for boys, on Agnietenstraat.

Continue along Agnietenstraat past the **Centraal Museum** (see below) and turn left down Nicolaasdwarsstraat to reach a 19thC park romantically laid out on the site of the old city walls. Turn right, walk through the tunnel and cross the road. You can then continue through the park, following the former moat N, and passing on the right a series of convivial 19thC working-class streets known locally as **De seven steegjes** (The Seven Alleys). Leave the park on reaching the snug medieval parish church, the **Geertekerk**, and turn right, then left along Springweg. At Springweg 110–30 is a row of 11 almshouses founded in 1583 by Cornelis van Mierop, Dean of the cathedral, while at Springweg 104 is the colorful 16thC gateway of the municipal orphanage.

At the end of Springweg, turn left and cross the square to reach a tiny doorway (no. 29) which leads into a maze of medieval alleys known as the **Mariahoek**. This eventually brings you to the cloister of the **Mariakerk**, all that remains of the Romanesque church that completed Bishop Bernold's cross of churches.

Churches

In the Middle Ages, Utrecht was the main religious center of the northern Netherlands, and although its skyline no longer bristles with spires, it still boasts numerous interesting churches. Most of these are open during the summer, and enthusiastic guides are on the spot to explain the curiosities. The cathedral, or **Domkerk** (*Domplein ☎ (030) 310403 ▣ ✗ ▣ open May–Sept 10am–5pm, Oct–Apr 11am–4pm, Sun 2–4pm*), begun in 1254, was still unfinished when a hurricane ripped through the town in 1674 and brought the inadequately buttressed nave crashing to the ground. All that now remains of the Gothic masterpiece is the soaring choir, built during 1254–1321 in the style of Cologne Cathedral, and the 15thC cloisters, with tympana showing scenes from the life of St Martin (who gave his cloak to a beggar), and a curious traceried window made to look as if it were held together with rope.

Utrecht also has two Romanesque churches, which formed part of a cross of four churches planned in the 11thC by Bishop Bernold. His favorite church was the **Pieterskerk** (*Pieterskerkhof 5 ✗ open Tues–Fri 10am–4.30pm*), built in 1048 of a distinctive grayish tuff, with vivid red sandstone columns in the nave. A peaceful mood is conferred by the arc of houses enclosing the **Pieterskerkhof**, which until the Reformation was a walled precinct that was immune from municipal jurisdiction.

Bishop Bernold's second church, the **Janskerk** (*Janskerkhof* ☎ *(030) 316440* �" *open Mon–Fri 9am–5pm*) was completed about 1250. The design was faulty, however, and the red sandstone columns later had to be enclosed by brick pillars (one of which has been exposed to show the original column). The choir was rebuilt in late Gothic style in the 16thC. After the Reformation, a chapel at the w end was converted into a guard house and adorned with gaudy military emblems.

Utrecht's oldest parish church is the **Buurkerk**, which now houses Utrecht's marvelous museum of mechanical musical instruments. The present building is a good example of a Gothic hall church, although the choir was demolished in the 17thC. The church tower, intended to rival the Domtoren (see below), attained only a modest height before funds ran out.

Another parish church, the **Nicolaikerk** (*Nicolaaskerkhof* �" *open May–Sept Tues–Sat 10am–5pm, Sun 1–5pm; enter through Centraal Museum*), was built at the s end of the city in

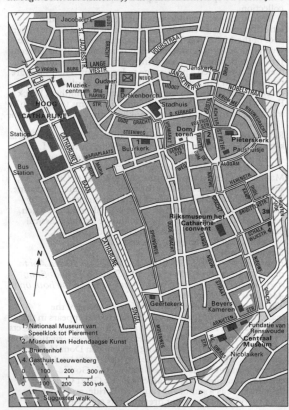

1: Nationaal Museum van Speelklok tot Pierement
2: Museum van Hedendaagse Kunst
3: Bruntenhof
4: Gasthuis Leeuwenberg

0   100   200   300 m
0   100   200   300 yds

---- Suggested walk

the mid-12thC. Romanesque details can still be seen in the
Westwork, although the interior was rebuilt under Bishop
David of Burgundy as a late Gothic hall church. The 12thC
Jacobikerk (*St Jacobsstraat* ☎ *(030) 317862* ▨ *open June and
Sept Tues–Fri 1–5pm, July, Aug Tues–Fri noon–5pm*), which
stands at the N end of the city, was also rebuilt in the 15thC as a
hall church. Its spire, recently restored after being brought
down by the 17thC hurricane, lends dignity to an otherwise
abandoned area of the city. The 19thC **Willibrorduskerk**
(*Minrebroederstraat 21* ▨ ✗ *open Mon, Tues, Thurs, Fri
10am–4pm, Wed noon–4pm*), contains an exuberance of
neo-Gothic detail in its murals, sculpture, iron-work, wood
carvings and stained glass.

Centraal Museum ★
Agnietenstraat ☎ *(030) 315541* ▣ ▨ *Open Tues–Sat
10am–5pm, Sun, hols 1–5pm. Bus 2 to Agnietenstraat.*
Housed in a 15thC convent, the Centraal Museum in Utrecht
is a confusing hodgepodge of collections brought under one
roof, including a costume museum, a set of period rooms in
Gothic, Renaissance, Classical and Louis XIV–XVI styles; a
Modern Art collection; a collection of Old Masters; a coin
collection; a department of applied art; and a Utrecht historical
collection.

Be sure to see the collection of paintings by the 16thC
Utrecht artist Jan van Scorel, which is displayed on the upper
floor of the 16thC **Agnietenklooster** chapel. These include
several early 16thC group portraits of members of the Utrecht
Jerusalem Brotherhood, carrying palm leaves to signify that
they had completed a pilgrimage to Jerusalem. Their faces are
rendered with a penetrating Netherlandish Realism, apart
from the face of the one woman – referred to simply as Dirck
Evert's daughter – whose fair complexion seems too good to be
true amid so many warts and wrinkles. Other works such as the
Entry into Jerusalem show the influence of the Italian
Renaissance, which Van Scorel encountered during his time as
keeper of the Vatican treasures under Pope Adriaen VI.

The museum also has works by Utrecht Masters such as
Abraham Bloemaert, whose early paintings are highly
Mannerist; Gerard van Honthorst, a follower of Caravaggio;
and Jan Both, who fell under the spell of the Italian landscape.
The 20thC collection includes several disturbing works by
Dutch Magic Realists such as Carel Willink and Pyke Koch.

Not to be missed is the 17thC dollhouse (in the Classical
period room), with its remarkably detailed furniture,
porcelain, Old Master paintings and globes.

Domtoren ★
Domplein ☎ *(030) 919540* ▨ ✗ *compulsory. Open Apr to
mid-Oct Mon–Fri 10am–5pm; Sat, Sun, hols noon–5pm;
mid-Oct to Mar Sat, Sun noon–5pm. Tours on the hour up to
4pm. Bus 2 to Domplein.*
This ethereal cathedral tower of Utrecht is one of the
masterpieces of Burgundian architecture and appears in the
background of numerous medieval paintings. Three architects
worked on the 112m (364ft) tower during its construction from
1321–82, the most notable being Jan van den Dom II, who
gave the octagonal lantern at the top its delicate lacelike
tracery. Not everyone was pleased with this Gothic
extravaganza, however; the ascetic monk Geert Groot
denounced it as a symbol of vanity and pride, and during its
construction had recurrent dreams of its collapse.

Yet even the hurricane of 1674 did not shake the Domtoren and it remains today a symbol of Utrecht's religious greatness, despite the unwarranted indignity of having buses pass through its arch.

Nationaal Museum van Speelklok tot Pierement ★
*Buurkerkhof 10 ☎(030) 312789 ▨ & 𝙆 compulsory ⚲ ▣
Open Tues–Sat 10am–5pm, Sun, hols 1–5pm. Guided tours lasting 1hr begin on the hr 10am–4pm. Commentary given in English, French or German on request. Bus 2 to Domplein.*

One of the most enjoyable museums in the Netherlands is the National Museum Van Speelklok tot Pierement (From Carillon to Barrel Organ), which is located in the 13thC **Buurkerk** (see above). The museum illustrates the development of mechanical musical instruments from the 18th–20thC.

What gives the museum its particular appeal is that many of the instruments are played during the guided tour, which is given by highly informed and enthusiastic music students. Among the more unusual instruments are a mechanical rabbit, a musical chair and an extraordinary "Phono-Liszt Viola" from a Berlin café, which conceals three pneumatic violins in its casing. The most striking exhibits, however, are the fairground and dance hall organs. It is worth ascending to the "promenade" floor to view the architecture and medieval frescoes of this hall church. There is also a small exhibition on the history of the church, including the story of Sister Bertken, who occupied a penitential cell in the choir for some 57 years, until her death in 1514.

Rijksmuseum het Catharijneconvent ★
Nieuwe Gracht 63 ☎(030) 313835 ▨ & ▣ Open Tues–Fri 10am–5pm, Sat, Sun, hols 11am–5pm. Bus 2 to Lange Nieuwstraat.

The history of Christianity in the Netherlands is the theme of this museum, located in an attractively restored 15thC monastery that once belonged to the Knights of St John. The highlight of the collection is the sculpture and painting from the Burgundian era, including several Renaissance works by Jan van Scorel of Utrecht, whose tomb is also displayed.

The museum is arranged thematically and the medieval works are mainly found on the ground floor of the *kloostergebouw* (convent building), which is reached from the entrance hall through a cellar passage. The Reformation and the theoretical quarrels of the 17thC are also covered in the *kloostergebouw*. Religious developments from the 17th–20thC are dealt with in the *grachtenhuis* (canal house).

≈ Utrecht is not well endowed with hotels and if you are intending to stay the night it is worth booking in advance. **De Pays Bas** (*Janskerkhof 10* ☎(030) 333321 ❶ 47485 ▨ ▭ ▣ ▣ ▣ ▣ *closed Dec 31, Jan 1*) is a distinguished hotel with a traditional flavor, close to the Dom. It boasts an airy Winter Garden. **De Stadhouder van Utrecht** (*J. W. Frisostraat 14–18* ☎(030) 521634 ▢ *closed Dec; bus 4 to Rosarium*) is a pleasing, friendly hotel in a rather elegant quarter of Utrecht near the Wilhelminapark, with an efficient bus service to the center of town. Rooms are spacious, airy and modern, but without bathrooms.

≋ Martin Fagel's **Café de Paris** (*Drieharingstraat 16* ☎(030) 317503 ▢ ▣ ▣ *closed Sun*) offers imaginative cuisine in an elegant setting; **Selamat Makan** (*Voorstraat 100* ☎(030) 322135 ▢ *last orders 11pm; closed Wed, Dec 24–31*) is a pleasant Indonesian restaurant offering dishes to please most palates. Enticing Italian *broodjes* piled high with salami, cheese and peppers are sold in large numbers at a stall on Oude Gracht near Café Oudaen.

📖 Utrecht's most distinguished café is **Stadskasteel Oudaen**
(*Oudegracht 99*), opened in 1986 in a renovated 14thC tower house.
Slightly dowdy, albeit extraordinary, is **Graaf Floris** (*Vismarkt 13*).
For a more typical brown café, try the pleasant, if somewhat dilapidated,
Tapperiji De Luifel (*Neude 36*), where flowers grace the tables and
sawdust is scattered on the floor. Student cafés, including the
picturesque **De Vingerhoed** (*Donkere Gaard 11*), are concentrated on
Donkere Gaard and Wed. **Café Zeezicht** (*Nobelstraat 2*) is a friendly,
modern café featuring art exhibitions, live groups and women's events.

Nightlife and the arts

Utrecht is a music-loving city, and scarcely a day goes by when there is
not a classical concert in the modern **Vredenburg Muziekcentrum**
(☎*(030) 313144*) or in one of the many churches. Concerts are
regularly given in the **Pieterskerk** (☎*(030) 311485*), the
Nicolaikerk (☎*(030) 315734*) and the **Domkerk** (*Sat at 3.30pm*
☎*(030) 310403*). Aug is a quiet month, but in early Sept the town
comes alive with the **Holland Festival Oude Muziek Utrecht** (*for
info: Postbus 734, 3500 AS Utrecht* ☎*(030) 340981*), which features
music from the Middle Ages to the early Romantics. Concerts are also
played on the Dom carillon every Thurs eve, and the cloisters are kept
open for listeners.

The cultural center **'t Hoogt** (*Hoogt 4* ☎*(030) 328388*) offers an
interesting film program; the **Oude Pothuis** (*Oudegracht 279*
☎*(030) 318970*) is a basement jazz café; and **Astaire** (*Voorstraat 102*
☎*(030) 319362*) is a café-disco that appeals to the 1960s generation.

The fortnightly *Uit in Utrecht*, available from the VVV, lists music,
films, theater and other events.

Shopping

Hoog Catharijne is a vast modern shopping center with shops of every
description; **La Vie** on Vredenburg is a more upmarket center. A large
pedestrianized shopping area spreads s of here. Lichte Gaard contains
some enticing shops in 18thC buildings, while Oude Gracht s of here is
good for interesting boutiques, avant-garde jewelers and art galleries.
The most inviting patisserie is **Noteboom** (*Oudekerkhof 9*), which also
contains a tearoom where you can sample the local specialty *botersprits*
(butter shortbread). Concealed in an alley beside the 't Hoogt cultural
center is a restored 19thC shop **Erven Betje Boerhave** (*Hoogt 6*
☎*(030) 316628*), which sells mustard, coffee and tea in traditional
wrappings, as well as old-fashioned sweets such as *drop* (liquorice) and
kerkpepermuntjes (church peppermints).

On Sat Utrecht is given over to markets, including a general market
on Vredenburg (also on Wed), a stamp market on Vismarkt (*noon–5pm*),
a flea market on Willemsstraat and around the Jacobikerk (*8am–1pm*),
an antique market in **De Ossekop** (*Voorstraat 19*) and a plant market on
the Janskerkhof. The most spectacular sight, however, is the flower
market, which spreads along Oude Gracht from Lange Viestraat to the
Stadhuisbrug, and reaches a peak of excitement around 5pm when
traders offer gigantic bunches of flowers at irresistible prices.

Volendam

*Map **3***A5. *Noord-Holland, 21km (13 miles)* N *of Amsterdam.
Population: 16,890. Getting there: By NZH bus 110; by car,
through IJ-tunnel, then E10* **i** *Zeestraat 21* ☎*(02993) 63747.*
Life in the small fishing town of Volendam has never been
quite the same since its discovery in 1873 by an art historian,
who described its quaint local costumes in the sort of glowing
terms reserved today for remote South Sea island paradises. A
few years later artists began to arrive in Volendam to paint
romantic scenes of fishermen in baggy black breeches and
women in curious peaked hats.

Much of Volendam is now tacky, with English fish-and-chip
shops and photographers specializing in group portraits in

local costume. However, the **Spaander Hotel**(see below) –
where the international community of artists was based –
retains an old-fashioned charm. The hotel café in particular
should be visited for its remarkable collection of 19thC
Romantic paintings gifted by former guests. The café
waitresses wear traditional costume.

The warren of streets behind the dike known as **Doolhof**
(maze) is also worth a glance.

≈ For an overnight stay in Volendam, the **Spaander Hotel** (*Haven
15–19* ☎ *(02993) 63595* ⊕ *13141* ▢ ≡ AE ⊕ ⊙ VISA *closed Dec 25*)
has bedrooms tastefully furnished in a modern style, many with views of
the IJsselmeer. The old part of the hotel is crammed with mementos of
the artists who stayed here in the late 19thC.

Zaanstad

*Map 3B4. Noord-Holland, 16km (10 miles) N of Amsterdam.
Population: 65,390. Getting there: By train, 10mins from
Amsterdam Centraal Station; by car, through Coentunnel,
then A8 i Gedemptegracht 76, Zaandam ☎(075) 162221;
also at the tea house, Zaanse Schans.*

The string of towns (now collectively known as Zaanstad)
along the river Zaan was a major center of industrial activity as
early as the 17thC. By the 18thC there were some 1,000
windmills in operation, supporting a diversity of industries
such as shipbuilding, paper-making, oil-milling and whaling.

The main town of Zaandam still reverberates with the
excitement of Czar Peter the Great's incognito visit in 1697,
which has something of the air of an old Russian fairy-tale.
Posing as the sailor Peter Mikhailov, the Czar came to
Zaandam to study local shipbuilding methods and lodged for a
few days in the humble dwelling of Gerrit Kist, a smith who
had worked in the Czar's service in St Petersburg.

Located in a baffling maze of streets near Zaandam harbor,
the **Czaar Peterhuisje ★** (*Krimp 23* ▨ ✗ *open Tues–Sun
10am–1pm, 2–5pm; closed first and third Sun of month*) – now
with a decided tilt and enclosed by a protective structure – has
become a shrine to which emperors (including Napoleon),
statesmen, poets and writers have paid homage. The concierge,
a Russian emigré, communicates an extraordinary store of
knowledge, and enthusiastically points out numerous
mementos ranging from the box bed in which the Czar slept to
a final demand for unpaid property tax sent to Czar Alexander
III, who was at one time the owner of the house.

On leaving the house, turn right, then left along Hogendijk
to reach the harbor and, slightly farther on, a statue of Peter
the Great working on a ship.

To obtain an idea of how the Zaan area once looked, visit the
Zaanse Schans (on the river Zaan at Zaandijk, a short walk
from Koog-Zaandijk railway station), where a number of
typical 17th–18thC houses and windmills have been
reconstructed. Some are open to the public (▨ *open Apr–Oct
daily, Nov–Mar Sat and Sun only*) and include a 19thC
grocery store, a museum of clocks, a furnished interior, a clog-
maker and an antique shop.

If all this seems somewhat artificial, cross the river to the
town of Zaandijk and visit the fascinating **Zaanlandse
Oudheidkamer** (*Lagedijk 80* ☎ *(075) 83628* ▨ ✗
*compulsory; open Tues–Fri 10am–noon, 2–4pm, Sat, Sun
2–4pm; ring bell for entry*), a local history museum located in

the early 18thC home of a Mennonite merchant. The 18thC rooms, toys, kitchen utensils and paintings of the Zaan are all of interest, but the best feature of the house is undoubtedly the room at the front overlooking the river. Since the river Zaan was once the main thoroughfare of the region, most of the houses face the river, and a boat excursion from the Zaanse Schans is therefore the best way to appreciate their eccentric green wooden gables.

De Saense Schans (*Lagedijk 32–34, Zaandijk* ☎ *(075) 211911* ▭ ⬛ ⇌ ♿ ▢ ⬜ ◀) is a comfortable modern hotel enjoying a panoramic view across the river to the windmills and green gables of the Zaanse Schans.

De Hoop op d'Swarte Walvis (*Kalverringdijk 15, Zaanse Schans* ☎ *(075) 165629* ▮▮▮ to ▮▮▮▮ 🆎 ⓪ ⓞ ⓓ 🎫 *last orders 10pm; closed Sun*) – the name means "In the Hope of a Black Whale" – is one of Holland's most idyllic restaurants, occupying a cluster of 18thC wooden buildings that includes the former orphanage from the village of Westzaan and a store for whaling gear. The restaurant, tastefully decorated with seafaring memorabilia, enjoys a splendid view of the river Zaan, and the French-style cuisine is excellent.

Cycle trips

An informative booklet, "Cycling in Holland," can be obtained from the Netherlands Board of Tourism 355 Lexington Ave, 21st Floor, New York NY10017 ☎ *(212) 370–7360; 25–28 Buckingham Gate, London SW1E 6LD* ☎ *(01) 630–0451.*

Amsterdam is such a neat and compact city that it is possible to cycle from the center to the outer edge in about half an hour. The N edge of the city is particularly abrupt, and after passing below the outer beltway you are suddenly surrounded by idyllic watery fields, with placidly grazing cows and red pyramid-roofed farmhouses buried in clusters of trees. This area – known as Waterland because of its numerous lakes and drainage ditches – is pleasantly dotted with small villages, such as Broek in Waterland. The towns on the edge of the IJsselmeer (the name for the Zuider Zee after it was enclosed by a dike in 1932) each possess a distinctive character, and although some have become swamped by tourism, others retain a traditional flavor far removed from the cosmopolitan bustle of Amsterdam. (See *Excursions*).

Amsterdam offers the cyclist two simple and relatively traffic-free routes to reach the open countryside to the S and N of the city. The first follows the winding river Amstel to Ouderkerk aan de Amstel, 10km (6 miles) from Amsterdam; the second follows the course of the raised dike on the N side of the IJ to Monnickendam, 16km (10 miles) from Amsterdam. There is also a pleasant route to the *Amsterdamse Bos*.

Getting around by bicycle

Holland is of course the land of the bicycle. There are 11 million bicycles in the country and 9,900km (6,200 miles) of cycle lanes. People of all ages use their bicycles in all weather to commute to work, to go shopping, to transport their children and exercise their dogs, quite apart from long-distance touring and racing.

Bicycles can be rented at more than 100 railway stations in

the Netherlands. Train travelers can obtain reductions on rentals at stations if they have a valid railway ticket to that destination – simply ask for a *fietsdagkaart* when you buy a ticket. There are hourly, daily and weekly rates and you will be required to pay a deposit. A passport or other identification is also required. You can expect to get a solid, one-speed fixed-wheel machine. Special attachable seats for small children can also be rented.

Before you set off check that the brakes, lights and bell are in working order. Be sure also to take a few minutes to get used to the bicycle – and in particular the brakes, which are operated by pedaling backwards – before you set off into the traffic. When planning a route, it is better to take meandering roads along rivers and dikes than straight routes along canals or across polders, which quickly become monotonous.

Proceed cautiously until you are accustomed to the rules of the road. Riding in bicycle lanes, designated by a blue sign with a white bicycle, or in cycle lanes marked *fietspad* or *rijwielpad* is compulsory. Routes particularly suitable for bicycles are indicated by signposts with a red bicycle. There are often separate traffic lights for bicycles, and you are permitted to cycle the wrong way down one-way streets if the no-entry sign declares *m.u.v. fietsen*. Finally, you should keep in mind that cars usually have priority when entering a road from the right.

If you leave your bicycle outside you should use a strong lock to attach it to something solid and remove all detachable parts such as lamps and pump. Most railway stations provide manned bicycle sheds where, for a small charge you can keep your bicycle locked up overnight or for longer periods.

You can take your bicycle with you by train, but you will have to pay rather a lot to do so. Rates for sending bicycles unaccompanied are considerably cheaper. Bicycles can also be taken on the Amsterdam metro – the fare is the same as for children.

Bicycle rental

Centraal Station　☎(020) 248391
Amsterdam Amstel Station　☎(020) 923584
Amsterdam Muiderpoort Station　☎(020) 923439
Amsterdam Sloterdijk Station　☎(020) 848409
Fiets-o-fiets　Amstelveenseweg, at main entrance to Amsterdamse Bos ☎(020) 445473
Heja　Bestevaerstraat 39 ☎(020) 129211 (some childrens' models)
Koenders Rent Shop　Utrechtsedwarsstraat 105
☎(020) 234657

Route 1/Amstelland

On warm Sunday afternoons, Amsterdammers set off down the Amstel in large family groups, with small children perched in baskets on the rear of a parent's bicycle, and grandparents following behind with folding chairs and fishing rods. The lure of the Amstel dates from the 17thC, when wealthy Amsterdammers built themselves country houses on the banks of the river. After the death of his wife Saskia in 1642, Rembrandt often wandered this route, sketching the landscape with a delicacy that seems more Japanese than European, and in the 19thC, the restful, watery landscape of Amstelland attracted Dutch Impressionist painters.

Beginning at the Blauwe Brug, head down the left-hand side of the *Amstel*, crossing the three main canals: *Herengracht*, *Keizersgracht* and *Prinsengracht*. On reaching Sarphatistraat, pass in front of the Amstel Hotel and through the underpass to reach Weesperzijde. Continue s past the Nieuwe Amstelbrug and cross the river at the Berlagebrug, with its distinctive red and black lampposts. Continue down the w side of the Amstel and turn left just beyond the Rivierstaete office, following the red cycle sign to Ouderkerk. The quiet treelined road follows the Amstel all the way to Ouderkerk aan de Amstel, passing the cemetery Zorgvlied, the attractive *Amstelpark* (where cycling is prohibited) the octagonal Rieker windmill that formerly stood on the Rieker polder, a statue of Rembrandt sketching, and the café **Kleine Kalfje**. On reaching the outskirts of Ouderkerk, turn left across the river, then immediately right and right again down Kerkstraat. On the left is the entrance to the **Portugees Israelitische Begraafplaats** (*Kerkstraat* ☒ *open dawn–dusk; closed Sat, Jewish hols*), a Jewish cemetery established in the 17thC and containing the exceptionally ornate, and romantically overgrown, tombs of prominent Amsterdammers, many bearing Hebrew and Portuguese inscriptions. Male visitors should, out of courtesy, wear a cap, which can be borrowed from the PIB Werkgroep office (*Kerkstraat 7*).

For those who wish to venture beyond Ouderkerk, the best route to follow is along the river Bullewijk, which is reached by crossing the bridge at the end of Kerkstraat and turning left. On reaching the Voetangelsbrug, choose one of two routes: either straight ahead to follow a circular route around the polder De Ronde Hoep (the round hoop), which eventually leads back to Ouderkerk, a distance of 13km (8 miles), or left along the river Holendrecht to the village of Abcoude, which is 6km (4 miles) from Ouderkerk. The energetic can continue N along the peaceful river Gein to Weesp, then follow the river Gaasp on the left-hand side (Provincialeweg) as far as the Loosdrecht Dreef. Turn left here and cycle through the Park Gaasperplas to reach the metro station Gaasperplas, which is 10km (6 miles) from Abcoude. You can then put your bicycle on the metro at a reduced fare and return to Centraal Station. Allow 2hrs for the return trip from Amsterdam to Ouderkerk and 4hrs for either of the longer trips.

Route 2/Waterland

Beginning at Centraal Station, use the underpass to the E of the station to reach De Ruijterkade, then turn left to reach the free ferry across the IJ, which departs from moorings behind the station (signposted *Pont naar Tolhuis*). Once across the IJ, follow Buiksloterweg, turn right at the café **Trefpunt** and keep to the w side of the Noord Hollandsch Kanaal until you come to a bridge. Turn right here to cross the canal and then the main road. Take care on this stretch as the traffic can move rather fast. Continue straight ahead down Havikslaan, turn left onto Meeuwenlaan and continue to the traffic circle, then turn right onto Nieuwendammerdijk. This quiet street follows an ancient dike eastward to join Schellingwouderdijk and then Durgerdammerdijk. Simply follow this dike to reach the pretty former fishing village of Durgerdam. The dike road then follows a pleasant meandering route to Uitdam, 6km (4 miles) from Amsterdam. If you are beginning to tire by Uitdam, cut the journey short by turning left to Zuiderwoude and then

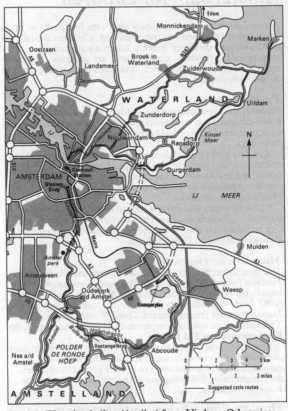

Broek in Waterland, 6km (4 miles) from Uitdam. Otherwise,
continue along the side of the dike about 3km (2 miles) until
you come to an intersection. From here take a short detour
right along an artificial causeway to reach the picturesque but
crowded village of Marken, or turn left and pedal for 5km (3
miles) to reach the unspoiled town of Monnickendam. Energy
permitting, continue along the dike road, ignoring the
horrendous Volendam, to Edam, which is beautiful; then
return by the main N247 (which has a cycle lane) to
Monnickendam. Most people, finding Monnickendam quite
far enough, return to Amsterdam via the lovely village of Broek
in Waterland, which is 3km (2 miles) by the main road. Here
you can reward yourself with a pancake in **De Witte Swaen**, a
restaurant popular with cyclists. Once rested, return the 6km
(4 miles) to Amsterdam by taking the underpass to reach the s
side of the main road, then following signs to Zunderdorp. The
route is marked *doorgaand verkeer* ("through traffic") and
enters Amsterdam just beyond Zunderdorp. Follow the road
straight ahead to return to Nieuwendammerdijk, then turn
right to retrace the route back to the ferry. Allow 3hrs for the
round trip to Broek in Waterland, 4hrs to Monnickendam and
5hrs to Edam.

Amsterdam for children

Amsterdam is a rather cramped city with few parks or open spaces where children can romp around. Children brought up in Amsterdam therefore quickly adopt adult pursuits such as visiting cafés, theaters, cinemas and art galleries. For more traditional children's activities, it is often necessary to venture outside Amsterdam.

Parks and zoos

Probably the top attraction for children in Amsterdam is *Artis*, a well-designed zoo with numerous indoor attractions – such as an aquarium and nocturnal house – to keep children amused on rainy days.

The best parks for children are the *Amstelpark*, which has a miniature train, pony rides, a farmyard, seals and a pancake house; and the *Amsterdamse Bos*, which can be reached on summer weekends by the *Electrische Museum Tramlijn* from Haarlemmermeerstation.

Children might also enjoy a visit to one of the children's farmyards (*kinderboerderijen*) in Amsterdam. These unusual city farms are found at Artis, the Amstelpark, next to the Okura Hotel and on Bickerseiland.

Museums and workshops

The most interesting museums for children are *Madame Tussaud* (waxwork figures), the *Spaarpottenmuseum* (piggy banks), the *Nederlands Scheepvaart Museum* (ship models), *NINT Technisch Museum* (push-button models) and the *Tropenmuseum* (reconstructed Third World villages). The Tropenmuseum also has a separate children's department, the **Kindermuseum TM Junior**.

Amsterdam children also seem to enjoy the modern art (and particularly the video shows) in the *Stedelijk Museum*. Although the *Rijksmuseum* is not really geared to children, they might enjoy following one of the trails described in the *Viewfinder* leaflets.

Theaters, films, circuses and other events

Children usually enjoy the spectacle of street theater, which flourishes in the summer months around *Leidseplein* and in front of the *Royal Palace* on the Dam. The *Uitkrant* (see *Local publications* in *Basic information*) has a special section, *Jeugdagenda*, devoted to children's events in Amsterdam, while Dutch-speaking children can also dial the *jeugdtheaterlijn* (☎(020) 222999) for a chatty recorded message informing them of coming events.

The main place for children's theater is **De Krakeling** (*Nieuwe Passeerdersstraat 1* ☎ (020) 245132, tram 7, 10 to Raamplein). Most shows will be in Dutch, but occasionally there is mime or music.

Films for children are screened at the **Kinder Film Centrum**, which is part of the **Amsterdams Filmhuis** (see *Nightlife and the arts*). The weekly film listings include details of children's matinees (*kindermatinees*). Most of these are dubbed into Dutch (you should look for the words "*Nederlands gesproken*").

Occasional shows are also put on by the children's circus. **Elleboog** (*Passeerdersgracht 32* ☎ (020) 269370, *telephone reservation essential, tram 7, 10 to Raamplein*).

Boat trips and tram rides

Canal boat trips are always fun, and most operators have
reduced rates for children. A more energetic way to explore the
canals is by canal bicycle (see *Sports and activities*). The
adventurous can also get to know the city by tram (see *Tram
rides* in *Planning*).

On summer weekends, old-fashioned trams run regularly to
the Amsterdamse Bos (see *Electrische Museum Tramlijn*). A
tourist tram also departs from Dam (*mid-Apr – Sept 10.30am–
6pm, every 45mins*) on a 70-minute tour of the city.

Walks

Certain areas of Amsterdam have details that might appeal to
children, such as the western islands (see *Zandhoek* in *A to Z
of sights*), a quiet, almost traffic-free area of narrow wooden
bridges and old boats. The center of the city is also packed with
interesting details (see *Walks 1* and *3* in *Planning*), such as the
facade stones on St Luciensteeg (see *Amsterdams Historisch
Museum*) and the curious barge moored near the
Muziektheater on the *Amstel*. Taking a trip on the free ferry
that departs from behind Centraal Station can also be
interesting.

Cafés and restaurants

In Holland, children are welcome in cafés, where they enjoy
chocomel (chocolate-flavored milk) and *warme chocolade* (hot
chocolate). Among the cafés that might appeal to children are
the **Américain** for its grand interior, **De IJsbreker** for
delicious hot chocolate (see *Cafés* for both), and the café-
restaurant of the *Amsterdams Historisch Museum*, which
contains 17thC wooden models of David and Goliath.

Some restaurants offer an inexpensive *kindermenu*
(children's menu), which usually involves dishes designed to
appeal to children, though they may horrify conscientious
parents with their emphasis on French fries, ice cream and
lemonade.

Amsterdam also boasts a children's restaurant, **Het Kinder
Kookcafé** (*Oude Zijds Achterburgwal 193 ☎ (020) 253257,
open Sat, Sun 3–6pm, reservation essential Sat noon–2pm, tram
4, 9, 14, 16, 24, 25 to Spui*), where meals are prepared under
adult supervision by children aged 6–12 years. Although most
of the diners are children, parents may, if they wish,
accompany their offspring.

Other ideas

Children will probably enjoy climbing a church tower for a
view of the city. The towers of the *Westerkerk*, *Zuiderkerk* and
Oude Kerk are all open to the public.

Energetic parents with small children can rent bicycles with
children's seats attached for short trips into the country.

Amsterdam has several swimming pools (the **Mirandabad**
has slides and artificial waves: see *Sports and activities*), a
roller-skate disco (see *Nightlife and the arts*) and several good
toy shops (see *Shopping*).

Excursions

Amsterdam is well located for excursions to surrounding
towns with attractions that might appeal to children. The
historic harbor towns N of Amsterdam are particularly
exciting. From *Hoorn* there are steam trains to Medemblik

and boat trips on the IJsselmeer. Boats also ply between the ports of *Monnickendam*, *Marken* and *Volendam*, and there are scheduled ferry services across the IJsselmeer from *Enkhuizen*. The Zuiderzee Museum in Enkhuizen allows children to roam freely through the reconstructed streets and houses, and younger children might enjoy **Sprookjeswonderland** (a park dotted with scenes from fairy tales) on the N edge of the town.

Den Haag has numerous major attractions for children, such as the miniature town of Madurodam, the pier and beach at Scheveningen, Omniversum, the Museon, and **Duinrell amusement park** (*Wassenaar* ☎ *(01751) 19212, bus 90 from Centraal Station*).

The main attractions in *Rotterdam* are the Euromast, the boat tours of the harbor, the zoo (Diergaarde Blijdorp), the maritime museum (Maritiem Museum Prins Hendrik), and the remarkable architecture at Oude Haven.

Finally, *Utrecht* offers the Nationaal Museum van Speelklok tot Pierement and the national railway museum, **Nederlands Spoorwegmuseum** (*J. van Oldenbarneveltlaan 6* ☎ *(030) 318514* 🚋 *open Tues–Sat, 10am–5pm; Sun, hols 1–5pm*).

See *Excursions* for further details of these towns and cities.

Sports and activities

Although the flat, watery and densely populated landscape of Holland may seem unsuited to outdoor activities, it is a perfect country for cycling, sailing and wind-surfing. The main recreation areas for Amsterdam are the *Amsterdamse Bos* to the SW for boating and cycling; the **Gaasperplas** to the SE for boating, wind-surfing and fishing (*metro to Gaasperplas*); and **Het Twiske** to the N for cycling, wind-surfing, rowing, canoeing, horseback riding, walking and bird-watching (☎ *(02984) 4338, bus 91, 92 from Centraal Station*).

Rowboats, canoes, wind-surfing boards, sailboats and bicycles can be rented at Het Twiske at the **Havengebouw De Roemer** (☎ *(02984) 4890*).

Bird-watching
The island of **Texel** (85km (53 miles) N of Amsterdam, reached by ferry from Den Helder) is particularly famous for its bird life. For information contact the tourist office: **VVV** (*Groeneplaats 9, 1791 CC Den Burg (Texel)* ☎ *(02220) 4741* ☎ *57573*).

Boating
Canal bicycles (*grachtenfietsen*) for 2–4 people can be rented at four locations on the main canals. These are: *Leidseplein*; *Westermarkt*; opposite the *Rijksmuseum*; and *Keizersgracht*, at Leidsestraat. (*For all* ☎ *(020) 265574, open 9am–7pm, summer 9am–11pm.*) Rowboats can be rented at the *Amsterdamse Bos* and **Het Twiske.**

Canoeing
Canoes can be rented at the *Amsterdamse Bos* and **Het Twiske.** For general information on canoeing on Dutch inland waters, contact the **Netherlands Canoe Association**

(*Postbus 434, 1380 AK Weesp* ☎ *(02940) 18331*). Good maps can be obtained from **Jacob van Wijngaarden** (see *Shopping*).

Chess

Chess is played in many cafés, particularly **Het Hok** (*Lange Leidsedwarsstraat 134*), just off Leidseplein.

Cycling

Cycling in Amsterdam can be stressful, but to the N and S are quiet roads that are ideal for short excursions (see *Cycle trips in Excursions*). The brochure *Cycling in Holland*, available from the **Netherlands Board of Tourism** (*355 Lexington Ave, 21st Floor, New York NY 10017* ☎ *(212) 370–7360; 25–28 Buckingham Gate, London SW1E 6LD* ☎ *(01) 630–1735*), contains practical advice for the cyclist, with recommended long-distance routes, and provides details of special package vacations.

Fishing

Information on fishing can be obtained from the **Netherlands Board of Tourism,** or from the **NNVS** (*Postbus 288, 3800 AG Amersfoort* ☎ *(033) 634924*).

Health clubs

One of Amsterdam's best equipped health clubs is the **Splash Sonesta Fitness Club** (*Kattengat 1* ☎ *(020) 271044*), where a one-day membership can be purchased.

Ice-skating

Amsterdam's ice-skating rink is the **Jaap Edenbaan** (*Radioweg 64* ☎ *(020) 949894*). A temporary ice rink is also set up on *Leidseplein* in winter; if it remains cold for long enough you can skate on numerous frozen canals, ponds and lakes around the city. Take your cue from the natives.

Roller-skating

Close to the Dam is the roller-skate disco **'t Nijlpaardenhuis** (see *Nightlife and the arts*).

Sailing

A country with so much water obviously offers excellent opportunities for sailing. The brochure *Holland Watersports Paradise*, available from the **Netherlands Board of Tourism** (see *Cycling* above), contains practical information and recommended itineraries. Traditional sailboats with crew can be rented in Amsterdam — contact **Stichting Het Varend Museumschip** (*De Ruijterkade 106* ☎ *(020) 270001*) — or in Enkhuizen — contact **Zeilvaart Enkhuizen** (*Zuiderhavendijk 101* ☎ *(02280) 12424* ✆*57689*). Charts and almanacs can be bought from **L. J. Harri** (see *Shopping*).

Sauna

De Kosmos (*Prins Hendrikkade 142* ☎ *(020) 230686, open Mon–Sat 10.30am–10pm*) is a friendly, mixed sauna with a small open-air pool.

Soccer

The main soccer club in Amsterdam is **Ajax** (*stadium at Middenweg 401; tram 9*).

Swimming
The most modern pool in Amsterdam is the **Mirandabad** (*De Mirandalaan 9* ☎ *(020) 446637*), which has artificial waves and slides. The **Marnixbad** (*Marnixplein 5* ☎ *(020) 254843*) is convenient for the Jordaan; the **Zuiderbad** (*Hobbemastraat 26* ☎ *(020) 792217*) serves the museum quarter; and the **Heiligewegbad** (*Heiligeweg 19* ☎ *(020) 236935*) is close to Muntplein.

Walking
The most pleasant areas for walking near Amsterdam are the dunes w of Haarlem (*train to Overveen*) and w of Castricum (*train to Castricum*), and the woods s of Hilversum (*train to Hollandsche Rading*).

Wind-surfing
Holland's inland waters are ideal for wind-surfing. The most popular areas close to Amsterdam are **Het Twiske; Gaasperplas** (SE Amsterdam); the *Amsterdamse Bos*; the **Gouwzee** (off Monnickendam); the **Kinselmeer** (NE of Durgerdam); and the **Hoornse Hop** (off Hoorn). Contact the Royal Netherlands Watersports Foundation: **Koninklijk Nederlands Watersport Verbond** (*Postbus 53034, 1007 RA Amsterdam* ☎ *(020) 642611*).

Yoga and meditation
Yoga, meditation and lectures on non-Western philosophy are organized by **De Kosmos** (*Prins Hendrikkade 142* ☎ *(020) 230686*).

Biographies

For a small country, Holland has produced a remarkable number of great scientists, scholars, navigators and merchants. The following selection deals mainly with people mentioned in this book. (Painters are listed separately under *Dutch art*.)

Barents, Willem (1550–97)
Dutch navigator and cartographer who made three unsuccessful attempts to discover a Northeast passage to China, and finally died after a winter on Novaya Zemlya. The expedition's camp and journal were found in the late 19thC.

Bicker, Andries (1586–1652)
Powerful Amsterdam merchant who, with his three brothers Cornelis, Jacob and Jan, monopolized city government in the 17thC. Andries served ten times as burgomaster; his brother Jan built and gave his name to Bickerseiland in Amsterdam.

Blaeu, Willem Jansz. (1571–1638)
Founder of an Amsterdam printing firm that specialized in maps and globes. His son Jan published the 11-volume *Atlas Major* in 1663.

Bredero, Gerbrant (1585–1618)
Satirical playwright and poet, author of *De Spaanse Brabander*.

Coornhert, Dirck Volckertsz. (1522–90)
Humanist, reformer, and proponent of tolerant penal policies at a time of Spanish atrocities.

Elsevier, Louis (1540–1617)
Refugee from the Spanish Netherlands, founder of a publishing house in Leiden which later moved to Amsterdam.

Erasmus, Desiderius (1466–1536)
Europe's foremost 16thC humanist, born in Rotterdam and later professor at Leuven University. He was a friend of Thomas More and opponent of the absolutism of Luther's doctrines.

Frank, Anne (1929–44)
German-born Jewish girl who, with her family, hid from occupying Nazi troops in a house on Prinsengracht. The family was eventually betrayed, and Anne died in Bergen-Belsen concentration camp.

Frederik, Henry (1584–1647)
The youngest son of William of Orange and his fourth wife Louise de Coligny. He was an able soldier, following in the footsteps of his brother Maurits (1567–1625), and a tolerant statesman.

Grotius, Hugo (1583–1645)
Jurist, statesman, poet and historian, born in Delft. He was imprisoned in 1618 for his support of the Remonstrant cause, but escaped to France with the help of his wife. His greatest work, *De Jure Belli ac Pacis*, is a cornerstone of international law.

Mata Hari (1876–1917)
The stage name of a Dutch dancer who was executed in Paris as a German spy during World War I.

Heyn, Piet (1578–1629)
Flamboyant Dutch sea captain who in 1626 captured the Spanish silver fleet, valued at some 12 million guilders, in the Cuban port of Matanzas. He was made an admiral, and died in a sea battle near Dunkirk.

Multatuli (1820–87)
The pseudonym of Amsterdam-born writer Eduard Douwes Dekker. He served in the Dutch colonial service in Java, and criticized its abuses in his most famous work, *Max Havelaar* (1860).

Louis Napoleon (1778–1846)
Brother of Napoleon I of France. He was King of the Netherlands from 1806–10, and converted the town hall of Amsterdam into one of his palaces.

Oldenbarnevelt, Johan van (1547–1619)
Statesman and lawyer who in 1609 concluded a truce with Spain. His support for tolerance at a time of religious strife brought him into conflict with the Stadholder, Prince Maurits, and resulted in his arrest and execution as a traitor.

Robinson, John (c. 1576–1625)
English religious leader, who fled to Amsterdam in 1608, and in 1609 settled in Leiden, where he established a church. Here the Pilgrim Fathers (as they later became known) worshiped before departing in 1620 for the New World.

Ruyter, Michiel Adriansz. de (1607–76)
Born in Vlissingen, he ran off to sea as a cabin boy and eventually rose to the rank of admiral. His most daring exploit was to sail up the Medway in 1667 and set fire to the English fleet. He died of wounds at Syracuse while fighting the French.

Six, Jan (1618–1700)
Son of a Huguenot merchant. He was a friend of Rembrandt (who painted his portrait in 1654) and wrote poetry and plays. He served as burgomaster and married a daughter of Dr Nicolaes Tulp.

Spinoza, Baruch (1632–77)
Jewish philosopher who was born in Amsterdam of Sephardic

parents. In 1656 he was expelled from the Jewish community for his Cartesian beliefs and was forced to earn a living polishing spectacle lenses. His greatest work, *Ethica*, used mathematical deduction to justify ethical beliefs.

Stuyvesant, Pieter (1592–1672)
Dutch governor of Nieuw Amsterdam (later New York). He was an unpopular leader and in 1664 was forced to hand the colony over to the English.

Swammerdam, Jan (1637–80)
Naturalist and collector, born in Amsterdam. He laid the foundations of entomology and was the first to observe red blood corpuscles.

Tasman, Abel (1603–c. 1659)
Dutch navigator who discovered Tasmania (originally named Van Diemen's Land) and New Zealand on a voyage (1642–43) in search of a route from the Dutch East Indies to South America.

Thorbecke, Johan (1798–1872)
Liberal statesman, architect of the 1848 Constitution.

Trip, Louis and Trip, Hendrick (1605–84 and 1607–66)
Dutch industrialists, famed for the manufacture of armaments and the development of iron and copper mines in Sweden.

Tromp, Maarten (1597–1653)
Admiral, born in Briel. He won several victories against the Spanish in the Eighty Years' War, fought in the First Anglo-Dutch War and died in a battle against the English off the Dutch coast.

Tulp, Nicolaes (1593–1674)
Physician and professor of anatomy, painted by Rembrandt in 1632. He was active in the city government and served four terms as burgomaster. One of his daughters married Jan Six.

Vondel, Joost van den (1587–1679)
Dutch poet and playwright of the Golden Age. He was born in Cologne of Anabaptist parents, but converted to Catholicism late in life. He worked in business and later in a pawn shop, using his literature to comment on political issues.

William of Orange (1533–84)
Also known as William the Silent. Brought up as a Catholic at the court of Charles V in Brussels, he converted to Protestantism in 1570 and in 1572 led the Dutch Revolt against Philip II of Spain. He was assassinated in Delft.

Witt, Johan de (1625–72)
Leading statesman of the 17thC, who guided the United Provinces through the First and Second Anglo-Dutch Wars. He became a scapegoat in the Year of Disasters (1672), and he and his brother Cornelis (1623–72) were lynched by an angry mob in Den Haag.

An introduction to Dutch

"Here, though destitute of what may be properly called a language of their own," wrote Oliver Goldsmith in 1759, "all the languages are understood, cultivated, and spoken." While it is certainly true that the Dutch are conscientious linguists (speaking good English, German and French), it is wrong to see Dutch merely as a corruption of German. Moreover, even as a casual visitor, it is rewarding to master the basic pronunciation and learn a few essential words.

In common with German, Dutch fuses words together into unwieldy compounds, but unlike German it has streamlined its case system and manages quite well with only two genders: *de* for masculine and feminine words and *het* for neuter. A curious habit of the Dutch is to reduce everything to diminutives by the addition of the suffix – *je* (e.g., *broodje*, a sandwich; *pilsje*, a harmless beer).

Vowels

Dutch vowel sounds are particularly baffling to foreigners, and some sounds have no equivalent in English. There is also a distinction between short and long vowel sounds. Words are divided into syllables, each syllable beginning with a consonant; e.g., Haar/lem, Ap/pel. If a syllable ends in a vowel, this will be a long vowel even if it is only a single vowel; e.g. E/dam. Double vowels will always be long.

a	(when short)	as the u in cut; e.g. Damrak
a	(when long) or aa	as the a in are; e.g. Haarlem
e	(when short)	as the e in bet; e.g. Delft
e	(when long) or ee	as the a in baby; e.g. Steen, Edam
i	(short)	as the i in sit; e.g. Prinsengracht
ie	(long)	as the ie in pier; e.g. bier
o	(when short)	as the o in dot; e.g. bos
o	(when long) or oo	as the o in no; e.g. Volendam, telefoon
u	(when short)	as the e in the (unstressed); e.g. brug
u	(when long) or uu	as the u in tune; e.g. Utrecht, buurt
eu		as the e in the (unstressed); e.g. Beurs
ui		a treacherous diphthong, close to the ou in out, but ending with a slight i as in item; e.g. zuid
ij or ei		another tongue twister, close to the i in light; e.g. Rijksmuseum, IJsselmeer, Leidseplein (but when ij unstressed at end of word, as the e in the (unstressed); e.g. Stedelijk
ou		as the ou in loud; e.g. oud
oe		as the ou in soup; e.g. soep
ieuw		similar to the ew in few; nieuw

Consonants

w	as the v in vole; e.g. Waterland
j	as the y in yawn; e.g. Jordaan
th	as the t in tea; e.g. thee
ch or g	as the ch in loch; e.g. Schiphol, Gouda
b and d	soften to p and t sounds at the end of words
n	when unstressed, becomes silent at the end of a word; e.g. Leiden

Reference words

Monday	maandag	Friday	vrijdag
Tuesday	dinsdag	Saturday	zaterdag
Wednesday	woensdag	Sunday	zondag
Thursday	donderdag		

January	januari	July	juli
February	februari	August	augustus
March	maart	September	september
April	april	October	oktober
May	mei	November	november
June	juni	December	december

189

Words and phrases

1	een	11	elf	21	eenentwintig
2	twee	12	twaalf	22	tweeëntwintig
3	drie	13	dertien	30	dertig
4	vier	14	veertien	40	veertig
5	vijf	15	vijftien	50	vijftig
6	zes	16	zestien	60	zestig
7	zeven	17	zeventien	70	zeventig
8	acht	18	achttien	80	tachtig
9	negen	19	negentien	90	negentig
10	tien	20	twintig	100	honderd

First	eerste	quarter-past	kwart over ....
Second	tweede	half-past one	half twee (i.e., half of two)
Third	derde		
Fourth	vierde	quarter to	kwart voor ....
.... o' clock	.... uur		

Mr	mijnheer	Ladies	dames
Mrs	mevrouw	Gents	heren
Miss	mejuffrouw		

Basic vocabulary

Yes	ja	Goodbye	dag/tot ziens
No	nee	Left	links
Please	alstublieft (formal), alsjeblieft (informal)	Right	rechts
		Straight ahead	rechtdoor
Thank you	dank u wel (formal), dank je (informal)	Day	dag
		Month	maand
Thanks	bedankt	Year	jaar
You're welcome	geen dank/graag gedaan	Here	hier
		There	daar
Sorry	sorry	Big	groot
Excuse me	neem me niet kwalijk (formal)	Small	klein
		Hot	warm
Good	goed	Cold	koud
Bad	slecht	Toilet/rest room	toilet/WC
Well	goed	I speak English	ik spreek Engels
Badly	slecht	Do you speak English?	spreekt u Engels?
And	en		
But	maar	I don't know	ik weet het niet
Very	zeer	I am American/English	ik kom uit Amerika/Engeland
All	alle		
Open	open	Do you have?	heeft u?
Closed	gesloten	Where is?	waar is?
Hello	hallo	How much does it cost?	hoeveel kost het?
Good morning	goede morgen		
Good afternoon	goede middag	What time is it?	hoe laat is het?
Good evening	goeden avond	Is there a ...?	is er een ...?

Signs decoder

Stadhuis	town hall	Verdieping	floor/story
Gracht/kanaal/singel	canal	Wisselkantoor	foreign exchange
Brug	bridge	Loket	ticket office
Straat	street	Nooduitgang	emergency exit
Laan	avenue	Noodtrap	emergency stairs
Steeg	alley	Geen toegang/toegang verboden	no entry
Poort	gate		
Perron/spoor	platform	Niet roken	no smoking
Station	station	Kassa	cashier
Ingang	entrance	Trekken	pull
Uitgang	exit	Duwen	push
Trap	staircase	Rondvaart	boat tour

Road signs

Doorgaand verkeer	through traffic	Parkeerplaats	parking/parking lot
Omleiding	detour	Parkeergarage	multistory parking lot
Centrum	center		
Uit	exit	Rijverkeer gestremd	no through road

Words and phrases

Uitrit vrijhouden **keep exit clear**
Niet parkeren **no parking**
Pas op/let op **danger**
Snelheid **speed**
Langzaam rijden **go slow**
Fietspad **cycle lane**
Voetganger **pedestrian**
Zachte berm **soft shoulder**

Vrachtwagen **truck**
Bromfiets **moped**
Motor **motorcycle**
m.u.v. **with the exception of**
Oversteken **crossover**
(Loodvrije) benzine **(lead-free)**
gasoline

Shops

Winkel **store**
Apotheek **pharmacy**
Bakker **baker**
Slager **butcher**
Groenteboer **greengrocer**

Boekhandel **bookstore**
Viswinkel **fish store**
Reisbureau **travel agent**
Postkantoor **post office**
Warenhuis **department store**

Food and drink

Breakfast ontbijt
Lunch lunch
Dinner diner
Glass glas
Bottle fles
Beer/lager bier/pils
Draft beer bier van het vat
Mineral water mineraalwater
Fruit juice sap
Orange juice sinaasappelsap
Apple juice appelsap
Tomato juice tomatensap
Milk melk
Buttermilk karnemelk
Red wine rode wijn
White wine witte wijn

Dry droog
Sweet zoet
Salt zout
Pepper peper
Mustard mosterd
Oil olie
Vinegar azijn
Bread brood
Butter boter
Cheese kaas
Coffee koffie
Tea thee
Chocolate chocolade
Sugar suiker
Steak biefstuk

Menu decoder

Aalbessen **red currants**
Aardappels **potatoes**
Aardbeien **strawberries**
Amandelen **almonds**
Ananas **pineapple**
Andijvie **endive**
Anijs **aniseed**
Appel **apple**
Asperges **asparagus**

Bami **egg noodles**
Banaan **banana**
Basilicum **basil**
Biefstuk **steak**
Bieslook **chives**
Bloemkool **cauliflower**
Borst **breast**
Bosbessen **bilberries**
Broodje **roll**

Champignons **mushrooms**
Citroen **lemon**

Dagschotel **dish of the day**
Deeg **dough**
Doperwten **peas**
Dragon **tarragon**

Eend **duck**
Ei **egg**
Erwtensoep **pea soup**

Fazant **pheasant**
Flensjes **small pancakes**

Forel **trout**
Frambozen **raspberries**
Fricandeau **cold, cooked lean**
pork or veal

Gambas **king prawns**
Gans **goose**
Garnalen **shrimps**
Gebak **cake**
Gebakken **fried**
Gebraden **baked**
Gekookt **boiled**
Gember **ginger**
Gepocheerd **poached**
Gerookt **smoked**
Gestoofd **stewed**
Gestoomd **steamed**
Gevogelte **poultry**
Gevuld **stuffed**
Groenten **vegetables**

Haas **hare**
Ham **ham**
Haring **herring**
Hazepeper **jugged hare**
Heilbot **halibut**
Hoofdgerecht **main dish**

IJs **ice cream**
Inktvis **squid**

Kabeljauw **cod**
Kalfsoesters **medallions of veal**
Kalfsvlees **veal**

191

Words and phrases

Kalkoen	turkey	Rauw	raw
Kaneel	cinnamon	Rijst	rice
Karbonade	chop/cutlet	Rode kool	red cabbage
Kerrie	curry	Rog	skate
Kervel	chervil	Rosbief	roast beef
Ketjap	soy sauce	Rozemarijn	rosemary
Kikkerbilletjes	frogs legs	Rundvlees	beef
Kip	chicken		
Knoflook	garlic	Salie	sage
Komkommer	cucumber	Sambal	very hot crushed chillies
Konijn	rabbit	Saté	meat on a skewer
Kool	cabbage	Saucijzebroodje	sausage roll
Kotelet	chop/cutlet	Saus	sauce
Kreeft	lobster	Schelvis	haddock
Kroepoek	prawn cracker	Schol	plaice
Kruidnagel	clove	Sla	lettuce/salad
Kwartel	quail	Slagroom	whipped cream
		Slakken	snails
Lamsbout	leg of lamb	Sneetje	slice
Lamsvlees	lamb	Snijbonen	runner beans
Lever	liver	Soep	soup
Linzen	lentils	Speculaas	ginger-and-spice biscuit
Loempia	spring roll	Spek	bacon
		Spekkoek	layered spice cake
Maatje	small, cured herring	Sperciebonen	green beans
Mais	sweet corn	Spinazie	spinach
Makreel	mackerel	Stokbrood	French bread
Marjolein	marjoram		
Meloen	melon	Tarbot	turbot
Mosselen	mussels	Taugé	bean sprouts
Munt	mint	Tong	sole
		Tonijn	tuna fish
Nagerecht	dessert		
Nasi	fried rice	Ui	onion
Nieren	kidneys	Uitsmijter	Fried eggs on bread with ham or cheese
Oester	oyster		
Ossehaas	fillet of beef	Varkenshaas	fillet of pork
Ossestaart	oxtail	Varkensvlees	pork
		Venkel	fennel
Paling	eel	Vers	fresh
Pannekoek	pancake	Vis	fish
Paprika	(green or red) pepper	Vlees	meat
Parelhoen	guinea fowl	Voorgerecht	hors d'oeuvre
Passievrucht	passion fruit		
Pasteitje	vol-au-vent	Wafel	waffle
Peer	pear	Waterkers	watercress
Perzik	peach	Wild	game
Peterselie	parsley	Witlof	chicory
Peulen	snow peas	Wortels	carrots
Pinda	peanut		
Poffertjes	tiny pancakes drenched in sugar and butter	Zalm	salmon
Pommes frites/patat	French fries	Zalmforel	salmon trout
Poon	gurnard	Zeeduivel	monkfish
Prei	leek	Zoetzuur	sweet and sour
		Zwezerik	sweetbreads

192

Index

General index   193
Gazetteer of street names   202

With the exception of a few of the most notable, such as the Pulitzer Hotel and De Bijenkorf department store, individual hotels, restaurants and shops have not been indexed, because they appear in alphabetical order within their appropriate sections. The sections themselves, however, have been indexed. Similarly, although most streets are listed in the gazetteer and not in the index, a few exceptions, such as Leidsestraat, are indexed as well.

The letters **ij**, when they appear together in Dutch (e.g., IJsselmeer, Bijbels Museum), sound as **y** and have been filed alphabetically as such (e.g., as if they were Ysselmeer, Bybels Museum).

Page numbers in bold type indicate the main entry.

193

Index

Index

Index

199

Index

Gazetteer of street names

Numbers after street names refer to pages on which streets are mentioned in the text. Map references relate to the maps that follow this gazetteer.

It has not been possible to name every street drawn on the maps, although all major roads, squares and canals are indicated. Some streets not named on the maps still appear in this gazetteer, however, with a map reference to show their approximate location.

A

Akoleienstraat, 179;
Map 10D2

Amstel, 26, 33, 79, 111,
114; Map 8G6

Amstelstraat, 45;
Map 7F5

Amstelveld, 70, 123;
Map 7G5

Antoniesbreestraat, Sint,
45, 57, 108, 120, 126;
Map 12D6

B

Baerlestraat, Van, 97, 111,
118, 124, 125, 126, 127;
Map 6I2

Barberenstraat, St, 103;
Map 11E5

Begijnhof, 17, 111;
Map 11E4

Berenstraat, 59, 122;
Map 10E3

Beulingstraat, 113;
Map 11E4

Binnen Bantammerstraat,
43; Map 12D6

Binnenkant, 40, 43, 67;
Map 12D7

Blauwburgwal, 44, 78;
Map 11C4

Bloemdwarsstraat, 1e,
118; Map 10D3

Bloemgracht, 58, 122;
Map 10C2

Bloemstraat, 127;
Map 10D2

Bolstraat, Ferdinand, 91,
95, 101, 109; Map 7H4

Breestraat, Van, 33;
Map 6H2

Brouwersgracht, 7, 39, 42,
54, 55, 59, 70, 107;
Map 11B4

Brouwersstraat, J. W., 92;
Map 6I2

Buiten Bantammerstraat,
67; Map 12D7

C

Ceintuurbaan, 110;
Map 8I6

Coenenstraat, J. M., 47;
Map 6J2

Cuypstraat, Albert, 123;
Map 7I4

D

Dam, 12, 14, 16, 27, 37,
38, 39, 60, 64, 65, 69,
90, 111, 116, 182;
Map 11D4

Damrak, 10, 16, 37, 43,
44, 45, 65, 68, 88, 89,
91, 117, 119;
Map 11C–D5

Damstraat, 37, 68, 121;
Map 11D5

E

Egelantiersdwarsstraat,
58; Map 10C3

Egelantiersgracht,
58, 107;
Map 10C2–3

Egelantiersstraat, 58;
Map 10C2–3

Elandsgracht, 45, 122,
123; Map 10E2

Elandsstraat, 103, 126;
Map 10E2

Enge Lombardsteeg, 69;
Map 11D5

G

Gasthuismolensteeg, 127;
Map 11D4

Geldersekade, 66;
Map 12C6

Gravenhekje, 's, 43;
Map 12D7

Gravenstraat, 44, 65, 104,
106, 120; Map
11D5

Grimburgwal, 40, 68, 122;
Map 11E5

Groenburgwal, 17, 40, 67;
Map 11E5

H

Haarlemmerstraat, 25;
Map 11B4

Harmoniehof, 47;
Map 6J3

Hartplein, Roelof, 47,
108; Map 6I3

Hazenstraat, 44, 58, 99;
Map 10E2

Heiligeweg, 26, 45, 65,
119, 125, 126, 127, 186;
Map 11E4

Heisteeg, 41, 45, 79;

Map 11E4

Herengracht, 17, 24, 25,
26, 32, 37, 41, 42, 53,
54, 60, 63, 69, 84, 88,
103, 112, 122, 180;
Maps 6, 7, 10, 11

Herenmarkt, 42;
Map 11B4

Herenstraat, 44, 59;
Map 11C4

Hobbemakade, 38, 100;
Map 6H–I3

Hobbemastraat, 97, 186;
Map 6H3

Hooftstraat, P. C., 90, 96,
98, 118, 120, 124, 125,
126, 127; Map 6H2

Huidenstraat, 45, 55, 121,
125, 127; Map
10E3

Huygensstraat, 1e
Constantijn, 47; Map
6G2

J

Jodenbreestraat, 30, 57,
71; Map 12E6

K

Kalverstraat, 39, 45, 50,
62, 65, 116, 117, 119,
120, 122, 124, 125, 127;
Map 11D–E4

Karthuizersstraat, 58;
Map 10B3

Kattengat, 92, 98, 112,
185; Map 11C5

Keizersgracht, 7, 15, 16,
24, 25, 26, 32, 33, 37,
41, 42, 54, 56, 59, 60,
69, 83, 89, 105, 110,
112, 115, 116, 117, 119,
122, 125, 126, 180, 184;
Maps 6, 7, 10

Kerkstraat, 95, 112, 115,
118; Map 6F3

Kloveniersburgwal, 24,
25, 37, 40, 66, 68, 100,
104, 113, 117, 118, 121;
Map 11E5

Koestraat, 66; Map
12D6

Kolksteeg, 108;
Map 12C6

Koningslaan, 17, 92;
Map 6H1

Koningsplein, 118, 124;

202

Gazetteer

AMSTERDAM

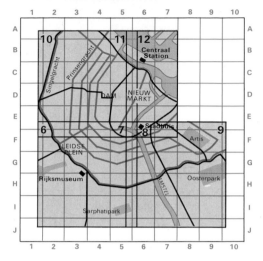

LEGEND

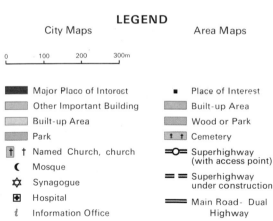

City Maps   Area Maps

0   100   200   300m

City Maps

- Major Place of Interest
- Other Important Building
- Built-up Area
- Park
- † Named Church, church
- (Mosque
- ✡ Synagogue
- ✚ Hospital
- *i* Information Office
- ✉ VVV Post Office
- ✋ Police Station
- ☎ Parking Lot
- Ⓜ Metro Station
- 6 Adjoining Page No.

Area Maps

- ■ Place of Interest
- Built-up Area
- Wood or Park
- ✝ ✝ Cemetery
- =○= Superhighway (with access point)
- = = Superhighway under construction
- Main Road- Dual Highway
- Other Main Road
- Secondary Road
- Railway
- ✈ Airport
- ♜ Castle

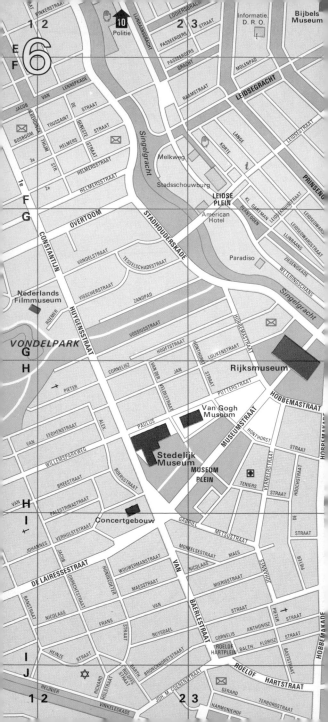

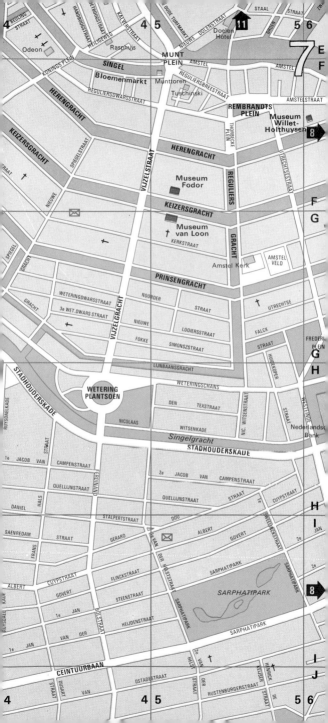

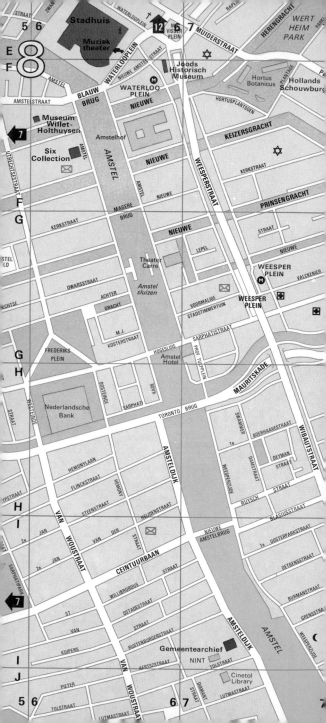

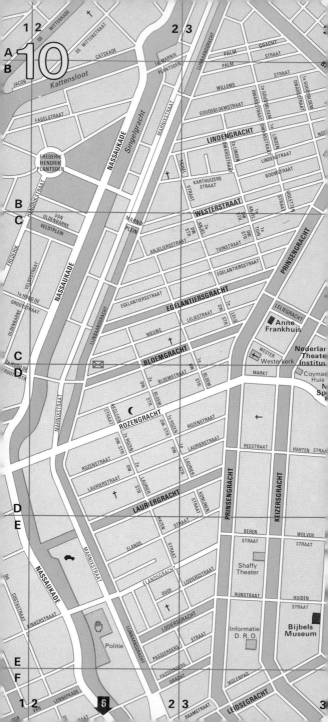

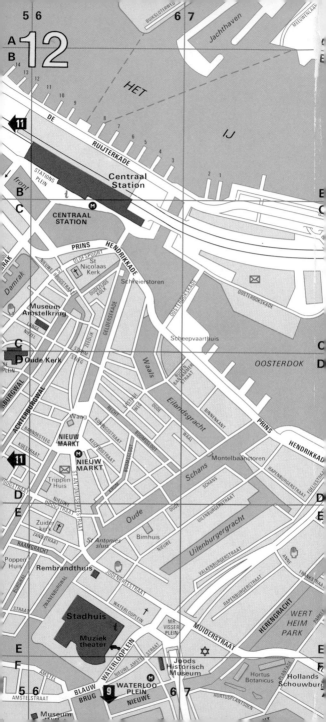